Brand
Meaning

"The least of things with a meaning is worth more in life than the greatest of things without it."

Carl Gustav Jung

Brand
Meaning

MARK BATEY

Psychology Press
Taylor & Francis Group

New York   London

Please visit Mark Batey's website at http://www.brandmeaning.com

The opinions expressed in this book are those of the author and do not necessarily represent the views or intentions of any company or advertiser cited.

Routledge
Taylor & Francis Group
270 Madison Avenue
New York, NY 10016

Routledge
Taylor & Francis Group
2 Park Square
Milton Park, Abingdon
Oxon OX14 4RN

© 2008 by Mark Batey
Routledge is an imprint of Taylor & Francis Group, an Informa business

Printed in the United States of America on acid-free paper
10 9 8 7 6 5 4 3 2

International Standard Book Number-13: 978-0-8058-6455-7 (Softcover) 978-0-8058-6454-0 (Hardcover)

Library of Congress Cataloging-in-Publication Data

Batey, Mark.
   Brand meaning / Mark Batey.
      p. cm.
   Includes bibliographical references.
   ISBN 978-0-8058-6455-7 (alk. paper)
   1. Branding (Marketing) 2. Product management. I. Title.

HF5415.1255.B39 2008
658.8'27--dc22   2007045418

Visit the Taylor & Francis Web site at
http://www.taylorandfrancis.com

and the Routledge Web site at
http://www.routledge.com

To Mum and Dad

Contents

Author

Mark Batey, a language graduate of Oxford University, has spent his career with leading international advertising agencies, working in areas as diverse as the United Kingdom, Central Europe, Latin America and the United States. His clients have included Coca-Cola, Unilever, Nestlé and Kraft Foods.

Preface

This book lays out new and fertile territory for the understanding of how brands both assimilate and provide meaning. It draws on the thinking of leading authorities in the industry on both sides of the Atlantic and considers the latest findings in newly associated fields, most of which have not traditionally featured in marketing and brand management literature. Its holistic, multidisciplinary approach befits the subject matter and encourages readers to reassess how they think of brands.

With its timely consideration of contemporary and emerging brand-related themes, such as sensory marketing, semiotics, archetypal theory, and neuromarketing, this volume, it is hoped, will be of interest to a diverse audience of academics, students, and practitioners. Primarily intended as a supplemental reader for undergraduate, graduate, and MBA courses, the book's scope should also make it rewarding and valuable reading for practitioners in the fields of marketing and advertising.

Introduction

Though companies create brand identities, people create brand meaning. The meanings people find in brands help them make sense of, and give shape to, the world around them. Brands help people to define themselves and their place in that world, or, rather, the different worlds and environments they inhabit—the workplace, the family nest, the social gathering and so forth. Meaning is at the heart of consumer behavior. Yet meaning is not a manufactured, concrete given. Meaning is up for negotiation and interpretation, and the role of the individual in the creation of meaning is a very active one. Structuralist semioticians like Roland Barthes have pointed out that individuals are not passive receivers of meaning created by some external agent or authority. Rather, they are actively involved in the process of *signification*—the production of meaning. Meaning can be elusive: It flows and drifts and is often hard to pin down. No matter—the search for meaning in all its forms is hardwired into our psyches. The millennia may have passed, but we are still hunters and gatherers—of meaning.

It is impossible to understand brand meaning without understanding consumer motivation, and it is impossible to understand consumer motivation without understanding human motivation—the needs we strive to fulfill, the values that inspire and guide us and the aspirations that drive us. Despite the complexity of these very human impulses, the concept of *consumer* is still largely defined in economic terms, as a seeker of purely utilitarian benefit or gain. The drawback of focusing on the more rational elements of consumer behavior and the decision-making processes involved in the purchase of goods and services is that the emphasis falls on buying rather than consuming in its broadest sense. Rationality is an important facet of the consumer psyche, yet it is just one of three dimensions involved in consumer behavior:

- Conscious rationality
- Semiconscious emotions
- Unconscious biological drives and "hardwired" instincts

The three dimensions do not operate independently of each other but are intertwined. This has been demonstrated by recent findings in the field of neuroscience and has crucial implications for the research and understanding of human behavior. The prevalence of cognitive branding models has tended to limit the consideration of emotions in consumption behavior to the role of affect in influencing attitudes within purchase dynamics. The result has been to underplay the intricate set of emotions that are engaged *during the entire consumption process*. Worse still, many contemporary branding models still preclude any recognition of the symbolic significance of consumption and consumption goods.

The exploration of brand meaning requires a holistic approach that extends well beyond the functional and, at a push, emotional constructs that are typically ascribed to brands in strategy documents—usually reduced to a simplistic "head and heart" dichotomy. Brands carry a deep reservoir of meaning in terms of the context of their use, the sociopsychological nature of their consumers and the cultures to which those consumers belong: "We understand the world and its meanings through cultural assumptions, shared meaning systems and taken-for-granted beliefs and values that are ideologically based and culturally reinforced" (Valentine 1995, p. 7). Valentine gives the example of a train that should have left at 8:30 but leaves fifteen minutes after schedule. The train does not become the 8:45; it becomes the "late" 8:30:

> The material reality of the departure time is subsumed in the taken-for-granted concepts of late and early—with all their connotations of proper and improper social behavior—that are circumscribing the way we think about this train.... An entire socio-cultural value system—all wrapped up in that little word "late" (ibid.).

Though brands derive meaning from the culture in which they originate and develop, they also themselves become mediators of cultural and symbolic meaning. To mine the insights that can unlock these meanings, researchers are turning more frequently to fields such as sociology, anthropology, ethnography and clinical psychology, besides category dynamics and the heritage of the brand itself.

There is, moreover, a sea change afoot in the nature of consumer–brand relationships. Whereas brands were previously selected for their capacity to confer values on the consumers who use them, it is increasingly and more pertinently the case that consumers are conferring values on the brands they use. More and more, "ownership" of brands is passing to consumers.

Implicit in this dynamic is the recognition that a brand comprises meanings from two different sources: (1) those codified and communicated by the brand originator, above all in the early stages of a brand's development; and (2) the brand meanings derived, created and attributed by consumers in their ongoing consumption environment. To quote Travis (2000, p. 18), "When a brand is first being introduced, there is a short period of time when marketers can influence its positioning. But after that, consumers decide what it means, and once they've decided, they don't like to change it."

In fact, *positioning* is a term that implies more precision than it can deliver in practice—particularly when it is used in the context of *brand* positioning. The term was "invented" by Al Ries and Jack Trout and first appeared—back in 1972—in an *Advertising Age* article titled "The Positioning Era." Ries and Trout (2001, p. 2) explained the concept thus: "Positioning starts with a product…. But positioning is not what you do to a product. Positioning is what you do to the mind of the prospect. That is, you position the product in the mind of the prospect." Product positioning was born, a concept that still has a lot of validity today. Yet much has changed since 1972. In the 1980s marketers gradually became aware of the enormous value of the brand as distinct from the product or service. At the same time, advances in manufacturing capabilities meant it became increasingly difficult to gain competitive advantage through functional product performance attributes. Marketers sought differentiation along more emotional lines. They began to build brands, endowing them with personalities and symbolic qualities. To capture these more complex entities on paper, marketers and agencies introduced intricate new tools—the brand onion, brand pyramid, brand wheel and so forth. And the word *brand* was conveniently substituted for the word *product* to give us brand positioning.

From the late 1980s onward, the previously unchecked omnipotence of brand owners has steadily been losing ground to the strength of major retailers. Then we have seen, from the nineties through to today, unprecedented media fragmentation and the evolution of new communication channels, in particular the Internet. Person-to-person Web sites, for example, provide consumers with a very public and accessible forum to directly exchange experiences and opinions of brands completely independently of the brand proprietor. The result of all this is that divergence between company-intended and consumer-perceived brand meaning is made all the more likely. As ownership of brands—and their meaning—has passed to consumers, those consumers have become far less susceptible to the type of conditioning implied in the term *positioning*.

Nor can the complexity of many brands be neatly enshrined in the marketing shorthand of *brand positioning*. Among numerous examples, Nike has never adopted a discernible single-minded positioning. Rather, its millions of advertising and promotion dollars have consolidated the enrichment of its brand meaning, turning it into a cultural icon along the way. What is Coca-Cola's single-minded brand positioning? In reality the so-called brand positioning statement is little more than the product positioning statement. It seeks to define the frame of reference (product category), key benefit and supporting attributes. All worthy exercises, but as an attempt to summarize what a brand means or should mean, it is wholly inadequate.

There are similar shortcomings with another piece of terminology and the concept to which it refers, which is routinely used by marketers today. The term *brand equity* is less than satisfactory due partly to its origination in accounting procedure and partly to its being used to describe so many different things. The term dates back to the mid 1980s, a time when, as described, the marketing and financial worlds were becoming aware of the huge monetary value of brands. It has become something of a cliché, a catch-all phrase that groups together several different, more or less interrelated concepts. Most commentators recognize three distinct senses in which the term is used. The first is in reference to the brand as a separable, financial asset on a balance sheet, or *brand valuation*. To distinguish them from this asset valuation meaning, the second and third, consumer-focused concepts are often referred to as *consumer brand equity*. They are *brand image* and *brand loyalty*.

Brand image is a description of the associations, beliefs and feelings consumers have about the brand. Brand image was the expression that brand equity came to largely replace with time. Brand loyalty is a measure of consumer attachment or commitment to a brand, often taking into account the price premium he or she is prepared to pay. Today there are numerous commercial methods from leading research companies for measuring and optimizing brand equity. Probably because it is more descriptive and less quantifiable, brand image and its components have received less attention than the evaluative aspects of brand equity. If an individual's preference or otherwise for a given brand is increasingly driven by what the brand means to that person, it follows that this brand meaning will determine brand loyalty, which in turn will directly influence brand valuation. It serves little purpose to try to lump all those aspects together under one umbrella term or concept. Rather, more time and resource should be devoted to understanding what lies at the heart of all this: brand meaning. Consider Keller's (1998, p.601) list of the five deadly sins of brand management (presented in the closing observations of his 600-plus page work). Top of his list? The biggest sin of brand management: "Failure to understand the full meaning of the brand." Failure to fully understand brand meaning.

The Structure of This Book

This book puts meaning front and center in the study of brands and encourages readers to think of brand management as brand meaning management. To anchor the concept of brand meaning, the brand meaning framework is set forth in Chapter 5. This framework is predicated on the way we as humans perceive and relate to the things that surround us and have importance for us. It reflects what has been called the "paradoxical kernel of brand meaning," namely, that a brand is both alive and not alive, a subject and an object (Brown, Kozinets and Shery 2003, p. 30). It is necessary to explore these issues before delving into the theme of brand meaning itself. Thereafter, the practical aspects of brand meaning can be addressed.

Though the history of brands dates back many years, recognition of their value is a relatively recent phenomenon. Chapter 1 reviews the development of brands and looks at what a brand is and is not. The concept of the *brand engram* is introduced in the context of how brands exist in our minds. Also discussed is the importance of the relationship between brand and consumer.

Chapter 2 examines the fundamental topic of human motivation and considers how and why we seek meaning as human beings. The needs and value systems that drive and determine human behavior are explored. The chapter also looks at means-end theory and the way this can reveal meaningful connections between consumers and products and categories. The topic of emotion is one to which we will return throughout the book. Here different theories and types of emotion are reviewed. The chapter next considers how brands and the meanings they provide are one way we seek to define ourselves and the world around us. Some brands achieve such profoundly meaningful resonance with consumers that they come to operate at a deep archetypal level within the human psyche. The theory and application of archetypal meaning are elaborated on in the final part of the chapter.

It has been said that perception is reality—and with good reason. We rely on our senses to pick up information about and to make sense of the world around us, including the products and brands with which we come into contact. How we perceive and process this information is the subject of Chapter 3.

Before exploring brand meaning in particular, it is useful to consider the meaning of things in general: objects, everyday items. Chapter 4 draws on the contributions of psychologists, semioticians and linguists in an attempt to unravel the way we find meaning in things. Concepts such as semantic space and the differences between connotation and denotation are analyzed, as are the tangible and intangible aspects of objects and the way objects take on both private and public meanings. Critical in the context of brand meaning is an understanding of how objects can come to be endowed with symbolic meaning. Also covered is the process whereby meaning gets into and is drawn from objects—the process of meaning transfer. Rituals, including consumption rituals, are important as they are a very concrete way we seek to fix meanings. The subject is discussed further here.

The core subject of brand meaning is analyzed in Chapter 5. The way brand information is received and processed is discussed, along with the brand associative network that results. The different dimensions of brand meaning are described and the brand meaning framework of primary brand meaning and implicit brand meaning is introduced. A section is devoted to the research of the difficult-to-access area of implicit brand meaning. The many diverse sources of brand meaning are also reviewed. Finally, the chapter considers the particular significance of underlying products and their categories with regard to brand meaning.

Chapter 6 focuses on the central role of brand meaning within brand strategy. Strategic areas such as brand extension, portfolio management and brand architecture are examined.

Brand meaning is invariably in a greater or lesser state of evolution. Chapter 7 describes the form that evolution takes and illustrates how today's fledgling brand may become tomorrow's iconic brand. The chapter also looks at the way successful brands are often able to break out of their categories and into mainstream culture.

Chapter 8 discusses the area of brand communication. It examines the role of advertising in the context of brand meaning and considers advertising from a semiotic viewpoint. The chapter also reviews how brand meaning is communicated through the whole range of touch points a brand has with its consumers.

1

About Brands

The Value of Brands

When Nestlé paid $4.5 billion to take over the Rowntree company in the United Kingdom in 1988 the financial community was staggered. The price tag was almost $1.5 billion more than the value being put on the company by analysts at the time. In the aftermath of dotcom mania, when the business world temporarily took leave of its accounting senses, it would be tempting to dismiss the seemingly exorbitant price as the result of a hyped-up bidding process. It was not. Nestlé simply evaluated the hidden assets of Rowntree's famous confectionery brands (e.g., Kit Kat, Quality Street, Smarties, Yorkie, Rolo) and equated these with its own ability to leverage them. It paid five times Rowntree's book value and has not looked back since. In a similar vein, when Ford bought Jaguar, the physical assets of the company represented just 16 percent of the value.

The next time you pour yourself a Coca-Cola from a dispenser machine, consider this: All that is happening inside the machine is that a dark syrup is oozing from a sachet and being mixed with water, the resultant carbonated fluid of which is flowing into your cup. Then reflect on the fact that Interbrand's 2006 survey of leading brands identified Coca-Cola as the most valuable brand name in the world, placing its value at $67 billion (Table 1.1). Brands command such huge values because they themselves allow their owners to charge very profitable margins—for products with ingredients as basic as water and syrup.

So what are the origins of branding, and what is a brand anyway, if not a product with a name?

TABLE 1.1   Most Valuable Global Brands 2006

Rank	Company	2006 Brand Value ($ billion)
1	Coca-Cola	67.000
2	Microsoft	56.926
3	IBM	56.201
4	GE	48.907
5	Intel	32.319
6	Nokia	30.131
7	Toyota	27.941
8	Disney	27.848
9	McDonald's	27.501
10	Mercedes	21.795

The History of Brands

Brickmakers in ancient Egypt are said to have put symbols on their bricks to identify them. In Europe the earliest signs of branding were the medieval guilds' efforts to require craftsmen and craftswomen to put trademarks on their products to protect themselves and consumers against imitation and inferior quality. In the United States cattle ranchers would brand their livestock to more easily identify them. Manufacturers began to burn their identities onto the barrels that carried their products using a *branding* iron. The Guinness harp and the Bass red triangle are among the world's oldest registered trademarks, being first registered in 1876.

There are other famous examples from around the same time. In 1862, Doña Amalia Lucía Victoria Moreau stepped into the small tin-roofed distillery recently purchased by her husband in Santiago de Cuba and noticed a colony of fruit bats living in the rafters. Doña Amalia was familiar with local traditions and knew that bats had great significance for the now extinct natives of Cuba, the Taínos. According to local lore, bats brought good fortune, health and family unity. Doña Amalia suggested to her husband that he should use the bat as the trademark for the new rum he was producing. Her suggestion was inspired and pragmatic. Besides the idea's originality, Doña Amalia knew that, because levels of illiteracy at the time were extremely high, a product needed a distinctive and memorable graphic logo—a trademark—to become identifiable and sell. News of the excellent rum soon spread, the verbal accounts enhanced by local storytellers who affirmed that the bat brought good fortune and gave magical powers to the drink. Doña Amalia's husband was delighted. He had every reason to be. His name was Don Facundo Bacardi, and today the Bacardi bat device is one of the best-known trademarks in the world.

What Brands Are

A name together with a trademark, then, is a classic example of branding at its most rudimentary: brand as both guarantee of authenticity and trustworthy promise of performance. The American Marketing Association's traditional definition of a brand back in 1960 emphasized visual features as a means of brand differentiation: "A name, term, sign, symbol, or design, or a combination of them, intended to identify the goods or services of one seller or group of sellers and to differentiate them from those of competitors" (De Chernatony and Riley 1997, p. 90). Branding, though, has evolved into something much more complex than its original purpose. It is why Mercedes is more than just a range of cars, why AT&T is more than just another telephone company.

In searching for a definition of what a brand is it is illuminating to consider the differences between a product and a brand:

- You buy a product for what it does; you choose a brand for what it means.
- A product sits on retailers' shelves; a brand exists in consumers' minds.
- A product can quickly be outdated; a brand is timeless.
- A product can be copied by a competitor; a brand is unique.

A product becomes a brand when the physical product is augmented by something else—images, symbols, perceptions, feelings—to produce an integral idea greater than the sum of its parts. A brand might be composed of a single product, or it might be made up of multiple products that span many categories. But at its core there remains a soul, a distinctive identity and image that resonates with its consumers and transcends its physical representation in terms of product format. Lysol is the brand; Lysol Anti-Bacterial Kitchen Cleaner is the product.

The first two aforementioned observations—that we choose brands for what they mean and that brands exist in consumers' minds—are absolutely fundamental to understanding brands and are central tenets of this book. The two points are interrelated, as the meaning that brands have for us is a function of the way brands exist in our minds.

How Brands Exist in Our Minds

It bears repeating that a brand is created, not only as a result of a marketer's activities (the stimulus or "input") but also, critically, as a result of the consumer's reading of and reaction to those activities (the "take-out"). From the marketer's perspective, a brand is a promise, a covenant. From the consumer's, it is the set of associations, perceptions and expectations existing in his or her mind. Brand associations are created, sustained and enhanced by every experience and encounter a consumer has with the brand. A TV commercial is an encounter with the brand. So is using or physically consuming it. These experiences and encounters with the brand over time build up into collections of associations, influencing brand perceptions and forming a brand associative network, or *brand engram*.
In *Searching for Memory*, Daniel Schachter (1996, p. 59) describes engrams thus:

> "Engrams are the transient or enduring changes in our brains that result from encoding an experience.... A typical incident in our everyday lives consists of numerous sights, sounds, actions, and words. Different areas of the brain analyze these varied aspects of an event. As a result, neurons in the different regions become more strongly connected to one another. The new pattern of connections constitutes the brain's record of the event: the engram."

Along with other scientists and theorists, Schachter (1996, p. 71) calls into question the traditional view that a memory is simply an activated engram of a past event. He disputes the direct one-to-one correspondence between a piece of information stored away somewhere in our brain and the conscious experience of a memory that results when this piece of information is activated. So memories are neither created from scratch each time (other than those formed when we are very young), nor do they constitute an activated picture of a past event: "We do not shine a spotlight on a stored picture" (ibid.). Rather, neural network models are based on the principle that the brain stores engrams by strengthening connections between different neurons that participate in the encoding of an experience. When we encode an experience, connections between active neurons are reinforced, and this specific pattern of brain activity constitutes the engram. When we later try to remember the experience, a retrieval cue will induce another pattern of activity in the brain, and if this pattern is sufficiently similar to a previously encoded pattern, remembering will occur (ibid.).

New information and experience connects with existing networks, with any of the thousands or millions of engrams in the brain. These patterns of connection have the potential to enter into awareness at any moment, though mostly they lie dormant. In the case of a brand associative network the information or input comes from the numerous and diverse encounters with the brand. Each such encounter is a stimulus that is stored in the brain and adds to the associative network already existing for the brand. New information about the brand passes down a neural pathway and modifies the brand engram. The more frequently a pathway is traveled the better defined it becomes. So the more frequently a given element is connected with a brand engram, the more strongly it tends to be associated with that brand in our mind (see Heath and Howard-Spink 2000). The opposite also holds true. In other words, though brand associations are strengthened and consolidated over time through repetition, they weaken over time if they are not repeated. In the latter case if lots of new, different pathways are created, existing associations suffer interference from the increased noise or traffic, potentially leading to what Schachter (1996, p. 79) calls "an increasingly blurred engram."

In neuropsychological terms, then, a brand is "the totality of stored synaptic connections…. A web of connecting neurons that 'fire' together in different patterns" (Gordon and Ford-Hutchinson 2002, p. 48). As these connections between brand associations are reinforced over time they effectively come to define the brand in consumers' minds. The collective, associated meanings of a brand thus resemble the structure of a neural network, as illustrated in Figure 1.1.

Neural networks and synaptic connections sound a long way away from the American Marketing Association's 1960 definition of

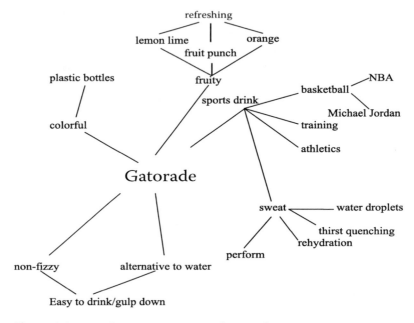

Figure 1.1   Brand as associative neural network.

a brand previously mentioned. The crucial difference is that today the concept of a brand is considered far more from the consumer's perspective than from the marketer's. For, ultimately, it is the consumer who assigns meaning to and therefore determines the fate of a brand, and consumers react not so much to reality per se but to their perception of reality. It is thus more accurate to describe a brand as *the consumer perception and interpretation of a cluster of associated attributes, benefits and values.*

Chapter 3 on perception will discuss how people perceive and interpret information and how this gives rise to meanings in our minds. Simplifying the previous statement, we can therefore arrive at a more concise definition of a brand:

> A brand is a cluster of meanings.

Though the nature of those meanings evolves over time, a brand remains always a cluster of meanings. Indeed, those meanings need to be constantly renewed, modified, burnished and, when necessary, rotated. Without brand meanings there is no brand: "Brands are first and foremost a bundle of meanings. Were it not for these meanings, it would be impossible to talk about brand images, brand personalities, or brand positions. When we craft brand experiences, we are doing so to communicate brand meanings" (McCracken 2005, p. 179).

The Brand Relationship

If a brand's foundations are composed of people's intangible mental associations about it, it follows that the stronger and more resilient the consumer's mental associations about the brand are, the stronger, potentially, is the intricate relationship between the brand and its consumer. Brands flourish or flounder on the strength of that relationship. The real importance of modifying a product formulation, amending the packaging or changing the advertising is the effect this will have on the consumer's relationship with the brand. Quite often people do not just buy one brand in a given category but swap among a repertoire of brands. Given the proliferation of brands available to them, they keep an open mind with regard to the brands they may potentially buy, maintaining a relatively wide consideration set. Once inside that evoked set, a brand must demonstrate that it is more relevant and appealing than its supposed peers by creating some advantage over its competition. Ultimately, through the special relationship that they forge with consumers, successful brands create a bond with those users, which secures their loyalty, ideally to the complete exclusion of the competition.

The way consumers relate to and interact with a brand both determines and is determined by what that brand means to its consumers. It is an ongoing, dynamic and multifaceted experience. As will be shown in the course of this book, the consumer's role in negotiating meaning from brands is a highly active one. Consumers turn to brands, among other resources, to help them affirm and construct identities. The nature of the brand–consumer relationship is defined by what the consumer looks for and expects from the brand. The resulting relationship may be similar to a personal relationship. With some brands this personal relationship is enshrined in the brand name—Uncle Ben's, Aunt Jemima's, for instance. The familiar abbreviation of Budweiser to Bud helps reinforce the way that brand is seen by its adherents. In a similar vein, a brand may be considered a confidante, like Tampax; a guide, like Microsoft ("Where do you want to go today?"); an advisor, like Charles Schwab; a protector, like

Legal & General and State Farm; or an ally, like Home Depot ("You can do it. We can help.").

Brands are about relationships, then, and relationships are about trust. According to the Henley Centre in the United Kingdom (1999), consumers place far more trust in the Kellogg's brand than they do in members of Parliament. The good will that people are prepared to invest in brands is immense. Even brands that suffer mishaps and make mistakes are "forgiven" by the public if it is felt that they act with integrity and are trustworthy. In 1982, seven people in the Chicago area died after taking Extra Strength Tylenol capsules that had been laced with cyanide. The capsules in question were each found to contain some 10,000 times the amount of cyanide that is necessary to cause death. Johnson & Johnson's handling of the Tylenol tampering crisis is considered a model of effective crisis management. The company immediately alerted the public nationwide and warned them not to take any type of Tylenol product. Advertising and production of the product were stopped and all Tylenol capsules were recalled from the market. The recall included around 31 million bottles of Tylenol, with a retail value of more than 100 million dollars. The company offered to exchange all Tylenol capsules that had already been purchased for Tylenol tablets. Although this move cost Johnson & Johnson millions of dollars more and there may not have been one microgram of cyanide in any of the capsules that were replaced, this initiative and the company's actions throughout the crisis illustrated its concern for the consumer, whose interests were put before financial considerations. As a result, Johnson & Johnson's reputation was preserved and further enhanced when it soon became the first company to introduce layers of tamper-resistant packaging to its products. Incredibly, not only did the Tylenol brand survive intact, but it also soon regained its original market share. Prompt and judicious action increased the perception of Tylenol's integrity and trustworthiness as a brand.

Such trust and confidence, though, have to be earned over time and through direct experience and interaction. Though it may be possible to buy awareness, a consumer's heart cannot be bought so easily. Many dotcoms found this out to their cost. They mistakenly believed that by throwing millions of dollars into events like the Super Bowl they could buy brand status and endear themselves to consumers. Of the first five dotcoms to advertise during the Super Bowl, four had disappeared not long afterward. Of course, goodwill, once earned, must be maintained. The trust deposited in a brand and the superior performance attributed to it derive from the brand's tangible and intangible qualities. These qualities are, and must be, experienced consistently over time by the consumer, both directly (through consumption) and indirectly (through, e.g., advertising and word of mouth recommendation). But if the covenant is broken— for example, if the manufacturer cuts corners by compromising on ingredients or lowering service levels or in any way jeopardizes the consumer's interests—consumer good will is soon withdrawn and the relationship turns southward.

The dependability that brands can offer has never been more relevant and attractive than in these times of failing social and financial institutions. The breakdown of the traditional family unit is a well-recorded global phenomenon. By way of example, the divorce rate in the United Status has increased from 25 percent in 1960 to its current level of around 48 percent. According to a report from the U.S. Census Bureau released in 2001, more than 20 million children, who account for more than 27 percent of young people in the country, were living in single-parent families around that time. Consistency over time, in both lived and mediated experience, creates a dependability and trust in brands of which consumers become highly appreciative and protective. Consider, for instance, the public outcry when Coca-Cola introduced New Coke in the United States and were soon forced to bring back Classic Coke. Or the uncompromising manner in which companies react to product contamination scares or the discovery of a technical fault in a product.

The ability of a brand to provide dependability in a less than perfect world was encapsulated in Volkswagen's famous slogan: "If only everything in life was as reliable as a Volkswagen." One of the TV commercials in which the slogan was featured is a 1987 U.K. commercial depicting a female protagonist defiantly casting off the material possessions her partner has given her—the earrings, the pearl necklace, the fur coat. She draws the line at the keys to the Volkswagen. The slogan is, of course, the generic brand promise of any strong, time-proven brand, but it is particularly apposite to a brand like Volkswagen whose consistent dependability at a product and mechanical level can and has been verified by consumers over the years. Brands of hotel chains are also well placed to deliver and benefit from the value of dependability. There is something very comforting about checking into a hotel far away from home, in an unknown city, without a hitch and safe in the knowledge that it will offer all the amenities that you always find with hotels of the same chain. Brands can be a source of comfort from change, transition and vulnerability. Brands such as Hovis bread in the United Kingdom or Pepperidge Farm in the United States evoke feelings of nostalgia and at the same time provide a sense of continuity and security: "Hovis. It's as good for you now as it's always been."

2

Human Motivation
How and Why We Seek Meaning

Introduction

Disney has been so phenomenally successful not because it branded a product but because it branded a meaning. Hallmark is a brand of greetings cards, but it is so much more. Hallmark enables us to give and receive love. Gillette amounts to something more than just a smooth shave. The phrase *Kodak moment* used (albeit sarcastically) by Lester Burnham's daughter Jane in *American Beauty* is instinctively understood by us all. This all sounds a long way away from antifriction blades, microfins, and multiformat picture taking. And it is. Until you think of ladders.

The highly insightful research technique called laddering investigates what connects consumers to categories and the products that compose them. Through a methodical system of probes laddering moves respondents from articulations of attributes that are relevant to them "up the ladder" to objective benefits, to more subjective benefits and, ultimately, to values. These "higher-order" values, such as self-esteem or pride in being a good mother, reveal the profound significance for consumers of a given product category. Personal values are important to understand because they have a strong influence on how we make decisions and are motivated to act the way we do. We will return to the specific technique of laddering later in this chapter.

Motivation consists of the drives, urges, wishes and desires that initiate a chain of events culminating in a given behavior. Need recognition occurs when a perceived discrepancy exists between an actual and a desired state of physical or psychological being. We then

11

act in response to that recognition and seek to fulfill and remove the need. Some motivational psychologists draw a distinction between needs and wants. Needs are seen as broad and basic biological and psychological requirements that propel behavior, whereas wants are described as the particular forms of consumption that are deemed to be capable of satisfying underlying needs—for example, the type of liquid that is sought to relieve thirst. In reality, though, there is little practical difference between the two: one person's needs are another's wants. The multitude of needs underpinning consumer motivation is complex and extensive, ranging from the raw physiological requirements for survival to needs of self-determination and definition. Understanding the needs to which consumers are responding and the values that ultimately guide them is a prerequisite to comprehending how those consumers derive personally relevant meaning from products and brands.

Human Needs

Consistent with the well-known hierarchy of needs devised by the American psychologist Abraham Maslow, it is possible to identify three basic categories or clusters of consumer needs: utilitarian needs, identity needs and emotive needs. Though less strong and primal than these three groupings, experiential needs lie somewhere between functional and emotive needs and are significant enough today to warrant inclusion in the following classification:

- Utilitarian needs are of a conscious, tangible and rational nature and have to do with specific tasks, physical processes and practical necessities.
- Experiential needs are primarily those that drive consumers to seek out stimulation of the senses.
- Identity needs are concerned with self-definition, social status, affiliation and affinity with certain social and cultural groups.
- Emotional needs are the least accessible to research and often lie deep in the psyche. Examples are the need for achievement or control. Whereas utilitarian needs and to an extent identity needs, form manifest motives for consumer behavior (motives known to the individual and freely admitted), emotional needs translate into latent motives and are either unknown to the individual or are such that the person is reluctant to admit them.

The interesting point to note here with regard to brand meaning is that, once basic needs have been materially satisfied, the more culturally meaningful aspects of consumption start to prevail and people become increasingly concerned with the more symbolic meanings of goods rather than with their functional use.

Needstates

The complex web of rational and, more often, emotional and unconscious needs that trigger consumer behavior is referred to as a needstate. An important distinction between modern-day consumer needstates and Maslow's model (and indeed similar models) is that, whereas the Maslow model is structured as a hierarchy and implies a progression, consumer needstates are in a constant state of flux, with different needs overlapping and intermingling. In particular, needstates are directly influenced by the context and situation in which an individual finds himself or herself: the atmosphere and environment and the individual's own mood, attitude and feelings—what we might call the individual's *moodstate*. It has been said that there are more differences between the same consumer making a brand choice on two different occasions than between two different consumers choosing the same brand on the same occasion (Gordon 1994).

Furthermore, our needs and priorities change over time. Take the oral care category. For many years Crest was market leader in the toothpaste category based on its cavity-reducing claim backed by the endorsement of the American Dental Association. People wanted to avoid getting holes in their teeth and needing to have fillings. Gradually this became less of an issue, thanks to the addition of fluoride to tap water, for instance. So people became more concerned about having fresh breath, reduction in plaque build-up and prevention of gingivitis. Today everybody wants to have white teeth, giving rise to a plethora of new products above and beyond toothpastes that offer extra whitening.

Brands succeed or fail on their ability to meet consumers' diverse needs. Indeed, brand benefits can be seen as the flip side of consumer needs, as illustrated in Figure 2.1. So, for instance, the functional features and benefits of a brand respond to consumers' utilitarian needs: convenient packaging, ability to shift stains without fading colors and so on.

Consumer needstates

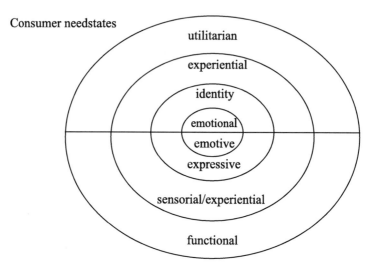

Brand benefits

Figure 2.1 Needstates/benefits.

Emotional and identity-related needs are met by the symbolic benefits that brands offer consumers. In particular, expressive benefits respond to identity needs and motives of self-definition, self-expression, assertion, reassurance and affiliation, among others. Consumers are, to a greater or lesser degree, conscious of such benefits: Status symbolism, for instance, is about the very deliberate and calculated acquisition of usually high-priced items to convey to others (and maybe reassure oneself of) a certain standing in society. More subtly and less consciously, a consumer may find himself or herself drawn to a brand that embodies values to which he or she also adheres. The deeply rooted, potentially suppressed, or unrecognized emotional needs we all have find a connection with the more subtle emotive benefits of brands.

Just as consumers are driven by a multiplicity of needs, so brands may simultaneously satisfy those needs at different levels. Thus, when Gillette proclaims, "The best a man can get," it is at once promising the most effective way to remove facial hair (functional benefit) and invoking some highly symbolic values (see p. 133 on Gillette). A woman approaching the ice cream cooler in a store may want to cool herself down and refresh her dry mouth. A fruity popsicle will appeal to her. Or, she may be hungry from having missed her lunch. A more substantial, creamy ice cream would be better.

A bit indulgent perhaps, but if she has worked through her lunch break she may feel she deserves a treat. Maybe she buys a small tub of Häagen-Dazs to take home and eat on the sofa, with a vague sense of its being "naughty but nice." Or perhaps she does not feel any guilt but, rather, feels fed up and unloved, in which case the ice cream serves as "comfort food." Whatever the origin of the need, the cabinet is full of products and brands offering her refreshment, nutrition, indulgence, comfort, compensation and sin—every one providing a different organoleptic experience: mouth-watering, smooth and creamy and so forth.

The Coexistence of Conflicting Needs

The "expression" versus "repression" polarities that are found in some brand mapping exercises have their roots in Sigmund Freud's psychoanalytical approach to human personality. According to Freud the *id*—uncoordinated, instinctual, pleasure seeking—is regulated by the *super ego*—our conscience, with its critical and moralizing influence over the guilt-ridden *ego*. To defend itself against guilt and angst, the ego develops mechanisms such as repression to send painful memories to the subconscious. Brands that would typically map toward the expressive end of the scale are feel-good, hedonistic brands providing sensual stimulation, such as perfumes. At the other, repressive, extreme of the dimension are do-good, utilitarian brands, which perform more serious roles and help relieve anxiety about personal health and well-being. Examples would be cold sore treatments or acne products. Most brands lie between these extremes, often combining do-good and feel-good benefits. Toothpastes that fight cavities or prevent gingivitis and at the same time offer fresh breath confidence are examples.

Implicit in the type of motivational hypotheses that Freud and Maslow put forward is the very complexity of the human psyche, for while one part of us may seek to belong and fit in, another may be hankering for self-actualization. The one drives us toward social affiliation and the other toward independence and individuation. Though these compelling urges pull us in opposite directions, there is nothing dysfunctional or schizophrenic about their coexistence within us. Similarly, most people have a strong need for safety and security: the reassurance of the familiar, the routine, staying within one's comfort zone. Yet at the same time we are enthralled by the potential excitement and reward of taking a risk and giving rein to our ambition, of challenging the status quo and putting ourselves to the test. As the saying goes, "You cannot discover new oceans unless you have the courage to lose sight of the shore."

Plotting these four instinctive urges along two axes gives us the needstate grid in Figure 2.2. In life we are permanently navigating our way along these axes, in a constant trade-off between opposing influences. When people branch out on their own, try their hand at something completely different or seek to fulfill their true potential, their actions are motivated by needs and desires represented in the bottom right quadrant. These have, at least temporarily, acquired the upper hand over the need for security and for conforming and sticking to the beaten path—urges that will force the psyche to seek some sort of balance. Similarly, when a brand identity corresponds to a particular quadrant or space within a quadrant, consumers will feel an instinctive pull toward that brand, according to their particular needstate. Because needs mapping is psychologically based, it offers consistency across different cultures and across demographics. It is "segmentation at source… before the constructs of personality, life-stage and socio-demographics…. The marketer is working with the raw stuff of human needs and motivations, the most solid material from which to create customer-driven marketing" (Goodyear 1996, p. 115).

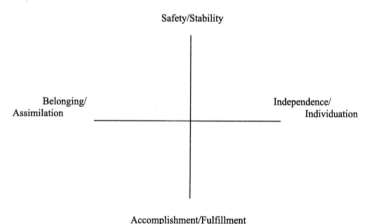

Figure 2.2   Needstate grid.

Human Values

In his book *The Nature of Human Values*, Milton Rokeach (1973, p. 5) defined a value as "an enduring belief that a specific mode of conduct or end state of existence is personally or socially preferable to an opposite or converse mode of conduct or end state of existence." Values are organized into value systems, which are hierarchies based on a prioritization of an individual's values in terms of the strength of those values. Values influence attitude and behavior, so one value system determines how we interact with friends and family, another how we behave in our work environment and so forth. Generally speaking, values are more stable and enduring than attitudes. The Rokeach Value Survey (RVS), designed by Rokeach to operationalize his value theory, is used to measure personal and social values. The RVS distinguishes two kinds of values:

1. Instrumental values reflect modes of conduct and behavioral characteristics that are ways of reaching terminal values.
2. Terminal values reflect end states of existence or a desirable end state in life that an individual would like to achieve. These values may be self-centered or society centered.

The 36 values identified in the RVS are shown in Table 2.1. Personal values play an important role in determining consumer behavior. "Freedom" as an important terminal value to an individual, for example, may imply a desire for freedom of choice and an interest in wide product lines and differentiated products. The instrumental value of "independent" might prompt a consumer to seek out customized or unique products that allow expression of his or her own personality and distinctiveness.

Other commentators have expanded on Rokeach's definition of values, notably social psychologist Shalom Schwartz (2003, p. 262), who summarizes the main features of basic values as follows:

1. Values are beliefs, cognitive structures that are closely linked to affect. When values are incited they become imbued with feeling.
2. Values pertain to desirable goals or end states, such as social equality or fairness.
3. Values transcend specific situations or actions. This characteristic of transsituationality differentiates values from narrower concepts like attitudes, which tend to be more situation specific.

4. Values serve as standards or criteria that guide selection and evaluation of behavior, policies and events.

5. Values are ordered by importance relative to one another, the result being a system of value priorities by which cultures and individuals can be characterized.

6. The relative importance of the set of relevant values guides action. The example given by Schwartz is how attending church might express and promote the multiple values of tradition, conformity, security and benevolence for a person—but at the expense of hedonism, self-direction and stimulation values.

The Schwartz Value Survey (SVS) (Schwartz 1992) is widely used by social and cross-cultural psychologists. Consistent with the definition of values as "desirable, transsituational goals, varying in importance, that serve as guiding principles in peoples' lives" (Schwartz 2003, p. 267), Schwartz and colleagues' global research has identified ten basic, universal values, or value types. These are derived from three universal requirements of the human condition: the needs of

TABLE 2.1 Instrumental and Terminal Values

Instrumental Values	Terminal Values
Ambitious	A comfortable life
Broad-minded	An exciting life
Capable	A sense of accomplishment
Cheerful	A world at peace
Clean	A world of beauty
Courageous	Equality
Forgiving	Family security
Helpful	Freedom
Honest	Happiness
Imaginative	Inner harmony
Independent	Mature love
Intellectual	National security
Logical	Pleasure
Loving	Salvation
Obedient	Self-respect
Polite	Social recognition
Responsible	True friendship
Self-controlled	Wisdom

TABLE 2.2   Definitions of Motivational Types of Values in Terms of Their Goals and the Single Values that Represent Them

POWER: Social status and prestige, control or dominance over people and resources (social power, authority, wealth, preserving my public image)

ACHIEVEMENT: Personal success through demonstrating competence according to social standards (successful, capable, ambitious, influential)

HEDONISM: Pleasure and sensuous gratification for oneself (pleasure, enjoying life, self-indulgence)

STIMULATION: Excitement, novelty and challenge in life (daring, a varied life, an exciting life)

SELF-DIRECTION: Independent thought and action-choosing, creating, exploring (creativity, freedom, independent, curious, choosing own goals)

UNIVERSALISM: Understanding, appreciation, tolerance and protection for the welfare of all people and for nature (broad-minded, wisdom, social justice, equality, a world at peace, a world of beauty, unity with nature, protecting the environment)

BENEVOLENCE: Preservation and enhancement of the welfare of people with whom one is in frequent personal contact (helpful, honest, forgiving, loyal, responsible)

TRADITION: Respect, commitment and acceptance of the customs and ideas that traditional culture or religion provide the self (humble, accepting my portion in life, devout, respect for tradition, moderate)

CONFORMITY: Restraint of actions, inclinations and impulses likely to upset or harm others and violate social expectations or norms (politeness, obedient, self-discipline, honoring parents and elders)

SECURITY: Safety, harmony and stability of society, of relationships and of self (family security, national security, social order, clean, reciprocation of favors)

individuals as biological organisms, the needs pertaining to social interaction and the survival and welfare needs of groups of people.

Each of the ten basic value types can be further characterized in terms of their central motivational goal. These are shown in Table 2.2 (Schwartz 2007, p. 166), together with (in parentheses) specific, single-value items that primarily represent each of the ten basic value types.

The important contribution of Schwartz's work is that it expounds the structural aspect of values and the dynamics of the relations among them. Behaviors that are motivated by a given value have

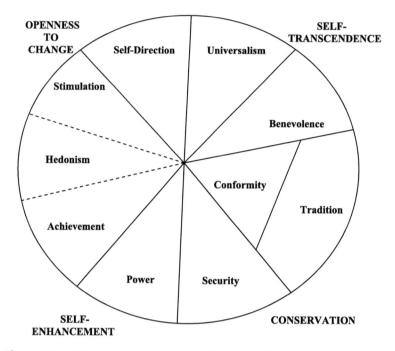

Figure 2.3 Schwartz's theoretical model of relations among ten motivational types of values.

social and psychological consequences that may either be at odds with or compatible with the pursuit of other values. Schwartz gives the example of how the pursuit of novelty and change (i.e., stimulation values) may adversely impact on the preservation of time-honored customs and practices (i.e., traditional values). Conversely, the pursuit of tradition values is congruent with the pursuit of conformity values, as both motivate behavior characterized by submission to external expectations (Schwartz 1992, p. 15).

Schwartz (2007, p. 167) plots these basic value types on a circumplex where the circular arrangement of the value types represents a motivational continuum. In this model (Figure 2.3) opposite value types are inversely related so that the more distant any two value types are from each other on the circumplex, the more incompatible and antagonistic their underlying motivations are. By the same token, the closer together two value types are in any direction around the circle, the more alike and compatible the underlying motivations. Schwartz further summarizes this integrated structure of values with two broad dimensions: self-enhancement versus self-transcendence and openness to change versus conservatism. With the former dimension, power and achievement value types (concerned with self-interests) oppose universalism and benevolence value types (concerned with the welfare and interests of others). In the case of openness to change versus conservatism, self-direction and stimulation value types (marked by independence of thought and action and disposition to new experience) oppose security, conformity and tradition value types (marked by self-restriction, order and resistance to change). Hedonism is deemed to contain elements of both openness to change and self-enhancement.

Besides determining consumer behavior on an individual basis as mentioned earlier, investigating and tracking values can both reflect and predict major social change and cultural currents in societies. We will return to the theme of cultural values and their significance for brands in Chapter 7.

Means-End Theory

Early approaches to the topic of product meaning tended to be from the product attribute perspective, whereby meaning was tied to the physical, observable characteristics of the product. This failed to recognize any type of personal meanings derived from those attributes. Given the limitations this implied, product meaning was expanded to take into account both the functional and nonfunctional benefits that attributes represented for the consumer. The focus was subsequently broadened further to cover yet higher levels of abstraction, that is, personal values. The application of the personal values perspective to consumer understanding finds optimal expression in means-end theory (Gutman 1982).

Means-end theory is an invaluable resource in investigating product meaning for two reasons: (1) Rather than concentrate on a particular level of meanings, it incorporates all levels into a conceptual framework; and (2) it focuses on the associations (i.e., derived meanings) between the levels. These associational linkages provide understanding of how consumers interpret product attributes ("means") as representing benefits to them (referred to as consequences) and how these benefits are ultimately translated into personal values ("ends"). It is this associational element of the means-end model that offers keen insight into the meanings that consumers derive from

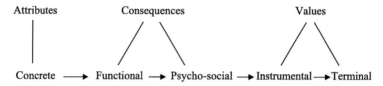

Attributes   Consequences   Values

Concrete ——→ Functional ——→ Psycho-social ——→ Instrumental ——→ Terminal

Figure 2.4   Means-end chain model.

products. Figure 2.4 illustrates a means-end model with three levels of abstraction.

The standard method for uncovering and assessing cognitive structure behind means-end hierarchy is laddering. Laddering refers to both the research process and the analysis methodology. The research entails in-depth one-to-one interviewing where the subject is probed, typically with the question, "Why is that important to you?" with the objective of identifying perceptual linkages between attributes (A), consequences (C) and values (V). For example, the ladder in Figure 2.5, beginning with a basic distinction among different types of snack chips, represents part of the data collection from a single subject in a study of the salty snack market (Reynolds and Gutman 1988).

Once all the laddering data are collected and analyzed, dominant connections can be arranged in a graphical representation of means-ends structures aggregated across all subjects (in "chains"), called a hierarchical value map (HVM). This cognitive map, with its connecting lines, shows the common pathways of meanings, representing the ways product attributes are related to personal values. Incidentally, after initial distinctions are obtained from perceived differences among particular brands of products, all subsequent higher-level elements are not brand specific. Although laddering charts the intrinsic meaning of product categories, as opposed to brands, consumers access categories through brands. Accordingly, it is instructive to consider the extent to which a particular

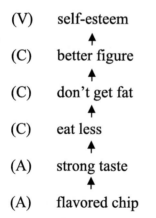

(V)	self-esteem
(C)	better figure
(C)	don't get fat
(C)	eat less
(A)	strong taste
(A)	flavored chip

Figure 2.5   Single-subject ladder from salty snack study.

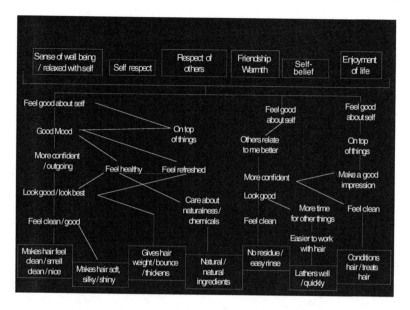

Figure 2.6 Hierarchical value map for the shampoo category.

brand may reflect the hierarchical linkages identified by laddering for its category. Close Up is an example of a brand that has been moved up the toothpaste ladder or at least one toothpaste ladder. In the beginning the brand communication was more attribute led, with visuals of the "mouthwash in the toothpaste" connoting freshness. Gradually it has moved up to social confidence and self-confidence values, with recent brand communication in some countries featuring complete strangers coming up to snatch kisses from unsuspecting women. It seems an appropriate ladder progression for a brand called Close Up.

The HVM thus presents a picture of consumers' underlying personal motivations in respect to a particular product category. Figure 2.6 shows an example of a HVM for the shampoo category. The HVM, though, is useful not only in understanding consumer motivation and meaning patterns of products and categories. It can also be used in the development and evaluation of product positionings in the marketplace. Each unique pathway from attribute to value represents a perceptual orientation and a potential product positioning. Untapped orientations may be discovered, offering an obvious positioning opportunity. Or it may be possible to establish ownership of a meaning by forging a stronger connection within an existing association that is relatively weak—or to develop new meanings by creating significant connections between two as yet unrelated elements (Gengler and Reynolds 1995).

Means-end theory and laddering clearly offer substantial benefits through the understanding they provide of the meaningful connections between consumers and products and categories. To quote Gengler and Reynolds (1995, p. 30), "... *the successful implementation of the Means-End approach to strategy is the realization that meaning is everything.*... Analysis of consumer perceptions of the reasons that drive decision-making behavior should be framed as a study of meaning." (italics in original)

Emotion

It is not without significance that the words *emotion* and *motivation* both have their roots in the Latin word *movere,* meaning "to move." Emotions are motivational in nature in that they arouse certain behavioral responses and patterns. They lie at the very heart of the way we experience life and all its vicissitudes. They determine our values and ethics, influence our judgments and give our lives color and meaning. Inputs from various fields and disciplines over the last few decades have broadened our understanding of emotions, but alternative and sometimes conflicting theories and definitions abound.

Before looking in more detail at what emotions are, their importance in a brand context should be emphasized. There are two key dynamics driving this importance. The first has to do with the fact that cognition and emotion are intertwined, as is discussed elsewhere in the book. What people feel about brands is integrated in what they think about brands. The second dynamic relates to the way memory works. When we experience something meaningful enough to be processed, the component parts of the experience are stored in different parts of our memory. Included in these components is any emotion associated with the experience. Emotional memories are stored in our unconscious. When a memory is triggered, all the component parts are reassembled in an instant, including the emotions associated with the memory. Brand encounters are part of our daily experiences and are thus characterized by the emotional memories associated with them. This is how brand meaning is imprinted in the psyche. Without emotions no mental connection is created. In the opposite case, a mental connection is made and brand meaning is imprinted.

So what is emotion? Emotion can be described as the subjective, internal experience by an individual of a complex pattern of bodily and mental changes in reaction to some situation (as opposed to the emotion being somehow consciously willed to occur). Psychologists have identified four components of an emotional reaction:

- A feeling or affective response, such as the experience of joy or anger
- A cognitive response: an interpretation of the situation, perception of the cause of the emotion and the label attached to the emotion
- A physiological response: physical changes in the body, such as elevated heart rate and blood pressure
- A behavioral response: a facial expression or a particular action

Cognitive appraisal occurs to evaluate whether the situation is of significance to our own well-being. Such evaluation often occurs unconsciously and has a biological or evolutionary origin—tied to our instinct for safety and survival, for example. Different emotions manifest themselves in different ways: For instance, fear, anger, disgust and surprise have distinctive facial expressions. It is also important to clarify that though the words are often used interchangeably, emotions and feelings are not the same thing. Feelings are the conscious experiences of emotions—the sensations we have when emotions become more conscious. Emotions and emotional drivers sit in our psyche ready for activation. Often, we are not even conscious of having emotional reactions or are unaware why we are reacting. This is because emotional reactions and emotional experiences can take place with little or no conscious or cognitive participation.

Theories of how emotional experience is produced tend to differ in terms of the sequential relationships they posit among emotion, cognition and behavior. The theories of Robert Zajonc are among the soundest. Zajonc's (1980) theory of emotion proposes that emotional reactions may occur both before cognition and without cognition and, furthermore, that emotional reactions may occur without any conscious registration of the stimuli. According to Zajonc, emotional reactions are quicker than interpretive and discriminative ones. In other words, emotions are autonomous reactions that occur before the emotion is interpreted. The suggestion that emotional reactions may be prewired helped fuel the debate on the relation between emotion and cognition.

Types of Emotions

How many different emotions do human beings experience? The answer depends on what system is used to classify emotions. Psychologists and philosophers have sought to identify the basic or primary human emotions. In 1650 René Descartes declared that there were six primary passions: love, hate, desire, joy, sadness and admiration. More recently, Robert Plutchik (1980) put forward a system based on eight primary emotions, each tied to some adaptive form of behavior or body process (innate or inborn emotions with survival value, so fear > escape, anger > destruction or removal of barriers, joy > attachment). Table 2.3 summarizes the groupings of basic emotions identified by different psychologists (Ortony and Turner, 1990).

Some commentators believe that the basic emotions have a biological origin, whereas others dispute this. Different nuances and intensities of these primary emotions may appear to be different emotions, but, according to Plutchik (1980), they are really similar to the primary emotion from which they derive. They simply carry a different label. So, for example, what we call *fear* when experienced at a medium intensity level is called *terror* when experienced at a high intensity level and *nervousness* or *apprehension* when experienced at a low intensity. Similarly, psychologists have proposed the idea of thinking of emotions in terms of dimensions or of families, with the primary emotion as the emotional nucleus and the members of the "family" rippling out from the core in various mutations (see, e.g., Goleman 1995). This is illustrated in Table 2.4. Additionally, some theorists have postulated that all emotions are to some extent and in some proportion, combinations of the basic emotions. So, for instance, according to Plutchik's theory of emotional blends and nuances, fear and surprise combine to produce awe, surprise and sadness to produce disappointment.

As Figure 2.7 depicts, moods lie in the outer reaches and tend to be milder and more subdued than emotions (Donaghey 2002). They are less spontaneous and more controllable than emotions. Far more enduring is temperament, the disposition to evoke certain emotions or moods that makes people happy-go-lucky or melancholy. Temperament becomes part of a person's psychological make-up and personality.

There is considerable debate over the extent to which emotions and emotional experiences are universal or culturally determined.

TABLE 2.3   Basic Emotions Identified by Psychologists

Psychologist	Basic Emotions	Basis for Inclusion
Arnold (1960)	Anger, aversion, courage, dejection, desire, despair, fear, hate, hope, love, sadness	Relation to action tendencies
Ekman, Friesen, and Ellsworth (1982)	Anger, disgust, fear, joy, sadness, surprise	Universal facial expressions
Frijda (1986)	Desire, happiness, interest, surprise, wonder, sorrow	Forms of action readiness
Gray (1982)	Rage and terror, anxiety, joy	"Hardwired"
Izard (1971)	Anger, contempt, disgust, distress, fear, guilt, interest, joy, shame, surprise	"Hardwired"
James (1884)	Fear, grief, love, rage	Involvement of the body
McDougall (1926)	Anger, disgust, elation, fear, subjection, tender emotion, wonder	Relation to instincts
Mowrer (1960)	Pain, pleasure	Unlearned emotional states
Oatley and Johnson-Laird (1987)	Anger, disgust, anxiety, happiness, sadness	Do not require propositional content
Panksepp (1982)	Expectancy, fear, rage, panic	"Hardwired"
Plutchik (1980)	Acceptance, anger, anticipation, disgust, joy, fear, sadness, surprise	Relation to adaptive biological processes
Tomkins (1984)	Anger, interest, contempt, disgust, distress, fear, joy, shame, surprise	Density of neural firing
Watson (1930)	Fear, love, fury	"Hardwired"
Weiner and Graham (1984)	Happiness, sadness	Attribution independent

Basic emotions are constant across all cultures. Where there is variance is in terms of societal or conditioned emotions and the display rules and regulation of emotions. Conditioned emotions are those that are molded by our status as societal beings. Emotions such as guilt, humiliation and pride are very much influenced by being in the pubic domain. Display rules—that is, when and how to express an emotion—are learned as part of socialization and enculturalization

TABLE 2.4   "Families" of Emotions

Anger	annoyance, irritability, animosity, vexation, resentment, indignation, acrimony, exasperation, vexation, wrath, hostility, fury, outrage and, at the extreme, pathological hatred and violence
Sadness	cheerlessness, gloom, melancholy, self-pity, sorrow, grief, dejection, despair and, when pathological, severe depression
Fear	apprehension, nervousness, concern, misgiving, wariness, qualm, edginess, anxiety, consternation, dread, fright, terror; as a psychopathology, phobia and panic
Enjoyment	contentment, amusement, relief, pride, satisfaction, gratification, happiness, joy, delight, thrill, bliss, rapture, euphoria, ecstasy and, at the extreme, mania
Love	acceptance, kindness, friendliness, trust, affinity, devotion, adoration, infatuation
Surprise	amazement, astonishment, wonder, shock
Disgust	distaste, aversion, disdain, contempt, scorn, abhorrence, revulsion
Shame	embarrassment, guilt, chagrin, remorse, regret, humiliation

and may differ from culture to culture as well as in different contexts or roles. Some degree of regulation of emotions is necessary in a society in which many people live together. In cultures that emphasize social interdependence, for example, negative emotions are rarely displayed openly. On the other hand, although keeping a "stiff upper lip" may be seen as an admirable trait by some, regulation of emotions and in particular repression of emotions, consumes a lot of energy as emotions occur automatically.

Although researchers acknowledge that words and language we use are not a totally adequate channel for probing or communicating the full gamut of emotion and emotional experience, they can reveal interesting cultural differences. Language enables us to become conscious of and to seek to convey our thoughts and feelings. Societies and cultures differ in their depiction and description of different feelings and emotions. All languages have lexically encoded different scenarios or states involving feelings and emotions. The meanings of these words are language specific and may often not match across languages and cultures. For example, there is no direct German translation for the word innocent (*unschuldig* means, literally, "unguilty"). Likewise, there is no English equivalent of the Russian word

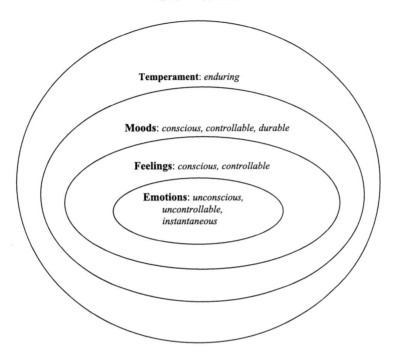

Figure 2.7   From emotions to temperament.

toska, meaning something like "melancholy-cum-yearning." The Portuguese word *saudade* has a similar but not identical meaning. The German word *Schadenfreude* means roughly "joy at somebody else's misfortune." The word *upset*, with its underlying metaphor of the upsetting of usual equilibrium (as in an upset vase), has no direct translation into other languages. Indeed, the very notion of *feeling upset* carries cultural baggage—the central concern being about losing balance, harmony, or control. Considering the dynamics of language and the emotions and meanings that words convey is important in the context of brand meaning. Over time, brands build up a brand vocabulary—the words that are associated with a brand, not just in its slogan but in its product descriptors, in print and online advertising and editorial, for instance.

Though there is not room to cover the subject here, research has examined the manner in which intervening emotional reactions to advertising mediate the relationship between advertising content and attitudes toward the ad or the brand being advertised. Holbrook and Batra (1987), for example, identified that the three emotional dimensions of pleasure, arousal and domination mediate the effects of advertising content on attitudes toward the advertising and that the combined result partially mediates the effects of advertising content on attitudes toward the brand itself. Whether through advertising or the direct use of a product or service, the role of emotion is fundamental to an understanding of brands and the meanings they have for us.

Self-Definition

Postmodern society is characterized by the recognition that individuals today are involved in the ongoing task of negotiating meanings from lived and mediated experiences in an attempt to create and sustain their identity. Amid the disintegration of nation states and political blocs, the waning of religious authority, the unreliability of other social institutions and the breakup of the nuclear family, individuals are often left facing uncertainty, fragmentation and ever more indeterminate meaning. In the face of what Giddens (1991, p. 201) rather bleakly calls the "looming threat of personal meaninglessness," the individual is thrown back onto his or her own resources as he or she seeks to construct an identity that will endure through rapidly changing times and circumstances: "A self-identity has to be created and more or less continually reordered against the backdrop of shifting experiences of day-to-day life and the fragmenting tendencies of modern institutions" (Giddens 1991, p. 198).

The existentialist Søren Kierkegaard in the nineteenth century and Jean-Paul Sartre in the post-World War II period had predicated a form of existentialist angst that comes with our being "condemned to be free," that is, free to determine our own essence by our temporary, transient choices of what we would like to be. According to existentialist thought, we alone are the source of whatever meaning or value the world has for us; we are responsible for giving meaning to our world. In a similar vein, Carl Jung contended that people are constantly compelled to search for meaning in life. In the postmodern world, the self is neither a given nor a fixed entity and nothing can be taken for granted. Rather, each of us must actively create our reality and identity and in so doing we are a product of sociocultural structures and circumstances. Social interaction is instrumental in the fashioning of identity, as we traverse myriad social situations, with yet more complexity accruing from the mediated experiences offered by the mass media. We are thus exposed to and engaged in

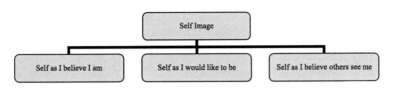

Figure 2.8   Self-image.

what Giddens (1991) terms a "plurality of lifeworlds," each with its own social roles, norms and values. This notion contrasts with the Cartesian concept of a highly individualist, autonomous and unitary self.

An individual's self-image is an amalgam of several dimensions: the self that I believe I am, the self that I would like to be (the ideal self) and the self that I believe others perceive me to be (Figure 2.8). This third conception of self, as perceived and influenced by the perceptions of significant others, peer groups, reference groups and so forth, is a critical component of identity. The sociologist Charles Horton Cooley coined the term "looking-glass self" to describe the way we develop a self-concept through our perceiving and imagining how others perceive and react to us. Viewed from this perspective, the self-concept emerges from social interaction. Other protagonists of the symbolic interactionism school of sociology added to Cooley's ideas. G. H. Mead later referred to Cooley's aforementioned process as the development of the "generalized other." For his part, Erving Goffman (1959), in *The Presentation of Self in Everyday Life*, described the principles of what he called "impression management" and the "dramaturgical performance" in which we engage, reminiscent of Shakespeare's lines:

> All the world's a stage,
> And all the men and women merely players ...

People tend to convey impressions that are somewhere between an accurate presentation of their self-image and one oriented toward their desired identities. One way individuals endeavor to establish identity (and it is but one way, which should be neither exaggerated nor underestimated) is through consumption patterns. As consumers become less preoccupied with buying provisions to satisfy physical needs, there is a shift toward a pattern of consumption whereby goods are increasingly used to create and express self-identity. Brands can play a role in this process—particularly when they are associated more with products that are likely to be on public display rather than those that are consumed privately. In a kind of self-symbolizing process, a person may buy and use a certain brand to affirm his or her actual self-concept or buy and use a brand to "lay claim" to a desired or idealized identity image. The latter is a form of what has been called symbolic self-completion (Wicklund and Gollwitzer 1982):

Actual self + Brand = Ideal self

Material goods, then, are consumed as symbolic signifiers of identity, lifestyle and taste. Belk (1988) writes of "extending the self" through ownership of material goods, and other commentators have highlighted the role of consumption in the context of what Gergen (1991) calls the "saturated self": a multidimensional self or assemblage of self-definitions into a "pastiche personality." The individual envisions a number of imagined possible selves and may create any variety of these within the framework of his or her particular socio-cultural context. Furthermore, we all have a variety of roles—a man may be a husband, a father, a police officer, a sports coach and a wine enthusiast. Each of these roles has a certain set of norms, values and characteristics attached to it. Often people engage in a prototype-matching process, seeking to make their social images conform as closely as possible to the prototypical characteristics of a given role (see Leary and Kowalski 1990). For each role people will have an associated self-image that they will feel the need to express. The self-expressive benefits of brands come into play here, helping us to express and define ourselves. See section on expressive benefits (Chapter 5) for examples.

As consumers use the symbolic meanings inherent in the cultural environment to create and maintain their multiple identities, they come to learn to accommodate shared meanings and also to develop individual symbolic interpretations of their own. Again, in this respect, the consumer "is nothing if not an actor in search of an identity.... The post-modern subject constructs itself around the image it projects for others in consumer culture. 'I am what you perceive me to be.' Consumption enables people to change hats as the occasion demands" (Oswald 1996).

The subtle but important difference between brand identity and personal identity in a brand context is worth underlining here. Organizations create brand identities (e.g., logos, packaging, design).

People construct identities for themselves employing a variety of means, including brands and the meanings that they come to hold for them. This conceptualization of what a consumer is and how a consumer behaves marks a radical departure from conventional wisdom. In particular, there is a huge divergence between the way traditional marketing theory considers the consumer and the more modern, holistic and multidisciplinary approach taken by commentators from the social sciences. As Grant McCracken (1990) suggests, the usual models of consumer behavior depict the consumer as a kind of proto-economic man or *homo economicus*, driven purely by concerns of economic advantage and benefit. The purely economic definition of what consumer means is no longer sufficient.

McCracken (1986), like the previously mentioned commentators, points out that a central tenet of postmodern consumer theory is that consumers make consumption choices not only for utilitarian gain (or even for reasons of brand likeability alone) but also for the symbolic meanings of these choices. People consume not only physical products but also—or, often, instead—the symbolic meaning of those products, in the creation and expression of personal and social aspects of identity. Self-definition is sought, in part, "through the systematic appropriation of the meaningful properties of goods" (ibid., p. 80). We will return to the theme of symbolic consumption and personal and social identity, in Chapter 4, in the context of the meanings that inhere in consumption goods.

So, we seek and achieve identity by inserting ourselves into a discourse or one of a number of discourses—what Valentine and Gordon (2000) call "moments of identity." By "romancing" its consumers, through the generation of an appealing and accessible narrative in which those consumers are invited to participate, brands can provide both the structure and the raw material for meaningful discourse. There is, perhaps, no better illustration than the Harley-Davidson brand, which is discussed in more detail in Chapter 7. Often, the discourses with which we engage in life, consciously or more usually unconsciously, are intertwined with the archetypal patterns running through our psyche. "I therefore claim to show," wrote structural anthropologist Claude Lévi-Strauss, "not how men think in myths, but how myths operate in men's minds without their being aware of the fact" (Lévi-Strauss 1983, p. 12). Let us look further at these archetypal representations and the myths or stories with which they are associated.

Archetypal Theory

Jung's Legacy

Maslow defined self-actualization, the highest level of human fulfillment, thus: "What a man can be he must be." The ideal finds expression in a previous advertising slogan for the U.S. Army's recruitment
campaign: "Be all that you can be." To hopeful young recruits, the
army signifies a lifetime opportunity to prove themselves and realize
their potential. It is a heroic call, reminiscent of John F. Kennedy's
"Ask not what your country can do for you. Ask what you can do for
your country." Or the film *Braveheart*. Or Frank Sinatra singing "My
Way." Or Nike, the winged Greek goddess of victory and the brand
that takes its name from her. We are, here, entering into archetypal
territory, an important potential area of brand meaning.

The deep and primal motivating forces within us, like the yearn-
ing to be heroic or the desire to go out and explore our world, are as
universal as they are timeless. Jung first identified these profound
psychic imprints as archetypes. His theory divides the psyche into
three parts. The first is the ego, which Jung identifies with the conscious mind. Closely related is the personal unconscious, comprising
anything that is not presently conscious but that can become so. The
personal unconscious corresponds to most people's understanding
of the unconscious in that it includes both memories that are easily
brought to mind and those that have been suppressed for some reason. The third part of the psyche identified by Jung, which sets him
apart from other psychologists and psychoanalysts, is that of the collective unconscious. This is our "psychic inheritance"—the reservoir
of our experiences as a species, a knowledge we are all born with. The
contents of the collective unconscious are called archetypes.

Jung wrote, "Archetypes are like riverbeds which dry up when
the water deserts them, but which it can find again at any time. An
archetype is like an old watercourse along which the water of life has
flowed for centuries, digging a deep channel for itself. The longer it
has flowed in this channel the more likely it is that sooner or later the
water will return to its old bed" (Jung, C.W. Vol. 10, p. 189). Archetypes represent fundamental aspects of the human condition. They
tap into our profoundest motivations and provide deep structure for
our sense of meaning. The archetypal imprints that are hardwired
in our psyches are described by Jung as unlearned tendencies to

experience things in a certain way, "forms which are unconscious but nonetheless active—living dispositions, ideas in the Platonic sense, that preform and continually influence our thoughts and feelings and actions" (Jung C.W. Vol. 9, part 1, para 154). The archetype thus acts as an "organizing principle" on the things we do or feel. The way a particular archetype is represented or its content, is not determined or inherited—only the form or "possibility of representation."

Take the mother archetype as an example. Our ancestors all had mothers. A mother or mother substitute was part of the environment in which we grew up. As vulnerable babies we depended on our connection to a nurturing protector for our very survival. Little wonder that when we enter this world we are preconditioned to need, want, seek and recognize a mother. The mother archetype, then, is our innate ability to recognize a certain relationship, that of mothering. According to Jung, as this is somewhat abstract we project the archetype onto the physical world and onto a particular person, usually our own mothers. In the absence of such a human form, we tend to personify the archetype, turning it into a mythological storybook character. This character symbolizes the archetype. The mother archetype is symbolized by Mother Earth, the motherland, and numerous mythological representations. The father archetype is often symbolized by a guide or an authority figure.

Archetypal representations surface in abundance in literature, art, mythology and film. They can be found in fairy tales, parables and songs. When we encounter an archetypal myth, symbol or character we instinctively feel an emotional pull. Consider the lover archetype in the Cinderella story, Mills and Boon romances, *Casablanca* and *Titanic*. Or outlaw figures in the *Godfather* or *Rebel without a Cause*. The mythological stories in which archetypes are brought to life are intrinsic to humankind, part of our inherited psychic make-up, as suggested by the aforementioned quote from Lévi-Strauss. Archetypal characters can also be seen in real-life figures whose personalities seem to take on larger-than-life significance: Florence Nightingale and Mother Teresa as caretakers, for instance. Some practitioners of archetypal theory refer to the mythological representations of archetypes—in Greek and Roman mythology, for instance—contending that the pantheon of the gods is populated by representations of our deepest psychic selves: heroic figures like mighty Heracles or the courageous Achilles; intrepid explorers such as Jason or Odysseus; or Aphrodite, the Greek goddess of love and beauty.

In his classic book *The Hero with a Thousand Faces* Joseph Campbell (1973) surveys the myths of ancient peoples and different cultures and concludes that they are all founded on the same archetypal plot line or monomyth: the archetypal hero story. The same hero appears in each myth—hence the book title. Campbell's work was the inspiration for George Lucas's *Star Wars*—it also inspired the American public at large; 30 million people are estimated to have seen *The Power of Myth,* the public television serialization of Campbell's ideas. And the story of Luke Skywalker is nothing more than the retelling of one of the world's oldest myths. It is always the story of a hero's journey and transformation. There is a call to adventure. The hero sets off. Along the way he meets a mentor who helps to guide and orient him. Then obstacles are encountered—there are evil dragons to be slain; Indiana Jones must confront the Gestapo, snakes and knife-wielding enemies. The hero, though, overcomes these difficulties and fulfills the quest, returning home triumphantly, transformed by his experiences and ready to share his new knowledge for the good of humankind. The essence of the hero is selfless courage. The hero will endure separation and hardship for the sake of his people, knowing that a price must be paid to achieve the goal. Real-life figures such as Martin Luther King Jr. and Nelson Mandela are the hero archetype made flesh and blood.

Brand Application

The relevance of archetypal theory in a marketing context is well expressed on the Web site of the Center for Applications of Psychological Type (https://www.capt.org/discover-your-archetypes/about-archetypes.htm):

> "Because archetypes are the meaning magnets of the psyche, they provide a bridge between the deepest human motivations and felt experience (including products and services) that fulfill, or promise to fulfill, basic human needs."

Brands that tap into deep, primordial experiences and motivations establish an emotional affinity and forge deep-rooted connections with consumers. They acquire a kind of meaning that is universal, iconic and larger than life—symbolic meaning, which, more often than not, turns out to be archetypal meaning. It is important to point out that, whereas strong brands are typically identified with one archetype, humans are much more multifaceted and a range of archetypes can appeal to us, depending on our needs and circumstances at any one time. The nature of an archetypal relationship between a brand and a consumer is that the brand, not the consumer, embodies the archetype or archetypal meaning. The connection occurs when the archetype appeals to the part of the consumer's psyche that is open and receptive to the archetype—when the trickster brand strikes a chord with the trickster part of us. "For the lover in you," "Brings out the hero in you," run the slogans. We are dealing here with human yearnings, often unfulfilled yearnings, that exert a strong motivational influence on our attitudes and behavior.

To quote a Harley-Davidson executive, "What we sell is the ability for a 43-year-old accountant to dress in black leather, ride through small towns and have people be afraid of him" (Ulrich, Zenger and Smallwood 1999, p. 38). There is no set limit to the number of potential archetypes, and their descriptions vary from one commentator to another. At any rate, the important thing is the meaning and nature of the archetype in question rather than its name. Let us look at some of the most commonly encountered archetypes in both a broad cultural context and a brand marketing framework, with some of their defining attributes and instances of brands that exemplify them.*

The Explorer/Seeker/Pilgrim

1. Attributes: Adventurous, restless, pioneering, independent, nonconformist; seeks fulfillment, change, excitement, a better world; values freedom, individualism, self-sufficiency.
2. Description: The explorer is constantly searching, always on a quest to find something: uncharted territory, new paths, self-knowledge or spiritual enlightenment. Since the beginning of time humans have displayed an elemental need to set out in search of new pastures, to discover what lies over the horizon. Real-life explorers like Marco Polo, Christopher Columbus and Scott of the Antarctic felt the irresistible urge to set out for the great wide beyond. In classical literature the narrator and protagonist of Dante's

---

* Many of these archetypes are discussed in great detail in *The Hero and the Outlaw*, Margaret Mark and Carol Pearson's (2001) ground-breaking book on archetypes and brands.

Divine Comedy provides a good example of the explorer archetype. The explorer's journey may equally be a figurative one: an
inner journey to find oneself, to discover where one's own boundaries lie. The explorer is a driven, rugged individual not averse to
enduring the loneliness and isolation that so often accompany a
personal quest. It is a price worth paying as the explorer helps us
discover our calling and to realize our unique potential.

3. Brand examples: Land Rover, Starbucks, Timberland, Trailfinders
   (United Kingdom).

The Caretaker/Protector

1. Attributes: Selfless, compassionate, empathetic, benevolent; offers
   sustenance and support to the needy and vulnerable; values gen-
   erosity and self-sacrifice.
2. Description: The caretaker archetype is dedicated to the safety,
   welfare and comfort of others. It may also appear as the helper,
   altruist or philanthropist. Often associated with, but not limited
   to, maternal and paternal figures (each of which is in itself an
   archetypal character), the caretaker nurtures and protects depen-
   dents and those in its charge. Like the Good Samaritan (and the
   Samaritans organization in the United Kingdom), caretakers will
   go out of their way to offer help and compassion to those in need.
3. Brand examples: Campbell's Soup, Mothercare (United Kingdom), Salvation Army, Oxfam.

The Lover

1. Attributes: Passionate, sensual, seductive, erotic; seeks true
   love and pleasure, follows its emotions; values loving and intimate relationships.
2. Description: This archetype is driven by the urge to give and receive
   love. Whether in friendship or romance the lover signifies affec-
   tionate commitment. From *Romeo and Juliet* to *Casablanca*, *Love
   Story* to *Titanic,* the lover archetype is as compelling as it is ubiquitous. The archetype is active when pleasure and fulfillment are
   found through intimacy or passionate commitment—to someone
   or something. The object of the devotion may be something ani-
   mate, like another person or an animal or something inanimate,
   like food, where sensuality and indulgence can be given free rein.
   Fragrance and cosmetics brands often embody this archetype.
3. Brand examples: Hallmark, Clairol Herbal Essences, Match.com,
   Ferrero Rocher, Estée Lauder.

The Trickster

1. Attributes: Playful, mischievous, irreverent; pokes fun, crosses boundaries, breaks taboos; values fun, change and spontaneity.

2. Description: The trickster or "Divine Joker," as Jung called the archetype, exists in all cultures: the Greek messenger god, Hermes, with his winged sandals and penchant for playing games and tricks; Mercury, his counterpart in Roman mythology, "mercurial" being a quintessential trickster descriptor; Loki, of Norse tradition, who changed himself into a salmon to escape the wrath of the gods; or Raven of the Eskimos and Coyote of western North American native peoples. The trickster appears as medieval jester, Shakespearean fool, joker, harlequin and clown and can be seen in entertainment figures like Charlie Chaplin, Steve Martin and the Marx Brothers.

   The archetype embodies the energies of mischief and the desire for change. It is "the spirit of disorder, the enemy of boundaries" (Kerenyi 1976). The trickster yearns for the fantastic and for escape from the humdrum routines of life. It is the part of us that pokes fun at the pompous, breaks taboos, questions the unquestionable and mentions the unmentionable. It appears when a way of thinking has become outmoded and needs to be overhauled and replaced by something new. It is thus destroyer and savior at the same time, good and evil, moral and immoral—a fool, but a wise fool. Brands in categories with few or no functional differences between competitors, which seek differentiation primarily along personality lines, may find embracing this archetype enhances their consumer appeal.

3. Brand examples: Miller Lite, Pepsi, Mountain Dew, The Comedy Channel.

The Creator

1. Attributes: Artistic, imaginative, innovative; strives to create something new that will last; values self-expression, that which is aesthetically pleasing.

2. Description: The creator archetype appears in the form of the artist, the writer, the musician and the inventor. Though the artistic world is the natural domain for the creator, the archetype is apparent in the various gods and goddesses described in the early creation myths portraying the very creation of the world itself. Fertility deities such as Isis or Ceres come to mind. The archetype is recognized through its promotion and undertaking of imaginative endeavors of all sorts—anything that allows us to express

ourselves by crafting something that is at once novel and of enduring value.

3. Brand examples: Crown Paints (United Kingdom), Crayola, Lego,
   HGTV, Home Depot.

The Outlaw/Outsider/Rebel

1. Attributes: Rebellious, revolutionary, disruptive, outrageous,
   iconoclastic; breaks the rules , dismantles outdated and oppres-
   sive structures; values liberation and counterculture.

2. Description: The outlaw exists on the very fringes of society and
   may be seen as a misfit, an outsider to the community. The archetype is galvanized into action by a feeling of powerlessness or
   resentment at perceived mistreatment, on a personal level or on
   behalf of a group. Robin Hood and Raffles, the gentleman thief,
   are more lighthearted, romantic examples, but there is often an
   undercurrent of brooding tension in the outlaw figure. Its rejection of prevailing convention and mores leads the outlaw either to
   affirm its alienation from the cultural mainstream through acts
   of outrage or to seek the destruction of what is seen as oppres-
   sive and restrictive. It is a complex archetype that requires careful
   handling in a brand or advertising context—as was demonstrated
   by a 1980s U.K. anti-heroin ad that backfired when its drug addict
   protagonist became a hero figure to heroin users.

3. Brand example: Harley-Davidson.

The Magician

1. Attributes: Intuitive, spiritual, holistic, charismatic; brings about
   transformation, turns visions into reality; values metaphysical
   solutions, the expansion of consciousness.

2. Description: The magician archetype also appears in the form of
   sorcerer, shaman, healer, witch/wizard and visionary. The powerful appeal to us of the archetype is witnessed in our fascina-
   tion with stage magicians, illusionists and hypnotists, as well as
   superstitions of all types. The instant appeal of Harry Potter is
   not difficult to fathom when you have observed a child's reaction
   to his or her first magic coloring book. Characters in tales and
   fables such as Thomas Mann's *Mario and the Magician*, Christopher Marlowe's Doctor Faustus, the Wizard of Oz and Merlin the
   Magician in the legend of King Arthur are examples from a rich
   tradition of literary and mythological figures gifted with special
   powers. More recently the archetype has surfaced in the genre of

magic realism made popular in Latin America through the writings of authors like Gabriel Garcia Marquez and by films such as *Like Water for Chocolate*.

Above all, the magician archetype is about transformation, be it physical or spiritual. With deep knowledge of the physical and spiritual worlds, the magician is able to harness the energies and forces around and within us, to transform situations and bring about change for the better.

The wonders of modern technology are often accompanied by and extolled with magical imagery. DuPont's slogan proclaims, "The miracles of science." When we download software we have a "wizard" to help us install it. Yet, despite the attraction of the magician, there are very few brands that truly embrace the archetype. This is in part due to consumer distrust and cynicism generated by disappointment at being let down by "miracle" products that fail to deliver on their claims. Disney is a brand in which two different archetypal representations exist together (more on this subject later): besides embodying the innocent it is also a magician brand.

3. Brand examples: Disney, Olay Regenerist.

The Sage/Wise Old Man or Woman

1. Attributes: Philosophical, reflective, informative; seeks truth, shares knowledge; values wisdom, objectivity.

2. Description: This archetype may appear as the oracle, expert, advisor, teacher or mentor. Notable sages have included Socrates, Albert Einstein and Confucius. The sage character is often portrayed as the guardian of truth and the source of wisdom. In the case where the sage appears as the wise old man or woman, the character's age symbolizes his or her experience and accumulated wisdom. By seeking and gaining a better understanding of the world around us, the sage enlightens us and helps us to progress and fulfill our potential.

3. Brand examples: *Financial Times,* Harvard University, *Encyclopedia Britannica*.

The Innocent

1. Attributes: Trusting, pure, wholesome, optimistic, happy; keeps hope alive, retains and affirms faith; values honesty, goodness, simple pleasures.

2. Description: Often appearing in the form of a child or naïve youth, as well as a saint or mystic, the innocent is characterized by great purity and faith. It has almost boundless optimism and, in the face

of whatever life throws its way, always manages to keep hope alive. Despite his intellectual limitations and naiveté or perhaps because of them, Forrest Gump manages to come through life's trials and tribulations—Vietnam, meeting presidents, the wild ways and eventual death of the girl he loves—and remain unscathed, with his endearing purity of spirit intact. To him life is as his mother says it is: "Life is like a box of chocolates; you never know what you're gonna get." On another occasion he comments, "I may not be a smart man, but I know what love is."

In its most child-like and naïve guise, the innocent tends toward dependency and a desire to be cared for. In its fuller, more mature manifestation it displays a mystical sense of serenity and one-ness. The innocent symbolizes belief in the promise of paradise, the existence of an idyllic, utopian world. Disney's motto, "The happiest place on Earth," perfectly corresponds to an innocent brand. The archetype is also active when there is a longing for a return to innocence, a warm nostalgia for the traditional way of doing things.

3. Brand examples: Coca-Cola, Ivory, Disney.

The Ruler

1. Attributes: Commanding, authoritative, powerful; strives to be in control, assumes leadership; values order, harmony, efficiency.
2. Description: The ruler archetype also appears as the leader, man-ager, king or queen. The ruler is driven to gain and keep control, to replace or ward off chaos by taking charge of situations and events. The archetype inspires people to take responsibility and to manage their personal and professional commitments in an orga-nized and efficient manner. Though sometimes surrounded by the prestigious trappings of position and authority, the ruler's focus is always power and control rather than mere status.
3. Brand examples: American Express, IBM, CitiBank.

The Hero

1. Attributes: Courageous, principled, determined, competitive; over-comes obstacles, rises to the challenge, rights wrongs; resolve in the face of adversity, moral integrity.
2. Description: Variations of the hero archetype include the war-rior, crusader and champion. The hero comes to the defense of the vulnerable, rescues those in distress. Heroes are motivated by the desire to prove their worth through courageous action and noble feats, particularly in difficult circumstances. They are will-ing to endure hardship and take knocks but are always confident

of prevailing for the good of humankind. Their readiness to make a stand and put their honor on the line means that heroes often find themselves in competitive situations. This archetype gives us energy and determination and inspires us to get the job done.
3. Brand examples: Nike, FedEx, U.S. Army, the Olympics.

Leveraging Archetypal Meaning

Leveraging archetypal meaning involves more than simply borrowing meaning in a one-off advertising campaign. Archetypal brands achieve their status by becoming an enduring and consistent expression of an archetypal identity that is intrinsic to the brand. Until recently one of the best examples was McDonald's, for a long time a classic embodiment of the innocent archetype both as a brand and as an organization. McDonald's was the company that liked to see us smile. It is an innocent desire that permeated everything the brand stood for—from Happy Meals to the Ronald McDonald character and promotions with Disney and toy manufacturers to the play areas it provides for children. Under the famous Golden Arches is an Eden-like place of "food, folks and fun." The brand became a paragon of archetypal consistency. The company then decided to adopt a more hip and cool persona and is currently of no fixed archetypal abode.

Few brands truly exploit their archetypal potential. It is common for brands to dip in and out of archetypal territory, usually unwittingly, leaving the brand with a schizophrenic identity. Take one of McDonald's competitors, Burger King. For a time the brand stumbled into ruler territory ("In the land of the burger the Whopper is king"). It has also flirted with the creator archetype. Recent campaigns have introduced at least two more archetypal identities for the brand: the trickster and the hero.

Another shortcoming that often occurs is the failure to have a brand progress past the lowest levels of a particular archetype. In fact, when this occurs, it is often not so much an archetype that is being invoked as a stereotype. Whereas an archetype is a universally familiar character or situation that transcends culture, time, place, status, age and gender, a stereotype tends to be specific to one or more of these facets and thus more limited in its expression and recognition. In a brand context stereotyping is the consequence of lowest common denominator segmentation and profiling methods, whereby the richness and depth of human motivations are over-looked in favor of a more reductionist conception of people as mere consumers. Generic claims and slogans, hackneyed story lines and unconvincing characters are the advertising corollary to archetypal impoverishment, undifferentiated brands its consequence.

Yet the concept of archetypal identity offers so much more. More-over, besides archetypal figures and characters there are archetypal objects, such as moon, sun, fire, water, chalice, snake; and arche-typal events, be they natural (e.g., birth, death) or rituals of all sorts, such as baptism, marriage, rites of passage; and archetypal tasks and activities. Considering products and categories from an arche-typal perspective can provide insights that in turn help to uncover a brand's actual and potential meaning. More often than not, there is an identifiable category essence—a fundamental, primal meaning underpinning a category—and, by extension, a category archetype. As will be discussed in Chapter 5, the essential meaning of a product category is determined largely by the original purpose of the prod-uct itself. When a brand both owns the category benefit (likely to be reflected in its primary brand meaning) and is emphatically aligned with the archetype that best represents category essence (reflected in its instinctually motivating symbolic brand meaning), that brand will be in an unassailable position in the market. (These distinctions in brand meaning will also be developed in Chapter 5.)

If "the best archetypal brands are—first and foremost—arche-typal *products*, created to fulfill and embody fundamental human needs" (Mark and Pearson 2001, p. 25, italics in original), it is how a product fulfills these needs, performs its function and provides its physical or emotional benefit that indicates with which particular archetype the brand may be aligned. In the analgesics market, for instance, there are brands that help soothe away aches and pains and other brands that forcefully attack the point of pain. In the former case, such a brand could embody the caretaker archetype, whereas in the latter the brand may be invoking the hero archetype. Similarly, in the household cleaning product category there are brands that display characteristics typical of the hero archetype, like the U.K. brand Domestos ("Kills all known germs. Dead."). Other brands in the category place greater emphasis on their more environmentally friendly natural ingredients, such as vinegar. This ecologically aware approach is more akin to the innocent archetype. Thus various archetypes may be appropriate and operational in the same category and archetypal identity can be used to achieve differentiation in highly competitive markets.

On the other hand, the same archetype may be at the heart of brands in totally different categories, yet those brands remain completely differentiated from each other. So, although the Coca-Cola and Ivory brands may be embodiments of the innocent archetype, there is nothing interchangeable and very little comparable between those brands. Two brands, or for that matter 200 brands, may tap into the same archetype, but the expression of that archetype may be rendered in numerous distinct ways. This is because, as outlined in the previous pages, there are many aspects to and therefore many manifestations of, a single archetype. The hero can be a warrior, always ready to enter the fray, or a champion or a selfless crusader for noble causes. Consider also the lover archetype, with its multiple nuances. The archetype is represented in classical mythology in figures such as Eros, Venus and Aphrodite and is seen in its erotic, sexual guise in lover brands such as Victoria's Secret, Durex and Givenchy.

Bailey's Irish Cream is a brand that has consistently aligned itself with the lover archetype. An early on-pack promotion offered a set of three "truth or dare" dice, one with different action commands written on its sides (e.g., *touch, caress, kiss*), one with adverbs like *passionately* or *provocatively*, and one with parts of the body. In a recent commercial for the brand three young men and a woman are playing pool. The woman sniffs her glass of Bailey's to savor its sweet aroma. She then takes her shot. When she returns to her glass she finds it empty. To discover the culprit she teasingly moves close to the lips of each of the men. When she reaches the third man she detects the aroma and kisses him passionately. "Let your senses guide you," runs the endline.

Then there are the less erotic, more romantic and even platonic guises of the lover archetype. The long-running Nestlé Gold Blend campaign (mentioned in Chapter 8) was romantic novel turned soap opera, with Cupid's arrows winging their way through the will-she, won't-she commercials. Hallmark Cards is a classic lover brand, one that helps people express their feelings toward others—whatever the nature of their relationship. In a wonderfully touching commercial an elderly, learned-looking piano teacher sits at the piano with his pupil, a young girl. As he opens the score sheet to begin the day's lesson he is taken aback to find an envelope hidden between the pages.

He reads the birthday card and realizes it is from his pupil, while a girl's voice sings, "So I'm giving you this Hallmark and I hope that you will see what I'm really giving you is a part of me." He struggles to contain his emotions and cannot resist a smile as she begins to play. Visit the Hallmark Web site and you can send flowers to the one you love ("Let love bloom") or e-cards to those you care about.

So two brands may be defined by the same master archetype yet may be differentiated by particular archetypal nuances that endow the brands with very different identities when it comes to executing the brand story. There might be secondary archetypes with which the brands are also aligned. Thus, although brand A and brand B may share the same dominant archetype—say the hero—brand A may embody elements of the caretaker, whereas brand B incorporates the outlaw as its secondary archetype. The Virgin brand is an example of the latter situation. The brand, its founder Richard Branson and the mythical figure, Robin Hood (Branson's "role model") all represent a tantalizing combination of champion of the underdog and irrepressible outlaw.

Finally, it should be noted that archetypes have a lighter and a darker side, a positive and a negative manifestation. So the ruler can be benevolent but can also be tyrannical, authoritative, domineering or a control freak. The caretaker can become smothering and prone to martyrdom. The magician can be a manipulator. In *Batman* the trickster appears in both positive and negative form: as Batman himself (positive side of the trickster—Bruce Wayne transformed into superhero in the guise of a black bat) and as the Joker (here as evil side of the trickster). The trickster as jester may become self-indulgent and a time waster. As an example a recent radio campaign promoting a call plan from a well-known cellular phone company tells potential customers they will have so many minutes under the plan that they will not know what to do with them—why, they will be able to call friends at work just to ask them what they are wearing.

Apple's famous 1984 Super Bowl commercial clearly associates competitor IBM with the dark side of the ruler archetype—here as an Orwellian Big Brother type. The genius of the commercial is that it uses archetypal imagery to infuse the brand with meaning and effectively cast a competitor in a negative light without so much as mentioning the competitor's name. Analyzing the competitive landscape from an archetypal viewpoint will reveal whether any competitor has become aligned with the negative side of an archetype, as well as highlighting opportunities such as unoccupied archetypal territory.

Given that consumer response operates simultaneously at several different levels, archetypal research in particular and symbolic research in general can be invaluable in accessing the more elusive and hidden depths of ultimate psychological motivation. Above all, research must fathom the underlying factors that determine why an archetype is apposite for a given brand. This requires profound knowledge of human motivation, a keen understanding of category dynamics and a thorough appraisal of the brand in question. If that can be achieved, archetypal meaning can be leveraged to greatly enhance the way people connect with a brand. Moreover, from the marketer's viewpoint archetypes are useful as metaphors capable of unifying the various elements of a brand into a single identity. Just as archetypes themselves act as organizing principles of the psyche, so an archetype can act as an organizing principle for a brand, providing inspiration, structure and coherence and giving creative teams more meaningful imagery to work with.

3

Perception

Introduction

The so-called sensorial benefits of a brand relate to the physical experience of that brand and derive from its sensorial properties—its look, taste, smell, texture, and so forth. They may be delivered through the intrinsic attributes of the product and its ingredients or through product design and packaging. Clairol's Herbal Essences is one brand that has built its appeal on sensory attributes. Starbucks is another brand that appeals to the senses. Food categories characterized by richness and creaminess are full of brands offering sensory satisfaction—the ice cream category, for example. The *organoleptic* characteristics of ice cream are leveraged by brands like Häagen-Dazs. Organoleptic refers to properties that are perceived by the senses, such as the flavor, mouth feel, or bouquet. Crayola has even trademarked the smell of its crayons, as believed to be an essential element of their brand. A Yale University study found that the scent of Crayola crayons is the eighteenth most recognized scent to American adults (coffee and peanut butter are first and second, respectively). Gillette razors, the Apple iMac, Absolut Vodka, and countless fragrance brands stimulate through their use of distinctive shapes and colors.

It is little wonder that so many companies are endowing their products and brands with overt sensorial properties. The computer age has brought with it greater efficiency and the ability to get things done more quickly, but it has done nothing to enrich our lives from a sensory perspective. Ordering a book on line is a very different experience to visiting our favorite bookstore, meandering down labyrinthine aisles, running our eyes over the colorful spines of a hundred interesting-looking books, plucking our desired title from the shelf and leafing through its pristine pages, with the aroma of fresh coffee lingering in the air. If sensory deprivation is one trade-off of the onslaught of today's technology, brands can fill the vacuum by offering the kind of sensory stimulation that energizes us as human beings. It means product and packaging design are more important than ever before, as will be readily appreciated by a quick overview of some of the latest products to be marketed in categories as diverse as bottled water, personal care, liquors, and high-end fragrances.

One complication with sensorial benefits is the difficulty of communicating them in advertising. Attempts to do so often consist of showing the effects of the sensorial benefits, sometimes using comic hyperbole, as in the case of Herbal Essences, where advertising usually features women in various states of ecstasy due to the "organic experience" of using the product. Advertising can represent sensorial benefits, but it is only when consumers come into sensorial contact with the physical aspects of a brand that these benefits can achieve their full impact. The sensation experienced when the sensory receptors respond to stimuli such as tastes, smells, or sounds does not even have to be a pleasant one for the brand to benefit. Listerine mouthwash built its success on the consumer perception that, with such a strong, harsh taste, it must have medicinal properties, which make it highly effective in combating bad breath and other oral hygiene problems. This is an example of the perceptual process in action.

Consumer perceptions are critical to the marketing of brands—whether those perceptions are accurate or inaccurate. Many brands of dishwashing liquid have been advertised for their gentleness to hands, whereas their main purpose is obviously to clean dishes. The reason for stressing mildness to hands is the consumer belief that any liquid so efficient in cleaning dishes must be harsh on the skin—something that is not necessarily true. The consumer's mistaken impression leads to the proposition concentrating on the hands and not the dishes (alongside other executions for concentrated strength of liquid and the like). In the United Kingdom, for instance, one of the most famous, long-running campaigns is that for Procter & Gamble's (P&G) Fairy Liquid. First aired in 1964, the campaign was still going strong several decades later and contains one of the best remembered jingles in British advertising: "Now hands that do dishes can feel soft as your face with mild gre-e-en... Fairy Li-quid!"

A quaint throwback to a time when it was considered acceptable to sing the strategy practically word for word.

The Perceptual Process

Although closely related, sensation and perception play different, albeit complementary, roles in how we interpret the world around us. Sensation is the immediate response of our sensory receptors (e.g., eyes and nose) to basic stimuli like light, sound, and texture. Perception is the process by which this sensory information is selected, organized, and interpreted. The raw data of sensations are sent to our brains for interpretation. What we add to or take away from these sensations as we assign meaning to them determines the outcome of the perceptual process. The process is illustrated in Figure 3.1.

The five senses referred to in Figure 3.1, which were first defined by Aristotle, are the ones with which we are most familiar. They are described in more detail later. Other senses that have been demonstrated include the sense of temperature and the sense of balance. Our sensory receptors translate physical energy from the environment into electrical impulses that are processed by the brain. For instance, light, in the form of electromagnetic radiation, causes receptor cells in our eyes to activate and send signals to the brain. But we do not understand these signals as pure energy. Rather, the process of perception enables us to interpret them as objects, people, threats.

The perceptual process is one characterized by subjectivity. The interpretations and meanings we assign to the sensory stimuli we receive emanate from our schemas—that is, the system of beliefs and feelings we each have. There is inevitably a cultural influence at play here. These schemas may predispose us to perceive some stimulus in a certain way. Take a look at the photo in Figure 3.2.

Sensory stimuli	Sensory receptors		
Sights →	Eyes ↘		
Sounds →	Ears	*Sensation*	*Meaning*
Smells →	Nose →	Exposure→ Attention→ Interpretation→Response	
Tastes →	Mouth		
Textures →	Skin ↗		

Figure 3.1 The perceptual process.

Figure 3.2   Metropolitan Police recruitment ad.

Do you see a white police officer chasing a black criminal? That was the intention behind the provocative ad, part of a campaign by the Metropolitan Police Force to increase recruitment among ethnic minorities in the 1980s. The two people shown in the ad are actually both police officers, one in uniform and one in plain clothes, pursuing a third party who is off camera. The ad is cleverly constructed to expose our own perceptual prejudice when confronted with the dramatic image. Of course, the ad also illustrates how our interpretation of a stimulus is socioculturally determined: The ad may be interpreted differently by readers in a different country or at a different time, where the problems facing the Metropolitan Police Force in the London of the early 1980s do not exist.

Sensory Systems

Vision   Although we depend in large measure on sight to navigate and make sense of the world, we do not actually see with our eyes. We see with our brain. Consider the sentence, "I see what you mean," or the word *insight*. The brain devotes about 35 percent of its power to the visual process. The eye is the light-sensitive organ that is the first component of the visual system that also includes the optic nerve and visual cortex of the brain. Like a camera lens focusing an image on film, the cornea and lens of an eye focus an image onto the retina. Unlike film, though, the retina is not a passive receptor of images but rather transforms them. Moreover, the image cast at the back of the eye is upside down and two-dimensional, having height and width but lacking depth. A huge amount of editing and processing takes place before the information that enters the eyes reaches the visual cortex. Much of this editing is based on our schemas and our belief in what is real.

There are two important points here. First, the visual process is less the passive reception of coherent images than it is the active process of construction and interpretation. Everything we see we construct: color, motion, shape, everything. Second, it is a personal, subjective process wherein our personal sense of reality becomes our experienced reality. To a large extent we see what we want to see. By way of example, imagine a dozen different people on the second floor of a Manhattan office block gazing out for a few seconds onto the busy streets below them. If each was then to recount what he or she saw, the details would be quite different. One person may comment that he or she saw a traffic cop waving down a car, another a Ford Mustang driving the wrong way down a one way street. One may have noticed the light blue sign of a Citibank across the street, another that a police officer was waving to the driver of a red, sporty-looking car. Yet another may have seen a large poster advertisement for Budweiser, whereas another may have seen a kiosk in front of some posters, including one for a beer. As the people looked at the street scene they were unconsciously selecting, discarding, and editing visual information, and their brains were comparing the selected information with stored records to ultimately generate visual images.

The constructive interpretation that is at the heart of the visual process has implications that reach far and wide and is of interest to those in fields as diverse as art, marketing, computer software design, and criminal law. With regard to the latter, consider the area of eyewitness testimony. As Donald Hoffman (1998, p. xiv) points out in *Visual Intelligence—How We Create What We See,* "The visual reality of an eyewitness is a constructed reality. Understanding the rules by which eyewitnesses construct visual realities can be critical to the proper evaluation of eyewitness testimony." We set great store by the outcome of the visual process. We depend on it for our survival and

Figure 3.3 Strand cigarettes miscalculated the overriding impact of visual content.

for an understanding of the world around us and our place in that world. Critically for marketers and particularly marketing communications, what we see is more important than what we hear. Perhaps one of the best examples of a brand learning this lesson the hard way was the case of a cigarette brand called Strand. In 1959, when it was still legal to advertise cigarettes on television in the United Kingdom, a commercial was aired for the brand (Figure 3.3). In the ad, a solitary young man dressed in trench coat, scarf and hat, lights up a cigarette under the lampposts of a central London street. There is no one else around. "You're never alone with a Strand," claims the slogan, suggesting the companionship of the cigarette brand. What viewers saw was a man all alone smoking a Strand cigarette. Not long afterward, the brand, by then associated with loners, was consigned to the big ashtray in the sky.

On the other hand, careful use of visual imagery in brand design and communication can be leveraged very effectively by brands, and offers particular advantages to global brands. One of the principal barriers to the expansion of global brands is that posed by the limitations of language—how to capture concepts in the vernacular of the country of origin and, further, how to render those words in a dozen other languages. The translation of slogans is notoriously difficult, which is why they are often paraphrased and why English-language slogans are sometimes simply left untranslated in international markets. Notwithstanding cultural influences and the perceptual subjectivity referred to previously, consumers in different parts of the world will cognitively process and respond to visual images in much the same way. A picture can be worth a thousand words.

Color: Marketing's Silent Language   What we call color is really the perception of the frequency, or wavelength, of light—in much the same way as pitch or a musical note is the perception of the frequency or wavelength of sound. It has been scientifically proven that, although some of our reactions to colors are learned behaviors, others are physiological responses. In fact, how we react to colors is influenced by a combination of physiological, psychological, biological, social and cultural factors. The green room of a concert hall or theater is where actors and performers relax before they go on stage. The color green is considered to have calming effects, which is why waiting rooms and hospital rooms are sometimes painted in a shade of green. Blue is also associated with relaxation and tranquility. Red is a color at the lowest frequencies of light discernible by the human eye. Because it is highly visible to us and easily catches our attention, it is used in stop signs, stop lights, brake lights and fire equipment. It is the color most commonly found in national flags. Yellow is another color with high visibility, also often used for hazard warnings. In soccer, referees brandish cards of two colors to caution and dismiss players: respectively, yellow and red.

Before reviewing some of the meanings colors have for us, consider how pervasive colors are in our everyday language. A *red-letter day* is one of special importance and good fortune. To *see red* is to be angry. *Into the blue* means into the unknown. *Out of the blue* means unexpectedly, as if from nowhere. Dealing in the *black market* is illicit or unregulated trade in goods or money. Interestingly, some idiomatic use of color vocabulary is consistent from one language to the next, whereas other expressions use different colors to convey the same sense. In English, *yellow journalism* refers to sensationalistic reporting. Spanish has the direct equivalent, *periodismo amarillista, amarillo* being the Spanish word for yellow. On the other hand, what in English is referred to as a *blue joke,* that is, risqué or indecent, in Spanish is a *chiste verde* (a green joke). Cultural considerations are of particular importance to global marketers. An exporter of white wedding gowns to China would soon be in the red; whereas in Western cultures white symbolizes purity and innocence, in China white signifies death and bereavement. Red is the predominant color for wedding gowns in China, where it is also the color of good luck and prosperity.

Note that colors can have both positive and negative associations. Table 3.1 lists the connotations that are prevalent in Western cultures. Most colors have more positive than negative associations. In

TABLE 3.1   Color Connotations in Western Cultures

Color	Positive Associations	Negative Associations
Red	Passion, love, sex, energy, speed intensity, strength	danger, anger, aggression
Blue	Relaxation, tranquility, dependability, stability, loyalty, coolness, conservatism, authority, water	depression, coldness, conservatism
Purple	Regality, nobility, ceremony, sensuality, creativity, spirituality	profanity, exaggeration
Green	Nature, fertility, environment, youth	inexperience, envy, illness, greed
White	Purity, innocence, reverence, peace, cleanliness, sterility, simplicity	coldness, sterility, clinical, surrender, cowardice
Black	Power, authority, formality, elegance, style, mystery	death, mourning, evil, darkness, mystery, fear

Western cultures the color that has the most negative associations is black. The physiological and psychological factors influencing this fact are varied, but key among them is the perception by humans of nighttime as dark, dangerous and devoid of the life-giving effects of the sun. The black–white, bad–good dualism is often manifested as a cultural shorthand: The bad guy in Westerns has the black hat; the witch is dressed in black. The meaning of colors is often also context dependent, as in the case of the conservatism of blue or the sterility of white in the chart in Table 3.1.

You cannot think of Avis or Home Depot or Milka without seeing their respective brand colors in your mind's eye. Pepsi is blue; Coke is red. In the United Kingdom the Silk Cut cigarette brand came to own the color purple. With increasing restrictions on tobacco advertising, the brand's advertising agency took the purple color from the pack and featured it in the form of purple silk, with a cut in it, in its print campaign that could not show the product and did not even mention the brand name. Certainly color is an important aspect of brand recognition. Yet, as the aforementioned associations and symbolic meanings of colors demonstrate, color can be used to achieve far more than simple differentiation. It can provide product cues, can evoke emotions and can help build connections at an unconscious level between brands and people. Color can influence perceptions of product properties such as taste. In a related piece of research, coffee in a yellow can was perceived as weak, coffee in a blue can perceived as mild, in a red can as rich and in a brown can as too strong.

Greens on packaging suggest naturalness and organic products. With its associations of purity, expanses of white on packaging is a good indication of low-fat or additive-free products. The use of black in product design adds high-end styling and sophistication. Several months after Motorola launched its state-of-the-art RAZR V3, what did the company do to build on the success of the model, update its product offering and underscore the cutting edge design ethos of the brand? It introduced a Special Edition Black RAZR V3. Black and style seem to go hand in hand. Think Mont Blanc pens. Colors along the red–orange–yellow part of the spectrum signify speed. Red and yellow are popular colors for sports cars—ideal colors, also, for one-hour film developing facilities and fast food outlets. In the latter case, these companies prefer to classify themselves as quick-service restaurants. The color symbolism still applies. Indeed, research has shown that reds and oranges stimulate people to eat quickly and leave. A number of large brand name companies actively consolidate the identification they have with their corporate colors. Blue signifies stability, dependability and conservatism. IBM, otherwise known as "Big Blue," incorporates blue in its logo, Web site, corporate materials and many of its products and programs: Deep Blue, Extreme Blue, Blue Logic and Blue Gene, for instance.

Further along the spectrum and somewhat neglected by the marketing world, is good old reliable, solid, and simple in a down-to-earth way brown. UPS was always well known for its package delivery credentials, but less so for some of its other services such as supply-chain management and financial services. In 2002 the company embarked on a brand overhaul aimed at unifying the identity of all its entities and at encouraging people to reconsider UPS's broader scope of business offerings. Leveraging its association with the color brown, the logistics company introduced a new tag line, dropping the corporate name and replacing it with "brown": "What can Brown do for you?" In its advertising the company is referred to simply as "BROWN."

Other examples of companies and their brands successfully tapping into the powerful properties of colors are the Crown Paints case mentioned in Chapter 8; Swatch watches, which used color and design to revolutionize the watch market; and Mars M&Ms, a brand that was revitalized by the more creative exploitation of one of its key

assets—color. The company ran a promotion in 1995 inviting consumers to vote for a new color. The winner was blue, polling some
54 percent of the more than 10 million votes that were cast. At the
beginning of 2004 color disappeared altogether from M&Ms and we
were left only with black and white M&Ms. On March 11 of that year
normal color was restored and a kick-off party held in Los Angeles,
where it was pronounced, "Chocolate is Better in Color!" The Web
site even allows you to customize your M&Ms in party favors.

Pharmaceutical companies are also realizing the benefits of using
color to differentiate their products. Esomeprazole magnesium is
something of a mouthful. Nexium is a little easier to pronounce but
may be still be easily forgotten. "The purple pill" is better recalled
by those seeking relief from heartburn symptoms of acid reflux dis-
ease, urged by TV advertising to "ask your doctor about the purple
pill." Such advertising has been possible in the United States since
the U.S. Federal Drug Administration (FDA) relaxed its restrictions
on direct-to-consumer marketing of pharmaceutical products. Print
advertising for AstraZeneca's product is predominantly purple, as
is the Web site. The use of color in tablets is of great practical value,
particularly to the elderly, who often fail to take their numerous
medications as prescribed. Those medications are often similar-look-
ing white tablets. Given the increasing number of medications now
available over the counter, such use of color will become ever more
important. It will also become more sophisticated, with pharmaceutical companies taking greater advantage of the symbolic properties
of color. As an example, though Viagra as a brand name probably
has slightly more resonance than its main competitor Levitra, the
color of Viagra tablets, pale blue, is a curious choice. It is a color
that seems more appropriate for a relaxant or sleeping tablet. Levitra,
co-developed and co-promoted by Bayer and GlaxoSmithKline, is a
more vibrant and energetic yellow-orange color (and its logo device
a flame), more in keeping with its purpose.

Before moving on to discuss the other senses, it is worth reflecting that the perception of color via the visual system is a process
characterized by subjectivity, imprecision and cultural influence. In
this sense, it is much the same as the broader area of signification.
For just as meanings do not have sharply defined edges (where does
"far" begin, how soon is "soon," and how much money do you have
to have to be "rich"?), so too with colors. Purple is any of a group of
colors intermediate between blue and red. I have half a dozen pairs

of "black" trousers in my closet, yet no two of them appear to be the same color. In English-speaking countries we split some hues into distinct colors according to their lightness. For instance, the pair of colors red and pink are seen as totally different colors, whereas objectively there is no more difference between them than there is between dark green and light green, which are considered subsets of the same color—green. An Italian makes the same red–pink distinction but also distinguishes between *blu* and *azzurro*, which English speakers would simply call dark blue and light blue. Different cultures assign different names to slightly different parts of the spectrum. One person's red is another's scarlet.

Sound   Are sound and meaning linked? Sound symbolism, or phonosemantics, refers to the process whereby the actual sound of a word conveys meanings. Although still a relatively obscure branch of linguistics, sound symbolism has a long history and was first referred to by Plato in the dialogues of Cratylus. Several ancient traditions refer to an archetypal relationship between sounds and ideas, and there is growing modern linguistic research that indicates a relationship between sound and meaning. Ferdinand de Saussure (1857–1913), considered the father of modern linguistics, seemed to pour cold water on the concept when he famously declared that "the sign is arbitrary." By that he meant that the words we use to indicate things and ideas could be any words—they simply represent a consensus agreed on by the speakers of a language, without possessing any inherent relationship to the things they describe.

Whereas most modern linguists assume sound symbolism plays only a minor role in language and that sound and meaning relate only arbitrarily, advocates of sound symbolism can draw on some convincing evidence. Research has shown that individuals, when presented with fictitious or unfamiliar words, consistently use sound symbolism to derive meaning from those words about the referenced object (Yorkston and Menon 2004, p. 43). Moreover, the phenomenon has been observed in speakers of several different languages, from native tongues to more developed languages. As a simple exercise, consider the interplay between sound and meaning in the following list of words, which are all different manners of walking: stride, stroll, strut, step, limp, totter, teeter, amble, saunter, prance, trudge. Notice the phonetic similarity among *stride, stroll and strut* and between *totter* and *teeter*. Do *amble* and *saunter* not suggest a leisurely, unhurried walk? Can you feel the difficult heavy-footedness of *trudge*? What about the precarious unsteadiness of *totter*? In short, do these words not sound like the actions they describe? The visual evocation of each word and the vividness of the meaning conveyed are undeniable. Sound symbolists would point out that there is nothing coincidental or arbitrary about that.

The best-known, but least interesting, form of sound meaning is onomatopoeia. This is simply the imitation of a sound and thus only applies to words that either refer to a sound (e.g., crackle, thud, tick-tock, rustle, pop) or that suggest something that makes a sound (e.g., the quack quack of a duck). Incidentally, if the duck was in Spain, it would go *cuá cuá*, and if in Argentina, it would go *cuac cuac*. Marketers sometimes make use of onomatopoeia in their communication, as in the case of Rice Krispies' *snap, crackle and pop* or Alka Seltzer's *plop, plop, fizz, fizz*. Again, the process here is a simple one of imitation of sound, in these cases as an effective mnemonic device for getting consumers to remember the products. Similarly, a campaign from the United Kingdom many years ago to encourage drivers to wear seat belts carried the memorable line, "Clunk, click, every trip"—a reminder to buckle up after closing the car door. Some brand names employ onomatopoeia—Schweppes, the carbonated beverages brand, for example.

The more important part of sound symbolism has to do with the phonetic structure of words. Language is a complex system composed of several levels. Individual sounds are called phonemes (i.e., speech sounds and letters). These phonemes are the basic building blocks of language and are combined to form morphemes. Morphemes are the smallest linguistic units having consistent meaning. There are more than 6,000 morphemes in the English language, including complete words (e.g., *man*, which can either be a free-standing word, or part of a word, as in *gentleman*), prefixes, suffixes and roots (e.g., *aero-, post-, -ology, -ly*). The brand name Compaq, for instance, was developed using morpheme combinations (Robertson 1989, p. 64). The morphemes and syllables formed by phonemes are in turn juxtaposed to form words. Words are then placed in context to create phrases that when put together form sentences.

The fact that phonemes, in certain situations, appear to be linked to specific meanings and even emotions is significant with regard to brand meaning. The implication is that brand names can serve as phonetic cues to brand meaning. Individual letters and phonemes in a brand name contain meaning that can influence attribute perceptions and trigger perceptual reactions to the brand name. Due to their soft sound, sibilants such as *s* and soft *c* suggest femininity, gentleness and serenity. They are often used in feminine products and perfumes (e.g., Silkience, Cerissa). Plosive and guttural sounds (i.e., the letters *b, c, d, g, k, p and t*) are harsher and tend to evoke toughness and masculinity (e.g., Kagool, Nautica, Cougar). One study revealed a relationship between properties of the letters in brand names and product characteristics. In the research, as consonant hardness and vowel pitch increased in hypothetical brand names for toilet paper and household cleaners, consumer perceptions of the harshness of the product also increased (Keller 1998, p. 140). The high, front vowel sounds *i* and *e* connote small size, whereas the low, back vowel sounds *a, o and u* suggest large size. For example, in a study where subjects were asked to plot *mal* and *mil* along the semantic dimension of size, some 80 percent of those subjects concurred that *mal* represented a large object and *mil* represented a smaller object (Tarte and Barritt 1971, quoted in Robertson 1989).

There are other ways sound is associated with brands. Advertising jingles are an obvious example, particularly when linked with a catchy brand slogan. "A Mars a day helps you work, rest and play," ran a famous jingle for Mars Bars in the United Kingdom. "The Quilted Quicker Picker-Upper," goes the Bounty paper towels slogan. Intel has successfully been using an audiovisual logo device as part of its co-op marketing program since 1991. TV commercials for computer manufacturers often include the animated jingle that displays the Intel Inside logo while playing the distinctive five-tone melody. Even the sound packaging makes when it is being opened can be important to consumers. A highly successful advertising campaign for Schweppes tonic water in the United Kingdom prominently featured the sound of a bottle of Schweppes being opened and the line, "Schhh…. You-know-who."

Taste By itself, taste is a somewhat unsophisticated sense. The receptor cells in our taste buds respond to only five basic tastes: sweet, sour, salty, bitter and a recently discovered fifth taste called umami. The latter, a loanword from Japanese, is a savory taste sometimes referred to as "more-ish." Ever noticed how a blocked nose, caused by a common cold, causes taste to all but disappear? It is because, despite the human tongue's having some 10,000 taste buds, as much as 90 percent of what we perceive as taste actually comes from our sense of smell. Sight also plays a role. Consider how wine tasting involves all three of these senses, but in reverse order. First, the wine taster observes the wine in the glass. Then, the nose lingers over the bouquet of the wine, and, finally, the liquid is tasted as it runs over the tongue. Research has shown that the color of food can greatly affect how its taste is perceived. Brightly colored food usually seems to taste better than more bland-looking food. We taste what we see. That is why much of what we eat today has a significant amount of color additives as well as flavor additives. Add food coloring to light-colored beer and consumers in taste tests will often describe it as heartier. Advertising and people's attitudes toward a brand can also affect their perceptions of taste. To counteract this, taste tests are frequently conducted both blind, where the brand is not exposed and with the brand name revealed.

Scientists now believe humans developed the sense of taste as a way to avoid being poisoned and ingesting harmful substances. Things have evolved since then and today the fortunes of major corporations—fast-food chains, beverage companies, snack-food companies—depend in large part on how their products taste. Coca-Cola's formula is a closely guarded secret and Kentucky Fried Chicken makes great play of the Colonel's secret blend of eleven herbs and spices. Such mystique only adds to the connection in consumer's minds and mouths between a brand and a taste. Consider also the extremely limited repertoire of words most of us have at our disposal to describe different tastes. Brands that can corner the market in a particular taste or that can bring unique tastes to consumers increase their chances of differentiating themselves against the competition. On the other hand, taste preference is not necessarily a guarantee of brand success, as the Coca-Cola Company discovered in the mid 1980s. Researchers at PepsiCo had learned that, in blind taste tests, consumers preferred the taste of Pepsi to Coke. This finding formed the basis of the successful "Pepsi challenge" campaign. In response, Coca-Cola spent millions of dollars in market research and conducted 200,000 blind taste tests of their own to verify that the reformulated "New Coke" outperformed both Pepsi and the existing Coke product. In 1985, New Coke was launched. As is well documented, there was public outcry and the company eventually reintroduced the original Coke formula as Classic Coke.

The New Coke case is often reviewed as an example of a gross marketing error. If it was the debacle that it is usually portrayed as, it provides a salutary lesson in what happens when companies concentrate on the product at the expense of the brand. Alternatively, if it was a premeditated gambit to rekindle Coca-Cola's declining sugar cola market share by stoking public affection for a brand they had always known and loved, it was a risky masterstroke. Either way, what it does illustrate is the somewhat paradoxical role of taste within the brand relationship. Intuitively, an improvement in taste should benefit the brand—and often does. But at the same time consumers will sometimes overlook taste factors in light of their overall evaluation of and loyalty to a brand.

Smell Back in the 1980s British supermarket managers began to realize that having an in-store bakery and allowing the smell of fresh baked bread to waft through the supermarket contributed to greater sales of bread and indeed everything else too. Olfactory marketing was born. Smell is the sense that has the most direct and unmediated access to the brain. Specifically, this most primal of the senses is the only part of the human sensory system that has a direct neurological link to the limbic system in the brain—which stores and regulates memories and emotions. Odors can thus immediately access emotional memories stored in our unconscious. We can usually recognize and respond in a fraction of a second to smells from our childhood, such as the first time we smelled a garden with mint growing in it, the smell of cakes baking in the oven, the musty aroma of a room in an unfamiliar house, the smell of clean bed sheets or of a freshly painted door. The memories of these smells are themselves resilient and enduring. Odor memory declines less rapidly than other sensory memory: People are able to recall smells with a 65 percent accuracy after a year, whereas the visual recall of photographs falls to around 50 percent after just three months (http://www.senseofsmell.org).

As a species, our nonreliance on smell has relegated the sense below those on which we depend far more in our day-to-day lives. Conversely, the social behavior of most animals is controlled by smells and other chemical signals. Dogs and mice, for example, rely on odors to find food, recognize kin, establish and identify territory and locate a receptive mate. Our sense of smell does not compare with that of our canine friends, yet human noses can still detect aromas present in quantities of a few parts per trillion. We can actually

**TABLE 3.2   U.S. Consumer Market for Scented Products 2001
versus 2006**

Product Category	2001 (in billions)	2006 (in billions)
Toiletries (soaps, bath and body products, deodorants)	$6.6	$9.6
Hair care products	$6.1	$9.5
Laundry care products	$6.1	$7.6
Men's/women's fragrances	$4.0	$5.8
Home fragrances	$2.3	$4.7

Source: Kline & Company Inc.

recognize up to 10,000 different odors. It is little surprise, then,
that marketers are finally waking up to the importance of smell in
their brand and retail management activities. The technology that
supports olfactory marketing has increased by leaps and bounds
in the last decade. Of course, stores like The Body Shop, Bed Bath
and Beyond and Starbucks have long benefited from the naturally
appealing fragrances of the products they sell. But now others can
create pleasant-smelling environments for their consumers, with the
help of various scent-generating devices. Environmental fragrancing
has expanded beyond the blanket perfuming of retail stores to more
customized applications, where products are displayed in a fragrant
ambience that is at once more compatible with and more evocative
of the nature of the products in question. The aromas of recently prepared food in the cookery equipment section of a department store,
the smell of freshly cut grass in the golf section of a sporting goods
store, or the unmistakable scent of suntan lotion in the swimwear
section are just a few examples. Airlines are using these techniques
in their members' lounges, as are hotels in their lobbies and restau-
rant areas.

Smell has always been an important element of some more obvious categories, such as personal care and the fragrance market, as
Table 3.2 shows (note the huge percentage growth in home fragrancing). Even with products where smell is not the primary benefit
sought (e.g., in the hair care category), smell plays a vital role. When
shoppers are selecting shampoos, they invariably flip the lid open to
check the fragrance. A pleasant smell will enhance the experience
of using the product, even though it will have no functional effect
on whether the shampoo delivers the three specific benefits most

consumers want to achieve from the product: clean hair, healthy hair and shiny hair. Colgate-Palmolive successfully conducted an olfactory marketing campaign for the launch of their new fabric softener Suavitel in France. The product's fragrance was diffused in major Parisian train stations for a week, giving 3.5 million consumers the chance to experience the scent. Nestlé went a step further in May 2004 when it combined the fragrancing of newspapers with that of train stations to entice customers with the scent of Nescafé.

Launched in 1969, the low-priced laundry detergent Gain had failed to attract a large consumer base and was facing declining sales when, in 1981, P&G decided to give the brand one last chance. Research indicated that scent was a particularly important factor in US Hispanic households, and the company decided to market Gain as a heavily fragrant detergent, hoping to appeal to the growing Hispanic population. Grass-roots events included giving away samples of Gain in laundromats in the Los Angeles area, with its high percentage of Hispanic immigrants. Highlighting fragrance enabled P&G to differentiate Gain from its other laundry brands, in particular Tide, Cheer and Era – marketed, respectively, for superior cleaning, color protection and stain fighting. Although the strong perfumes did not have mass appeal, and the approach of targeting a narrow audience was unusual for P&G, by 2007 annual sales of Gain had broken the $1 billion mark for the first time, and the brand occupied the number two slot in the laundry detergent market, behind Tide.

Interestingly, sometimes aroma trumps taste: In the United States, for example, whereas a huge majority of more than 90 percent love the aroma of coffee, only 47 percent actually like the taste (Rapaille 2004). For reasons already mentioned, when it comes to food products, our perception is largely determined by what we smell when we open the package. Is there anything better than inhaling the aroma of fresh coffee beans on opening a pack of your favorite java? Yes—being able to sample the aroma before you open the pack, or, more pointedly, buy it. Some brands of coffee have started to cleverly design their packs of premium coffee with special valves so that, by gently squeezing the pack, a foretaste of the invigorating brew can be savored—that's right, foretaste. The fact that smell and taste are virtually inseparable has implications and offers opportunities for product packaging design. Crest Whitening Expressions toothpaste comes in a variety of intense flavors such as Extreme Herbal Mint, Cinnamon Rush, Fresh Citrus Breeze and the winner of a recent consumer poll,

Lemon Ice. Special packaging with scratch-and-sniff panels allows consumers to compare the smell of the different flavors in store and to get a good idea of the taste of each toothpaste. The technology used means the shelf life of these scratch-and-sniff panels is quite long. It is like a permanent sampling program right there at the point of purchase. Similarly, when P&G introduced Mountain Spring Tide it included a scratch-and-sniff feature in its print advertising to allow consumers to experience the new scent before purchase.

Touch   Coke and Pepsi taste different. They look different—Coke is red; Pepsi is blue. Yet, increasingly, the two brands feel the same. The color of the cans may be different, but they have the same feel. The classic curved Coke bottle was the result of a very single-minded brief back in 1915—the bottle should be distinctive enough to be recognized by touch. It became an icon, a visual and tactile representation of "the real thing." Most consumers believe that Coke tastes better in a glass bottle than in a can. Though still used in many markets, the bottle has gradually been replaced by the generic can format and a strong sensory association has fallen by the wayside.

The largest organ in our body, the skin, is responsible for the sense of touch. Touch is the earliest sense to develop in the fetus. We use touch to detect the presence of something harmful—an object that is too hot, or sharp. But we also use touch to appreciate textures and physical forms. Tactile properties cue symbolic meanings. We associate the textures of fabrics and materials used in clothing, bed linen and upholstery with certain product qualities. A fabric that is "smooth as silk" has a luxurious feel about it. Touch can indicate and foster emotional closeness. It can be the gateway to a sense of well-being, as the millions who visit spas and receive therapeutic and recuperative massages can attest. Touch is used metaphorically in phrases such as *in touch with somebody* or *touched by something.*

In a retail environment we are first drawn to attractive packaging visually. If the packaging has a pleasing tactile appearance, we are more likely to pick it up from the supermarket shelf, and once we have it in our hand its tactile properties begin to influence our overall perception of the brand. Sleek, ergonomic design and tactile appreciation go hand in hand today, whether it be Gillette razors or the latest impossibly slim flip phone. Communicating product benefits that are most apparent through the sense of touch calls for innovative use of media. L'Oréal recently ran a major print advertising campaign in the United Kingdom. The advertising took up two pages. The first page was wrinkled and rough to the feel; the second was smooth and silky. The texture of the paper used reinforced the message: L'Oréal gives you smooth, wrinkle-free skin.

We are becoming more and more used to having touch screens in the devices we use every day; think ATM machines and, lately, mobile phones: It is estimated that by 2012 some 40 percent of new mobile phones could have touch screens (Anonymous 2007). Apple's recently launched iPhone has accelerated the trend: The phone uses the screen as an input device instead of the usual keypad. A launch ad for the product (see color insert following p. 76) shows the iPhone and a user's hand against a stark black background, accentuating the bright, crystal clear display screen. Ghost-like fingers move up and down the screen. Besides the visually arresting image, the copy line provides a nice twist on an old adage: "Touching is believing." Replacing physical buttons with virtual ones has one potential drawback. We like to feel some confirmation (tactile or audible) that our instructions have been received. On an ATM machine we hear a beep when we push a digit or "balance inquiry" on the screen; with keypad phones we feel the subtle click of the buttons. Phones like Samsung's SCH-W559 touch-screen phone offer a solution (ibid). It provides tactile feedback in the form of tiny vibrations. The phone's handset fools the user's sense of touch and imitates the feeling of pressing a mechanical button. It is an example of *haptic* technology being applied to the digital world. Haptic means pertaining to the sense of touch and haptic technology refers to the simulation of pressure, texture, vibration and other sensations related to the sense of touch. Among other things the technology is found in joysticks and game controllers.

Making Sense of Brands

Just as we depend on sensory information to interpret and assign meaning to the environment around us, so brand meaning is fundamentally influenced by the sensorial stimuli we pick up from our interactions with brands. Brands that manage to leverage multiple sensory touch points with their consumers leave a stronger, more vivid sensorial profile in the minds of those consumers. Millward Brown recently conducted a global study into branding and sensory

TABLE 3.3   Loyalty Impact Scores for Dove and Irish Spring Soaps

Sensory Perception	Dove	Irish Spring
Smell	0.11	0.17
Touch	0.10	0.06
Sight	0.08	0.07

awareness. The 5 Senses Study investigated the extent to which brands make use of and appeal to the different senses. A further consideration was the extent to which they do so synergistically.

The soap category provides an interesting example. In the U.S. survey, soap brands Dove and Irish Spring were included. The two are quite distinct and use the senses to create very different brand experiences. Dove is positioned as a moisturizing beauty bar, whereas Irish Spring is a deodorant soap. At a category level, smell was considered the most important sense in choosing between soap brands (71 percent of respondents). As Table 3.3 shows, smell is a more important driver for Irish Spring than for Dove. For Irish Spring users, the smell is usually referred to in terms of freshness. Dove's smell is described as more subtle, more pure.

It is along the touch dimension that Dove really differentiates itself from Irish Spring. A greater number of Dove's devotees believe that the feel of their brand is more positive and distinctive. When asked if their brand feels soft and creamy 91 percent of Dove users agreed, compared to just 56 percent for Irish Spring users. When it comes to sight the two brands again differ in the sensory experiences they offer, but in each case there is synergy with the brands' other sensory associations, enhancing and adding clarity to the overall brand experience. Irish Spring's green-and-white striations connote freshness, whereas Dove's whiteness cues purity and its oval form triggers positive associations with regard to touch. These findings are illustrated in the sensogram in Figure 3.4.

How We Process Sensory Information

Exposure   The first stage of the perceptual process is that of exposure. Exposure occurs when sensations come within range of our

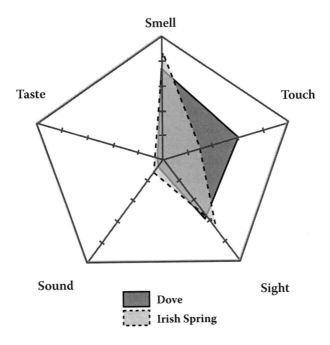

Figure 3.4 The sensory profiles of Irish Spring and Dove Soap brands.

sensory receptors. How close does a bumblebee have to come for us to hear its buzzing? How near must a brewing coffeepot be for us to detect the aroma of coffee? How much must the percentage of fat vary for us to taste the difference between the reduced-fat and regular versions of our favorite cookies? These questions and their answers are related to what are termed sensory thresholds. Psychophysics is the field of science that studies links between the physical properties of stimuli and people's experience of them. It determines the lowest intensity of a stimulus that can be detected by a sensory receptor, that is, the threshold for that receptor.

The absolute threshold refers to the minimum amount of stimulation that can be detected by a given sensory receptor. Absolute thresholds vary with demographic factors and may increase due to physiological reasons. Females are said to have a better sense of smell than males—particularly younger ones, as our sense of smell declines with age. Some examples of approximate absolute thresholds are given in Table 3.4. Note that in the case of the candle flame, for

TABLE 3.4   Some Approximate Detection Threshold Values

Sense Modality	Detection Threshold
Light	A candle flame seen at thirty miles on a dark clear night
Sound	The tick of a watch under quiet conditions at twenty feet
Taste	One teaspoon of sugar in two gallons of water
Smell	One drop of perfume diffused into the entire volume of a three-room apartment
Touch	The wing of a bee falling on your back from a distance of one centimeter

instance, the qualifier is "on a dark clear night." The term *noise* is given to any irrelevant and competing stimuli. In this case, if there were other sources of light or bad air pollution the threshold would be significantly lower.

The differential threshold is the smallest physical difference between two stimuli that can still be recognized as a difference. The minimum change in a stimulus that can be detected is also referred to as the just noticeable difference (JND) threshold. JND differs from absolute threshold in that the former is concerned with changes in sensations, not minimum sensations. Marketers who decide to make a change in some aspect of a brand—for reasons of harmonization, cost-cutting, modernization, market opportunity and so on—must determine whether they want the change to be perceived by consumers. Normally, if the change is deemed to be advantageous to the consumer it will be communicated in some way, perhaps on-pack, or through advertising, or via a promotion. Consumers are very sensitive and largely resistant to changes to their favorite brands. Changes that have the potential to adversely affect brand perceptions are often pitched just below the JND threshold. Reducing the number of chocolate chips in a brand of cookie that is loved for its abundance or updating packaging or modernizing a logo or brand icon for a brand that has been around for some time are examples that can have a detrimental impact on brand loyalty. Price increases and product resizing are other common examples. Figure 3.5 shows several of the face-lifts undergone by Shell's famous "pecten" emblem, one of the best-known brand symbols in the world.

Perceptual Selection   Because of the brain's limited capacity to process information, people tend to filter and to select only a small

1948   1955   1961

1971   1992   1999

Figure 3.5   Gradual modifications to Shell's famous emblem. (See color insert following p. 76.)

amount of the stimuli to which they are exposed for conscious processing. Without perceptual selectivity we would become overwhelmed by the noise and clutter that bombards us. Although our inclination is to prevent sensory overload, certain factors increase the chances of our selecting stimuli for further processing. One of these is concerned with consumers' needs, motives and goals. People are more likely to attend to information that is relevant to and instrumental in the achieving of goals and the satisfying of needs. This type of need-specific attention is called perceptual vigilance. Note that these needs may be conscious or unconscious. Someone who rarely pays attention to advertising for cars will suddenly start to notice car ads when he or she is in the market for a new car.

The nature of the stimulus can also have an impact on perceptual selection. Size, color, position and novelty are properties that can make a difference. Involuntary attention is an innate response that can occur when something surprising, unexpected, or threatening elicits attention automatically. As a general rule, any type of perceptual surprise may increase the probability of selection. This may be the deliberate and creative use of contrast, or scale, in advertising, for example.

Perceptual Organization   People do not perceive individual stimuli in isolation but, rather, organize the isolated parts of a stimulus into a meaningful totality. The human brain tends to relate incoming sensory information to imagery of other experiences and sensations stored in the memory. A number of perceptual principles determine how this sensory information is organized. These organizational principles form the basis of Gestalt psychology. The word *Gestalt* has no direct equivalent in English and literally refers to how something has been put or placed together. It is usually translated as *shape, form* or *configuration*. To Gestalt psychologists the whole is different from and greater than the sum of its parts. The brain makes a cognitive leap from the registration of the parts to the interpretation of the whole. The perceptual tendencies or principles identified by the founders of Gestalt psychology are most often applied to visual perception, though these principles are also valid for perception in the other senses. Underlying all these principles is the general principle of simplicity, by which people prefer the simplest, most stable of possible organizations.

The principle of closure leads us to perceive an incomplete form as complete. We tend to fill in the blanks when faced with an incomplete object based on previous experience. This principle is closely related to our basic impulse as humans to find meaning as well as to our innate inclination toward harmony and completeness. The IBM logo in Figure 3.6 is a good illustration of the principle of closure. The fact that we mentally fill in the gaps in incomplete images and insert letters and words when they are missing from a text makes the

Figure 3.6   IBM logo: An illustration of the principle of closure. (See color insert following p. 76.)

Figure 3.7 Rubin's famous face/vase.

principle of closure one much loved by advertisers. Readers are thus drawn into the advertising and actively participate in its construction, increasing involvement and, if done well, enjoyment.

Other perceptual principles of Gestalt psychology are illustrated in the Appendix.

The concept of figure and ground is another important element of Gestalt psychology and its application to perception. As a process of organizing and grouping incoming stimuli, perception also involves distinguishing an object from its surroundings. The figure–ground relationship means that we group some sensations into an object, or figure, which stands out from the background. The well-known Rubin face-vase figure shown in Figure 3.7 features an ambiguous

Figure 3.8   The FedEx logo exhibits a subtle example of figure and ground. Can you spot the "hidden" arrow?* (See color insert following p. 76.)

figure–ground relationship in which figure and ground can be reversed. We perceive the same stimulus as two different things: either a vase on a black background or two faces in profile on a white background.

There is an interesting and very subtle example of figure and ground in part of the FedEx logo shown in Figure 3.8. The "hidden" arrow is suggestive of speed, precision, and accuracy, qualities the company would be happy to be associated with. Can you spot the arrow?

Interpretation   Interpretation refers to the meaning people assign to the stimuli they perceive. These meanings may derive from the stimuli themselves or from people's minds. Context also plays a critical role in shaping our interpretations. Indeed, it has been said that there is no meaning without context. Context may be of a personal, situational, or sociocultural nature, for example. In the same way that people differ in terms of the stimuli they perceive in the first place, so the meanings that people assign to stimuli may be different as well. Two people may perceive the same event but interpret it very differently. This is particularly so when they have different backgrounds and cultures. Or the same person may derive very different meaning from the same set of stimuli depending on the context in which they are encountered.

The importance of the context in which thought and action occur cannot be overstated with regard to brand meaning. The physical and social setting of brand experience can influence the brand's frame of reference. It can also help explain why the same person may view a brand differently at different times. The context in which a

* Look between the E and x.

brand is viewed may prompt the foregrounding of one interpretation over another. Thus, a duality or even paradox may exist in the way people perceive a product or service (see Zaltman 2003, pp. 70–71). In the same way that a shower may be considered stimulating and refreshing first thing in the morning yet relaxing in the evening, so Coca-Cola may be described as invigorating in one setting yet relaxing in another—or as an American symbol in another context.

To help in the assignment of meaning to stimuli and thus make sense of things, we draw on our schemas. As mentioned earlier, a schema is a kind of mental template, an organized structure that reflects an individual's knowledge, experience and expectations of a given aspect of the world. For instance, most people have a staircase schema, which helps them recognize and climb an unfamiliar stairway. Archetypes, stereotypes and social roles are all examples of schemas. Schemas can guide the encoding and retrieval of information. But although they can aid recall, they can also introduce errors, where the schema leads us to "remember" something that was not there but would have been consistent with our schema.*

---

* An experiment on the influence of schemas on visual perception and memory used a room designed as a graduate student's office (Brewer and Treyen 1981). However, items were included that did not fit into that setting, such as a skull, a toy top and a picnic basket. Each subject on arrival was asked by the graduate assistant to wait in his office while he checked on the prior subject. After thirty-five seconds, the subject was escorted to a conference room and asked to write his or her recollections of the room. Of interest is that eighty-eight objects were recalled by one or more subjects, of which nineteen were objects not found in the room. Among the nonpresent items named by the subjects were books, a filing cabinet, coffee cup (a coffee pot was in the room), pens and a lamp. These objects were highly relevant to the schema "office"; thus, the researchers concluded that schema knowledge became integrated with actual information about the room.

Figure 3.5 Gradual modifications to Shell's famous emblem.

Figure 3.6 IBM logo: An illustration of the principle of closure.

Figure 3.8 The FedEx logo exhibits a subtle example of figure and ground. Can you spot the "hidden" arrow?

iPhone launch ad: a nice twist on an old adage related to perception.

4

The Meaning of Things

Introduction

The nature of meaning has been debated since the time of Plato and Aristotle. Philosophers, logicians and linguists have all wrestled with the elusive topic. Important contributions have been made in recent times by semanticists and semioticians. Semantics is the study of meaning in language. Semiotics is the study of signs and their role in signification. Both fields provide useful illumination and important lessons for the understanding of product and brand meaning as well as brand communication.

Semantic Space

In 1957, a pioneering and hugely influential book called *The Measurement of Meaning*, by American psychologist C. E. Osgood and colleagues G. Suci and P. Tannenbaum presented a new method for the measurement of meaning. The technique has come to be used in empirical research in fields such as clinical psychology, social psychology, linguistics, mass communications and political science. The authors of the book used *Roget's Thesaurus* to help construct bipolar scales based on semantic opposites, such as *strong–weak* (on the rationale that semantic opposition is common to most language systems). They called these scales "semantic differential" scales, the name indicative of their view that it was possible to analyze meaning into a range of different dimensions. The aim was to locate a concept in semantic space so that its meaning is defined as that point in the semantic space specified by a series of differentiating factors.

Concepts were plotted along numerous seven-point scales with the opposed adjectives at each end, such as good–bad, important–unimportant, awkward–graceful and regressive–progressive. Difference in the meaning between two concepts would be a function of the differences in their respective allocations within the same semantic space.

Several interesting findings emerged from the studies conducted by the authors. First, three factors, or dimensions, proved predominant in individuals' assessments:

1. The individual's evaluation of the object or concept being rated, as measured by scales such as good–bad, beautiful–ugly, clean–dirty, valuable–worthless, kind–cruel, pleasant–unpleasant, happy–sad, nice–awful, fragrant–foul, honest–dishonest
2. The individual's perception of the potency or power of the object or concept, as measured by scales such as strong–weak, large–small, heavy–light, thick–thin
3. The individual's perception of the activity of the object or concept, as measured by scales such as active–passive, fast–slow, restless–quiet

The relative weights of these three major factors—evaluation, potency and activity (EPA)—were found to be fairly consistent, with evaluation counting for approximately double the amount of variance due to either potency or activity and these two in turn being approximately double the weight of any subsequent factors. The relative importance of the various dimensions of semantic space is illustrated in Figure 4.1. These factors (EPA being the major ones) thus represent dimensions of meaningful discrimination when considering the meaning of objects or concepts.

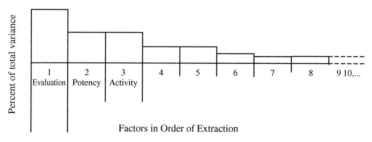

Figure 4.1   Relative importance of semantic space dimensions.

Attitude and Behavior

According to Osgood et al. (1957, pp. 190–191), "It seems reasonable to identify attitude ... with the evaluative dimension of the total semantic space.... Obviously every point in semantic space has an evaluative component.... Therefore, every concept must involve an attitudinal component as part of its total meaning." The semantic differential may thus be used as a generalized attitude scale; however, the authors make a critical point with regard to its use in predicting actual behavior in real-life situations. They point out that behavior can seldom be predicted from knowledge of attitude alone. The meaning of a concept to an individual is far richer than what is revealed by his attitude or evaluative score alone: "So two people may have identical *attitudes* toward a concept (as determined by allocation to the evaluative dimension alone) and yet have quite different meanings of the concept (as determined by the profiles as wholes)" (ibid., p. 198, italics in original).

Osgood et al. (1957) quote an example where one respondent rated a subject as unfavorable (E), strong (P) and active (A), and another rated the subject as equally unfavorable (E) but also as weak (P) and passive (A). The contention is that the former respondent would behave differently in a real-life situation, possibly with fear and avoidance, than the latter. So whereas it is true that different attitudes imply different behaviors toward the objects signified it does not follow that the same attitude automatically implies the same behaviors (ibid., p. 199).

On a related issue, research in social cognition has shown that semantic consistency dominates evaluative consistency during the formation of trait inferences. For instance, somebody who is described as thrifty (a desirable trait) is more likely to be judged as stingy (an undesirable but conceptually consistent trait with thrifty) than generous (a desirable but conceptually inconsistent trait with thrifty) (Broniarczyk and Alba 1994).

For similar reasons to those discussed in the foregoing paragraphs, a brand's overall meaning to a consumer extends beyond that revealed by simple tracking of likeability ratings (e.g., "My kind of soft drink"). The ultimate meaning the brand will have, though connected in large measure to the consumer's attitude toward the brand, is an aggregate of various factors. This meaning will effectively determine real-life behavior. Many marketers with big enough budgets to allow television advertising seek to use humor as a device for creating an engaging brand personality and affecting attitude ratings toward their brand. Done well and as part of an overall brand strategy, it can be very successful, but too often such humor is used as an expedient and seems somehow disconnected from the brand or only obliquely attached to it. Besides rarely being differentiating at brand level, such advertising, which seems so prevalent today, will seldom do much more than to nudge attitude ratings along the positive scale (if it achieves that). On its own this is never enough. As the previously quoted example illustrates, it is even possible to have a favorable rating while at the same time falling into negative territory on the other dimensions that measure meaning. As an example, Millward Brown uses "passive–active" as a key criterion in its advertising research methodology. Indeed, the EPA factors established by Osgood and his associates (1957) underpin many of the research practices widely used today in marketing and other fields. The validity of the three dimensions has been demonstrated and upheld across time and across cultures and is seen as contributing significantly to the definition of the underlying meaning structures of brands.

Denotation and Connotation

Osgood et al. (1957) believed their measurement system provided a valuable means of getting a handle on meaning. Yet there was one important qualification to be made. Osgood acknowledged that the semantic differential taps the connotative aspects of meaning more immediately than the denotative aspects. Denotation is a definitional, literal meaning. Connotation is what is implied by, for example, a word, in addition to its literal meaning. Connotative meaning is more variable, figurative and subjective. It includes the feelings and emotions a word evokes in people and the sociocultural and personal associations that arise from that person's race, class, gender, religion and so forth.

> "Denotation and connotation therefore represent two vocabularies using the same set of words. The denotative usage presents the thing in its essential and objective meaning. The connotative usage presents it enriched by associations and feelings which, though not susceptible of being pinned down, are nonetheless real" (Weaver 1974 pp. 239–240).

Meaning includes both denotation and connotation. Consider, for example, the following definition of meaning: "the denotative and connotative associations produced as a reader decodes a text" (McQuarrie and Mick 1992, p. 181). *Text* here is used in its broad, semiotic sense of something that can be read or decoded like a painting or an advertisement. Incidentally, the term *associations* needs to be treated carefully. In *The Measurement of Meaning* Osgood et al. (1957, p. 17) states flatly that the notion that meaning and association can be equated is wrong. Exaggerating to make a point, he notes that *black* does not mean "white" any more than *needle* means "sew," despite these being the most frequent respective associations. What is actually at issue here is the associative value of a stimulus such as *needle*. Though there is some overlap, due to the common mediation process (elicited by the same stimulus), Osgood observes that the responses one receives when asking what something means are usually quite different from those obtained when asking for associations (e.g., the other things that *needle* makes the respondent think of). It is beneficial to bear this in mind when researching brand meaning and to always consider what is orienting one toward brand meaning and what is orienting one away from it. In other words, if we accept that meaning can be accessed via associations, it is imperative to identify which are the associations that most define the meaning of an object or a brand.

Semiotics

In the context of meaning in general and denotation–connotation in particular, there are useful theories and interpretations to be found in the field of semiotics, especially in the work of Roland Barthes (1915–1980). Semiotics is the study of signs and the way they work to generate meaning. Barthes's predecessor, the Swiss scholar Ferdinand de Saussure (1857–1913), known as the father of modern linguistics, was first to systemize his views on language as an example of a sign system. *Course in General Linguistics* was reconstructed from students' notes after his death and was first published in 1916. His work founded modern linguistic theory and his new method, known as structuralism, has since been applied to areas as diverse as anthropology, architecture and folklore. Saussure was interested in the structure of language and the nature and relationships of linguistic signs. His focus was on the linguistic system itself and not on the connection between that system and the reader and his or her sociocultural context and personal experience.

Barthes pointed out that Saussure's model of the sign focused on denotation and neglected to account for connotation. In *Eléments de Sémiologie* Barthes (1964) redressed the balance and expounded his theory on the connotative dimension of meaning. Central to Barthes's theory is a model of meaning construction based on different orders of signification (Barthes 1987). The first order, or level, of signification is that of denotation. The second order of signification is connotation. In *Image—Music—Text* Barthes (1977) suggests photography as an example where the difference between denotation and connotation is clear. For Barthes, in photography the denoted (i.e., first-order) meaning is conveyed through the mechanical process of reproduction. Connotative (i.e., second-order) meanings are introduced by human intervention—through lighting, pose, camera angle and so forth. As John Fiske (1982, p. 91) puts it, "Denotation is *what* is photographed; connotation is *how* it is photographed." He cites the instance of a photograph of a street scene. The photograph would denote that particular street, just as the word *street* denotes a road or thoroughfare with buildings on either side. But the same street can appear very different according to how it is photographed: "I can use a color film, pick a day of pale sunshine, use a soft focus and make the street appear a happy, warm, humane community for the children playing in it. Or I can use black-and-white film, hard focus, strong contrasts and make this same street appear cold, inhuman, inhospitable and a destructive environment for the children playing in it" (ibid.).

This may seem similar to the form versus content distinction, but it is more subtle and fundamental. Like Saussure, for Barthes a sign consists of a signifier and a signified. The signifier is the physical or material carrier of the meaning (e.g., sounds, images, objects, words), and the signified is the mental representation, or concept. Thus, the signified is not "a thing" but a mental representation of the "thing." The signified of the animal cow is not the animal cow but its mental representation, the concept of a cow as it exists in your head. The signified is more than just a mental picture, as it may well incorporate representative elements perceived through other senses—smell or sound, for instance.

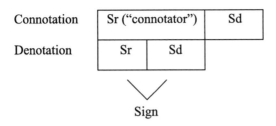

Figure 4.2 Connotation according to Barthes (Sr = Signifier, Sd = Signified).

This basic relation of signifier to signified is denotation, or the literal meaning of a sign. In Barthes's theory the signifiers of connotation, the "connotators" are made up of signs (i.e., signifiers and signifieds united) of the denoted system. Connotation, then, uses the denotative sign as its signifier and attaches to it an additional signified. This is illustrated in Figure 4.2. Denotation can therefore lead to a chain of connotations.

So in the example in Figure 4.3 the sign "rose" (signifier #1 and signified #1) becomes the signifier (#2) for a secondary signified, that of "love." Of course the image of the rose in Figure 4.3 is not in itself the signified but is rather another sign being used to signify the signified: what exists in your head.

Barthes maintains that these two orders of signification combine to produce myth* or ideology, which others (though not Barthes himself) have referred to as a third order of signification. He illustrates his theory in "Myth Today," the final essay in his book *Mythologies* (Barthes 1987), using the now-famous example of the photograph on the cover of a copy of *Paris-Match,* showing a young black soldier saluting what is presumed to be the French tricolor. The photograph, like all photographs, would appear to present a literal, transparent meaning: A young black soldier salutes the national (French) flag. According to Barthes's semiotic reading, though, the photograph shifts between different levels of meaning. One level is simply the historically specific image as presented in the photograph, of an individual soldier saluting the French flag. The mythic meaning has

---

* Barthes' use of the term *myth* here is a specific one. The term can refer, as it does here, to something that is fictitious, imaginary or invented, particularly as part of an ideology. Elsewhere in this book the term is used in its other sense of a traditional and popular story or belief that illustrates a cultural pattern of behavior or the customs or mores of a society.

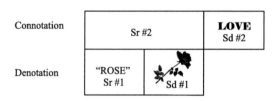

Connotation	Sr #2	**LOVE** Sd #2
Denotation	"ROSE" Sr #1	Sd #1

Figure 4.3 An example of connotation.

to do with the unified French nation, with all her sons, regardless of color or origin, happy to serve under her flag.

The third, mythological or ideological, order of signification reflects substantial cultural concepts and values such as freedom, independence, individualism, femininity and so forth. Another practical illustration of the three orders of signification in the context of a photograph of Marilyn Monroe is provided by Susan Hayward (1996) in her book *Key Concepts in Cinema Studies*. At the denotative level it is a photograph of the particular film star Marilyn Monroe. At a connotative level the photograph conveys to us Marilyn Monroe's qualities of glamour, sexuality and sensual beauty (or, if it is a photo taken later in her life, her depression and drug taking). At a mythic level we encounter the operation of the myth of Hollywood: the dream machine that produces glamour in the form of movie stars that can be destroyed just as quickly.

So with second-order signification (i.e., connotation) and in particular with third-order signification (i.e., the realm of mythology or ideology), we are dealing with the invocation of meanings deeply rooted in our culture. It is here a question of the cultural meaning of signs, meanings that derive not from the sign itself but from the way a given society employs and values the signifier and signified. For Barthes, in the example of the picture of the young black soldier just mentioned, it is the ideological import of the photograph that matters. This is determined by the way the photo relates to and draws on the prevailing sets of myths that serve as organizing structures in a society and influence the meanings we attach to signs.

In *Mythologies* Barthes (1987) applies to food, like steak and chips, his methodology for examining the spectrum of meanings that common objects can invoke. The hamburger provides an equally valid example (see Slater 1997, p. 139). It can refer to a particular kind of food, in relation to other items in a food code, such as sausage, bun, chips, lettuce. But it can also signify broader meanings, such as

American culture—as opposed to lasagna, TexMex, or sushi—or, yet broader, American cultural imperialism. So *hamburger* can denote or signify a slab of grilled beef; or it can serve as a signifier within another system, or level, of signification, for example, one comprising different national cultures and the types of values they represent (e.g., American fast-food culture or commercial dominance, European high-brow culture, eclecticism). "'Hamburger' can therefore connote Americanism, modernity or other values which are not in any literal sense perceptible in the object. It is denotation which gives mythological power to the connoted values: the latter appear to be natural properties of the former" (ibid.). This is a key characteristic of what Barthes refers to as myth.

Tangible and Intangible Properties

Things, consumption objects, or products have both tangible and intangible properties. Tangible properties are those capable of being perceived through the senses. They reside in the object itself and can be touched, seen, smelled, heard, or tasted. They thus have an objective quality as they exist independent of the mind. Intangible properties exist only in the mind of an individual. They emanate from the mind of the subject, or individual, rather than from the object being observed. Intangible properties are therefore subjective in nature, being mental constructs of the individual. They represent subjective associations brought about by previous direct and vicarious experience. So, as Figure 4.4 shows, whereas tangible properties emanate from the object to the individual's mind via the senses, intangible properties emanate from the individual's mind and are projected onto the object.

Research has suggested that consumers, when mentally grouping products into categories, tend to operate at the lowest level of abstraction, using surface properties of products to determine physical similarity. It is useful to understand how consumers categorize or cluster products in their mind, as this indicates what meanings these products have for consumers. Needless to say, consumers do not perform the same type of rational, detailed analysis that marketers and researchers do. The marketer will ask, "What does this product compete with, or substitute for?" Frame-of-reference models are usually organized along hierarchical lines, with competitive sets operating at a number

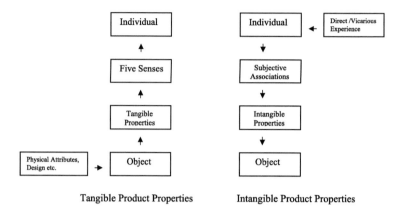

Figure 4.4   Tangible and intangible properties.

of different levels. Consider Sprite as an example. At the product-type level, it competes with other carbonated non-cola soft drinks. At the product-category level it competes with all other soft drinks. At the product-class level it competes with all beverages, including tea, coffee and milk. The closest the consumer will come to this type of analysis will be in forming—instinctively, rapidly and, for the most part, unconsciously—a consideration set of options at the moment of deciding what to drink. Something hot? Cold? Sweet? Sharp? Flavorful? Neutral? As discussed elsewhere, much will depend on what that person feels like or is in the mood for.

Besides an object's physical attributes and usually resulting from those attributes is the other key dimension of object meaning: its performance or performance potential (Kernan and Sommers 1967). Whereas an object's attributes refer to the physical dimension of meaning, to perceptions of an object's palpable characteristics (e.g., baking soda is white and powdery), performance refers to the functional dimension of meaning, to perceptions of what the object actually does, or could do—its action potential (e.g., a refrigerator deodorizer, antacid, or dentifrice, in the case of baking soda) (Kleine and Kernan 1988). It has been argued, for instance, that similarity of meaning within a category is largely determined by performance—by the functional consequences of a product's attributes—that is, that natural categories would appear to consist of objects that do the same thing. Along similar lines, a popular observation on consumer behavior maintains that what consumers seek are benefits rather than features.

So consumers will perceive features, but what they seek are the benefits of those features. Moreover, even though they may recognize the product-class type of product category used by manufacturers and retailers, consumers are capable of creating further categories based on product functions. For instance, although product-class product categories such as toothpaste, mouthwash, chewing gum and mints are well defined, consumers could create a category of breath fresheners that would include products from all of these product classes and maybe more besides (see Gutman 1982).

The meaning of an object to an individual is thus an amalgam of tangible, objective properties emanating from the object itself and subjective, intangible properties associated with it in the mind of the individual. Influencing these tangible and intangible properties of object meaning is the crucial element of context. Objects have a greater or lesser degree of what Kleine and Kernan (1988) call "contextual sensitivity." The context in which an object is perceived will affect the meaning ascribed to that object: "Contextual sensitivity suggests that the meaning of a turkey on a Thanksgiving Day dinner table probably differs from that of a turkey placed on a dinner table during mid-May" (ibid., p. 498). As we have seen earlier, in positioning their products marketers must decide what market context (i.e., frame of reference) is the most appropriate. Later we will see how advertising agencies frame and modify brand meaning through their choice of context for the brand in its communication.

The origination of intangible attributes warrants further description. Some of these intangible attributes will be widely shared across members of a particular society or culture. Others may be shared only among members of a subset of that culture—that is, a subculture. Finally, there are intangible properties that are idiosyncratically associated on a highly individual basis. Any object or product thus possesses, potentially, several strata of meaning—ranging from a high degree of shared meaning to a low degree. This is represented in Figure 4.5. Depending on the object and individual in question, there may be a greater or lesser degree of conventional (i.e., societal) meaning and of idiosyncratic meaning.

Common objective meaning consists of direct sensory impressions such as size, shape, weight and sound, which are largely verifiable and invariable across all people. Culturally shared subjective meaning derives from thoughts and images that most people in a culture associate with an object. Subculturally shared subjective

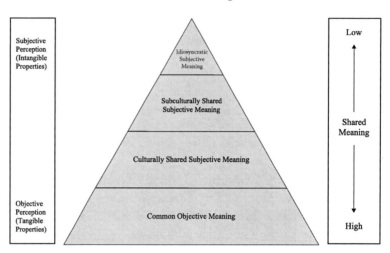

Figure 4.5   Multilayered meaning.

meaning arises from the thoughts and images that members of a specific group within a culture associate with an object. Finally, idiosyncratic subjective meaning derives from unique, highly personalized experiences with an object, generating personal meaning that varies from one person to the next.

Pulling all these components together, the complexity of an object's meaning can be appreciated, as summarized in Figure 4.6.

Private and Public Meanings

The meanings ascribed to objects by individuals are important because they contribute to the value of those objects above and beyond economic value. Possessions have both private meaning—assigned by the individual owner—and public meaning. Public meanings, also called social meanings or cultural meanings, are the subjective meanings ascribed to an object by others in society. They are meanings shared by society at large. The society into which we are born and in which we are raised, creates the meanings in our lives. As we grow up and become more integrated into society we realize that things have associations connected with them that impart meaning on them quite apart from their physical attributes. The contexts of these associations and the source of these meanings vary; they may originate at school, at church, at home with the family, the workplace.

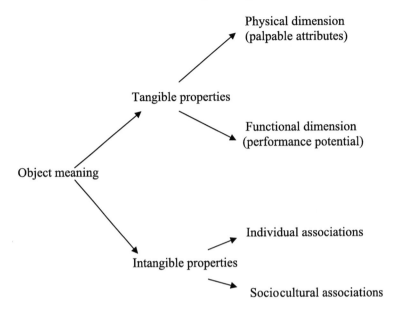

Figure 4.6 Components of an object's meaning.

Though the public meanings of some things remain constant over time, the public meanings of others may be prone to modification. Take candles as an example. The function of candles is to provide light. In centuries gone by, before electricity and electric light bulbs and hand torches, they were indispensable as a way of lighting the home so people could see what they were doing. Today, power cuts notwithstanding, this utilitarian meaning of candles has morphed into one more to do with ambience setting than illumination. Candles are still found in most homes. The difference is that now they are used in a decorative, aesthetic context. Their basic physical dimension has remained unchanged for centuries, yet their functional dimension has been reframed and their public meaning has been substantially modified. More recently, the market for scented candles has broadened their meaning.

Watches provide another example. In bygone centuries, when we were not surrounded by electronic clocks, stoves with clocks, cable boxes with clocks and computers with clocks, the timepiece was the only accurate way of keeping track of the passing hours and minutes. Nowadays, watches have also become fashion statements and accessories and indispensable status symbols. Even in the economic downturn of the beginning of this century luxury watches were commanding prices anywhere from $10,000 up to $1 million. Piaget watches average $15,000 and run as high as $4 million. Often, technological advances are responsible for the meaning shifts in everyday objects. Not that long ago a radio was a piece of furniture.

The private or personal meanings of an object are those subjective meanings assigned to it by a particular individual. These meanings may incorporate facets of the object's public meanings, but the owner's personal circumstances and experiences with regard to the object are the determining factors. Private meaning is cultivated over time through repeated interaction with an object and the psychic energy invested in it. Jewelry, an old toy and a vintage car are examples. A special pair of earrings, worn only on certain occasions and perhaps a gift from a husband or parent, will hold vivid associations for a lady.

Symbolic Meaning

> Symbols are the imaginative signposts of life.
>
> Margot Asquith (1934)

The various meanings that goods hold for us are of particular interest in the context of personal identity and social communication. Yet contemporary marketing thinking has been painfully slow in assimilating the implications of this dynamic. Commentators such as McCracken (1990, p. 4) contend that traditional consumer behavior theory disregards the connection between culture and consumer practices because it refuses to take on board the topic of meaning. He laments that the possibility that the consumer might turn to consumer goods as sources of cultural meaning is rendered unthinkable. In 1959, Sidney J. Levy wrote along similar lines: "The things people buy are seen to have personal and social meanings in addition to their functions. To ignore or decry the symbolism of consumer goods does not affect the importance of the fact. The only question is whether the goods are to be symbolized thoughtfully or thoughtlessly" (p. 117). In essence, symbolic consumption is the process by which people endow products and objects with meanings above and beyond those that inhere in the objects themselves. An understanding of this process—and of the way objects can take on symbolic meanings—will throw more light on the connection among self, culture and consumer behavior. The implications for the role of brands and brand meaning will be evident. First, though, it is necessary to clarify what is meant by symbolism and in particular the term *symbol*, a term intimately connected with the concept of meaning itself.

The word *symbol* is derived from the Greek verb "to throw together." The corresponding noun *sumbolon* originally referred to each of two matching pieces of some object—a ring, a piece of pottery, or a tablet, for example—that two people entering into an agreement or contract would break between them and retain as proof of identity. So the earliest symbols were two essentially similar things that matched and belonged together. This characteristic of the term would change somewhat with time, yet implicit even in the original use of the term is the important aspect of the two parts, when joined, pointing to something else, to some meaning, or understanding, lying beyond the reassembled object itself.

Dictionary definitions usually refer to a symbol as an arbitrary sign that represents something else by association, resemblance, or convention, especially a material object used to represent something invisible. Such a definition touches on all the key facets of symbolism that have been advanced and debated by the various fields of which it forms an important part, notably semiotics, psychology, anthropology and philosophy. Some theorists have classified symbol as a special kind of sign. Semioticians such as Charles Peirce, the father of semiotics in America, typically hold this view, stressing that symbols are characterized by the fact that the relation between signifier and signified is arbitrary. In other words, there is no strict material, physical, or biological connection between symbol and symbolized. Nonarbitrary, or motivated, signs, on the other hand, depend more on similarity and contiguity for the understanding of their meaning, as in the case of the sign of a tap indicating water or smoke being a sign of fire.

Others contrast the direct nature of signs with the indirect nature of symbols. Still further commentators distinguish between (usually two) different types of symbols—for instance, conventional versus nonconventional symbols. The symbols of logic, morse code and mathematics have been established by agreement or convention. What the symbol means, or stands for, has to be learned. Yet there are other instances of symbols, symbolism and symbolic manifestation—for instance in the areas of literature, myths, fairy tales, folklore, art and dreams—in which these symbols must be interpreted and construed and in which that interpretation is not set by convention. At most, there are cultural, historical, or habitual guidelines, but the meanings of such symbolic phenomena are open to debate and contention.

Symbols evolve, gain or lose strength and sometimes fade away. Objects that in one context are highly charged with symbolic significance may be devoid of such significance in another. Or they may have a different significance—for symbols are multivalent and multimeaning, the variation in their meanings usually a function of cultural differences. The red cross is a symbol of protection during armed conflicts. When nations gathered to approve the first Geneva Convention in 1864 they adopted a red cross on a white background—the reverse of the Swiss flag—as the official sign of the humanitarian aid services. However, disputes soon arose. Muslim countries claimed the symbol signified the Christian Crusades. In the Russian–Turkish war of 1877–78 the Ottoman Empire decided to use the red crescent instead of the red cross and today the symbol and name Red Crescent is used by Islamic countries. When there is a change in the sociocultural, political, or economic conditions that originally provided a symbol with its associations and resonances, the symbolic reference may become obscure or forgotten and the symbol may lose its meaning. Conversely, precisely because such contexts may change continually, the common cultural pool of meaning may come full circle and symbols may effectively be reborn. Other symbols seem to endure with relatively little modification to their meaning.

The world has recently witnessed the literal demise of a symbol that will be familiar to every reader of this book. During the dedication ceremony to his greatest construction, Japanese American architect Minoru Yamasaki said of his creation that it had "a bigger purpose than just to provide room for tenants." Rather, he saw it as "a living symbol of man's dedication to world peace … a representation of man's belief in humanity, his need for individual dignity, his beliefs in the cooperation of men and, through cooperation, his ability to find greatness" (http://architecture.about.com/library/61worldtrade02.htm). It took just minutes for the physical object of that symbolism to be brought crashing to the ground on September 11, 2001. It is impossible to talk of the terrorist attack on the World Trade Center without talking of symbolism. The Twin Towers had become a symbol of American economic might. As such, they became a target for members of the al-Qaeda network. There was even a macabre symbolism about the date of the attack—"nine eleven," or 911—the emergency number in the United States. In the days and weeks following the attack, the symbolism surrounding the site evolved poignantly. The gaping hole in the landscape, with its debris and twisted metal, became a symbol of America's sudden and unaccustomed sense of vulnerability and insecurity. On the six-month anniversary of the attack two massive beams of light were sent up into the night sky from a site just north of where the towers had once stood—a symbolic "Tribute in Light." It was a light of hope and spirit. In the aftermath of the destruction, proposals were invited for what, if anything, should replace the towers. Some suggested a memorial in honor of those who lost their lives. Others suggested a new skyscraper, even higher than the World Trade Center—a new symbol, in this case one of defiance.

Whether the symbol in question is a building or structure, like the Statue of Liberty or the Taj Mahal, or something far smaller and more modest like a ring or a rose, symbols are all around us and an integral part of our lives. We will see that symbolism is an important part of brand meaning and communication and exerts a strong influence on consumer behavior. As long ago as 1899 the American economist and social critic Thorstein Veblen asserted that clothing, particularly that of the wife of the bourgeois gentleman and other categories of material culture carried status meaning and were thus objects of "conspicuous consumption," a phrase he coined in *The Theory of the Leisure Class*. Today such goods are referred to as status symbols—though the symbolism is hardly subtle or complex. As Veblen observed, these articles simply provided good prima facie evidence of income.

In a semiotic sense status symbols may be seen as positional or relational goods, their value residing in their semiotic ability to position their owners within a social structure (see Slater 1997, p. 156). When goods mark social status by being part of the trappings and lifestyle of a certain social sector (be it the Rolls Royce of the affluent or the Barbour jacket of the British country set), they are acquired by others laying claim to the same status through emulation of their manners, style and possessions. There is, of course, an in-built futility in the process, which becomes a self-defeating game of catch-up. The prestige attached to aspirational goods or services depends precisely on their exclusivity. As Slater puts it, "A holiday in Marbella or a taste for nouvelle cuisine has a certain cachet until ten million other people are consuming it in packaged form" (ibid.). Once everyone else has joined the club, it loses its appeal, by which time the trendsetters and social elite have moved on. Needless to say, the media and fashion worlds perpetuate and thrive on this circular pattern of differentiation–distinction, emulation–conformity. The market is constantly renewing itself as the latest look, trend, or fad becomes obsolete.

It is worth making reference to the views of the eminent French philosopher and social theorist Jean Baudrillard (1968) with regard to consumption and the meaning of goods. Baudrillard argues that we no longer consume goods but only signs. This is an extreme semiotic extrapolation of Veblen's concept of the function of goods being to signify and differentiate status. In other words, utilitarian value is entirely displaced by sign value. Even with the ultimate example of status symbolism it is difficult to conceive of a good whose value is purely as a sign, with no functional purpose. Rolls Royces still carry their drivers from A to B; fur coats still keep their wearers warm, despite the fact that Barthes, as we have seen, would dismiss these utilitarian uses as "alibis," as ways of "naturalizing" the cultural order and conspiring to make something as culturally arbitrary as a status symbol (eg., a fur coat) appear to have a natural and rational function (e.g., protection against the cold). To Barthes, function "mythologizes" (Slater 1997, p. 145).

It is a characteristic of affluent societies that, having covered fundamental needs such as those indicated at one extreme of Abraham Maslow's hierarchy, people, whether consciously or not, are more sensitive to and influenced by the subjective and sociocultural meanings attributed to goods: "Once the satisfaction of basic needs has been materially secured, the meaningful or cultural aspect of consumption comes to predominate and people become more concerned with the meanings of goods than with their functional use to meet a basic or 'real' need" (Slater 1997, p. 133). Indeed, given the long-recognized pervasiveness of status symbolism, for example and the fact that almost all cultures display the characteristic of using objects to signify status, it is surprising that more investigation has not been forthcoming as to other possible meanings, particularly symbolic meanings, of objects. Whereas sociologists seem stuck in the status symbol groove, psychologists are wont to reduce everything to the level of sexual symbolism, where anything longer than it is wide is a phallic symbol (even Sigmund Freud said sometimes a cigar is just a cigar). The way society and its consumers endow objects with meaning and link product and consumption meanings is infinitely more interesting and complex than this, as the relatively few research programs into the subject have revealed.

What Our Possessions Mean

The objects with which we surround ourselves, whether branded consumer goods or common household items, are rich and diverse in meaning. We develop connections to our possessions for a variety of reasons and they become a material part of our existence. As consumer researcher Russell Belk (1988, p. 139) noted, "We cannot hope to understand consumer behavior without first gaining some understanding of the meanings that consumers attach to possessions. A key to understanding what possessions mean is recognizing that, knowingly or unknowingly, intentionally or unintentionally, we regard our possessions as part of ourselves."

The heading of this chapter, "The Meaning of Things," is taken from the title of the work by Csikszentmihalyi and Rochberg-Halton (1981), a study of the symbolic relationship between home and self—more particularly the meaning of objects found in homes and the reasons for people's attachments to those objects. Interviews were conducted in 1977 with more than 315 members of households in 82 families in the Chicago Metropolitan area. The authors were interested in fathoming the deep-seated meaning of the artifacts in homes: "The real meaning of a possession, like that of a dream, does not lie in its *manifest* content but, rather, in its underlying *latent* content" (ibid., p. 23, italics in original).

The classification of objects and meanings into categories was based on respondents' conceptions. The 1,694 objects mentioned were grouped into 41 categories, such as furniture, visual art, books, photos, stuffed animals, trophies, toys and plants. The thirty-seven meaning categories, reflecting the meanings embodied in the objects for the respondents, were further classified into eleven meaning classes; so, for example, the categories memento, recollection, heirloom, and souvenir were all combined in the class memories. Other meaning classes were personal values and accomplishment.

It should be noted in passing that a total of 7,875 significations were recorded for the 1,694 objects; in other words, each object was coded as having an average of four separate meanings. That meant that the same object could appear in different categories. Polysemy is a characteristic of object meaning and refers to the fact that a given object can mean many things—for instance, as mentioned earlier in this chapter, baking soda can be an antacid, a refrigerator deodorizer, or a dentifrice.

Some interesting demographic differences emerged from the Csikszentmihalyi and Rochberg-Halton (1981) study. Among the reasons given for cherishing items, children would often reflect enjoyment and egocentricity, adult women would stress social networks and adult males would emphasize accomplishment and abstract ideals. The authors suggest two broad categories for all objects: objects of action and objects of contemplation. The former involve some type of kinetic activity and physical involvement with the object (e.g., instruments, sports equipment, vehicles, stereo systems), whereas the latter do not require physical intervention (e.g., art, photos, silverware). Typically, males cherished objects of action more frequently; and females tended more toward objects of contemplation. In this respect the female pattern is closer to that of the grandparents and the male pattern is closer to that of the children. To complement the polarity of action–contemplation, the authors propose another dimension, with the polarities self-differentiation–other-integration. Typically, males emphasize action and self in contrast to females, who value contemplation and relationships with others. Broadly speaking, household objects can be classified along these two dimensions of meaning (ibid., p. 113). This is illustrated in Figure 4.7.

The overriding conclusion from the study is that meaning, not material possessions, was the ultimate goal of the respondents. Things were cherished not because of their intrinsic value or for the material comfort they provide but rather for what they convey about the owner and his or her ties to others. "Things can have meanings that may transform the very world in which we live. But things by themselves alone cannot help us; only in the way we relate to them is their symbolic energy released" (Csikszentmihalyi and Rochberg-Halton 1981, p. 247). Whereas on the one hand people are not passive consumers, on the other they are never fully conscious of their motives. The social and personal meanings that goods carry for people lie somewhere between these two psychological states (Bourdieu 1984).

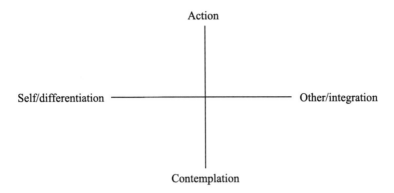

Figure 4.7   Dimensions and categories of object meaning suggested by Csikszentmihalyi/Rochberg-Halton.

Ordinary household objects substantiate the self-definition and reaffirm the identity of the owner by providing a familiar symbolic context for daily life. Books, for example, can connote learning and education. Some people like to display books as a sign of being well read. Professionals often like to be surrounded by the books of their trade. Some use books more or less for decoration purposes in the kitchen or on coffee tables. Or consider the example of a humble T-shirt. Its core meaning would be functionally oriented—a short-sleeved, collarless item of clothing. If it had an Armani logo on it, its symbolic meaning might be that of a status symbol. If it had a slogan written on it, representing some ideological standpoint, it would have a different symbolic meaning for its wearer. If it carried the date and location of a march or rally, or a marathon its owner had competed in, or if it was bought at a rock concert of a favorite group several years ago, it would again have a different symbolic significance. Or it may have been given to its wearer by a loved one. Notice that in these instances meaning spans the spectrum of conventional, socially shared meaning through to idiosyncratic, personal meaning.

The way things, objects, can carry diverse layers of meaning provides insight into how brands take on meaning. Consider what the meaning might be of *Christmas tree*: At the manifest level it is an evergreen or artificial tree decorated with tinsel and lights. Its symbolic meaning may be Christmas spirit, family togetherness and harmony, the rekindling of childhood memories. Similarly, the word *church* may mean a stone-walled building with wooden doors or an institution, but it may also mean a sanctuary or a mystical oasis. Champagne, even that produced using the genuine méthode champenoise, is basically sparkling wine, made from the same types of grape as still wines, such as chardonnay. Yet no drink in the world has the same symbolic resonance that champagne possesses. It is synonymous with joyous celebration, as well as carrying connotations of affluence.

Symbolic Consumption

The cultural, social dimension of consumption patterns refers to the way our social milieu influences the perceptions we form and the choices we make. Our own personal decisions are never quite as self-determined as they seem. There is always the consideration of what other people (e.g., whom we like, admire, want to impress) will think of our behavior. This in part stems from a need for reassurance, but it is actually symptomatic of a far more substantial phenomenon. For, as we have seen, through our consumption behavior—through what we consume and how we consume it—we are constantly defining our position within society and our relationship with that society. Alcohol and its consumption provide an example. The consumption of alcohol is an important social activity in most cultures. Alcohol, in its vast array of different formats, has an extensive network of meanings. Its physical properties can induce relaxation, libidinousness, aggression, inebriation. It is intricately associated with age, gender, taste, social standing. It can procure social approval and facilitate social interaction but also connote irresponsibility. It also has a strong ritualistic element: It often accompanies celebration (e.g., to raise a glass, toast the newlyweds) or commiseration (e.g., to drown one's sorrows). It can mark initiation into adulthood. It is an integral part of voodoo and *santería* ceremonies, where its ingestion lubricates the transition to another life or state of being.

A study of the symbolic meaning of alcohol consumption was conducted in Australia (Pettigrew 2002). Beer is the most popular form of alcohol in Australia and has traditionally been associated with masculine symbolism. Although Australian females generally prefer wine to beer, they are increasingly turning to beer as a means of communicating their desire for equality. This is having the effect of attenuating the masculine association with beer consumption. The particular focus of the Australian study was male and female attitudes regarding female alcohol drinkers. Projective techniques were used and a total of 65 interviews were conducted. Respondents were asked to imagine two females, both resembling Australian actress and model Elle McPherson, sitting at either end of a public bar. The only difference between the two was their choice of beverage—one was drinking wine and the other beer. Male participants were asked which of the Elles they would prefer to ask out on a date, whereas female participants were asked which Elle would be approached to request change for a call on the public telephone. In addition, female respondents had to guess which of the two Elles was more likely to be asked out on a date by males.

Solely on the basis of a difference in alcohol consumption, the two Elles were construed as being very different people, both in terms of social standing and personal characteristics. It emerged that there is a definite division between the alcohol consumption expected of males and that expected of females. Males were expected to consume relatively large quantities of masculine beverages like beer and spirits, whereas females were expected to exercise more restraint in their consumption of alcohol and to limit it to drinks considered to be more feminine, especially wine. The beer-drinking Elle was even perceived as being less feminine than Elle herself.

The projected differences in femininity between the two Elles were reflected in descriptions of the clothing they were considered likely to be wearing. The wine-drinking Elle was often visualized as wearing a dress, whereas her beer-drinking counterpart was felt more likely to be wearing jeans. These projections indicate the more feminine associations of wine relative to beer and also the association of wine with the context of a more formal social gathering compared to the more casual drinking situation associated with beer. The wine-drinking Elle was also perceived to be more physically attractive and was considered to be a better prospect for a long-term partner, due to her higher levels of social propriety apparent in her choice of alcohol. The beer-drinking Elle was described by some as being overweight and less image-conscious. On the other hand, she was felt to be more approachable, more likely to accept an invitation and more fun to be with on a date.

Though gender considerations tended to muddy the waters in terms of class attributions (e.g., to be sophisticated is to be more feminine and of a higher social class), the general impression was that the beer-drinking Elle was of a lower social class. That said, respondents were reluctant to ascribe their preference for the wine-drinking Elle to her perceived superior social standing. It should be stated that those beer-drinking females who were interviewed, though aware of the negative associations evident from the research, stated that they were prepared to accept such negative stereotyping to communicate their equality with males. The values of equality and liberation are important to these females, who see themselves as social leaders.

What the study does underline is the extent to which the symbolic meanings of products are culturally determined. Sociocultural conditioning is a strong force, even in the more libertarian, individualistic Western economies. It tends toward adherence and conformism. Yet it does not preclude individual discretion and creativity in assigning and selectively employing the symbolically meaningful properties of goods.

Symbolic consumption, then, helps the consumer in the tasks of self-definition and self-categorization in society. It provides some sense of continuity. The creation and cultivation of the individual self and the social self proceed in parallel. The symbolic meaning of consumer goods is a factor in both. Self-symbolism is concerned with the construction of individual self-identity and is derived in part from the personal and private meaning of goods. Social symbolism has to do with the construction of a shared, social identity and is influenced by the public meaning of brands. This is depicted in Figure 4.8. In this context, the theme of the multidimensional self mentioned in Chapter 2 should be kept in mind.

As mentioned earlier, symbolic consumption may also serve in the process of so-called symbolic self-completion, (Wicklund and Gollwitzer 1982) in which people who perceive that they are lacking in a certain quality attempt to plug the gap by using material symbols, among other strategies. The process of self-completion

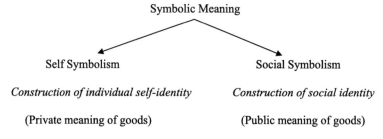

Figure 4.8 Self symbolism and social symbolism.

through consumption can be problematical. Sometimes individuals seek meanings from goods that simply cannot yield these meanings. More seriously, some people attempt to construct their identity and lives purely on the basis of the meaning of goods. Though self-definition can be partially achieved through the meanings that goods can provide, this is only one source. Person–object relations are not more important than direct person–person relations. Family ties, friendships and relationships, religion and work all contribute to what we are and what we may become. Also, a good deal of consumption is of a very habitual, routine nature and hardly lends itself to any greater signification.

Nonetheless, if self-definition in a personal and social context is linked in part to the meanings inherent in the consumer goods we choose, the implications of this and its importance for brands must be recognized. Moreover, this has always been the case—even before the advent of the complex branded environment we inhabit today. The ubiquitous brands of the twenty-first century are simply the modern-day equivalent of the diverse objects of consumption and possession that were the receptacles of similar meaning centuries ago. Like those objects, brands today are one of the more important ways we codify, define and structure the world around us and our place within it.

The Process of Meaning Transfer

The process of meaning attribution and derivation is a dynamic one. A well-known systematic approach to charting the trajectory and circulation of this movement of meaning is McCracken's (1988) meaning transfer model (Figure 4.9). Meaning originates in the culturally constituted world. This meaning, though, is restless and mobile and seeks other outlets for its expression. One of the places to which it is transferred is the consumer good. But meaning remains restless and is soon drawn from the consumer good to the individual consumer whose life it enters. According to the model, there are thus three locations of meaning (the culturally constituted world, the consumer good and the individual consumer) and two phases of transfer (world-to-good and good-to-individual).

There are several mechanisms involved in the stages of meaning transfer. Advertising is the key one in world–good transfer. Also

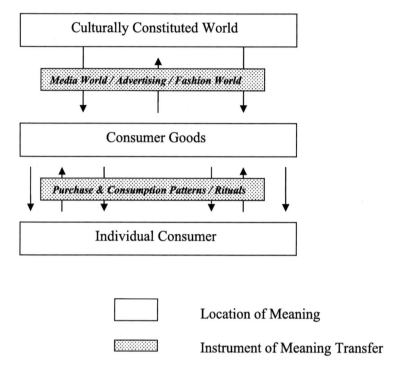

Figure 4.9   Meaning transfer model.

instrumental is what McCracken (1988) calls the "fashion system," which covers more than the title literally suggests. In good–consumer transfer the individual consumer effects meaning transfer via consumption and various rituals. Advertising achieves meaning transfer by combining the consumer good and a depiction of the culturally constituted world within the context of an advertisement. Objects and situations that convey the same meanings as it is desired that the good will carry are selected and given representation in the advertising. When and if the individual as viewer–reader successfully decodes these meanings the process of world–good transfer is complete.

Though this illustrates the primary mechanism for meaning transfer, it should be reiterated that individuals are not just passive receivers of meaning but actively participate in its creation. Individuals, through their own experience, history and social context, endow objects with meaning from their own world. Although these meanings may be highly idiosyncratic, at times they are absorbed, if not into the mainstream, at least into a subculture. In *Subculture: The*

Meaning of Style Dick Hebdige (1979) describes the dynamics of subcultural consumption. Through a process called bricolage, subcultures and other groups appropriate for themselves and manipulate the cultural resources at their disposal—clothes, consumer objects, music, leisure pursuits. The meanings of these resources are reorganized, with the normalized and preestablished meanings being subverted and reassembled into newly meaningful patterns, or styles. This has the effect of drawing attention to these objects as they appear in a new context of cultural signification. British Mod culture, for example, was characterized by parka coats with Union Jacks, Italian suits and scooters, short hair cuts, soul music and an almost dandyish preoccupation with sartorial style and neatness of dress. Mods thus differentiated themselves from others in society, as well as other subgroups such as Teddy Boys and rockers with their long hair, leather jackets and unkempt looks. Later, punks would take to wearing plastic trash bags and safety pins as fashion accessories.

Given the polysemic (i.e., multimeaning) nature of things and the sociocultural appropriation of their meanings, many commentators see consumption as a creative, recreational process whereby consumers are involved in the negotiation of meaning from goods—goods that come to serve as the raw materials and symbolic resources of everyday life. This contrasts with the conception of the simple acquisition and consumption of goods with a closed meaning predetermined by a manufacturer. The reality lies somewhere between the two views. Though the consumer will always be the final arbiter and will thus preserve his or her interpretative freedom, this is inevitably qualified by the nature and structure of the consumer object, the sociocultural context of its user and the manufacturer's intentions. There will be greater or lesser collusion between manufacturer and consumer and more or less potential for negotiation of meaning. Besides, divergent or subversive consumer meanings are often reappropriated by manufacturers and absorbed back into the capitalist mainstream. For instance, by appropriating an existing consumer good such as a scooter and endowing it with meaning in accordance with its own aims, the mod subculture created a new market and a new set of meanings that manufacturers could take advantage of and use to expand their market.

In the 1990s the Smith Kline Beecham company faced a challenging and unforeseen situation in the U.K. soft drinks market. Their Lucozade product (mentioned in later chapters) had been positioned since its launch as an energy-providing carbonated drink. It had extended this product platform to address the opportunity in sports drinks, using well-known athletes in its advertising. In 1993 the company decided it wanted to more specifically target teenagers as it was not commanding much share among this market. Though teenagers were aware of Lucozade's sports drink profile, the product's energy properties had in the meantime been reinterpreted in the rave scene and in the country's young black community. It had thus been endowed with a kind of underground street credibility by certain sections of the teenage population. Although the identification of young black people with the brand was possibly due in part to the fact that most of the athletes used in the advertising were black (e.g., Linford Christie), there was certainly nothing in the marketing of the brand to link it with the rave culture, nor was there a specific marketing intention to target black teenagers. This was an example of a particular group investing a certain meaning in a brand—a meaning appropriated from their own cultural milieu. This is another example of the fact that, quite often, it is not so much brands that confer meaning and values on consumers but consumers that confer meaning and values on brands. Incidentally, in the case described, Smith Kline Beecham ended up introducing a subbrand, Lucozade NRG, to take advantage of the teenage opportunity.

The transfer of meaning can thus be seen as a two-way process. Furthermore, when consumers give certain meanings to brands, these meanings will often subsequently influence advertising for the brands and will pass into the prevailing (sub)culture. Meaning is thus always in circulation and flux. Taking this into account, the adaptation of the meaning transfer model in Figure 4.9 illustrates the flow of meaning in the consumer society.

Changes in style, attitude and values originating in fashion entities such as clothing and fragrance houses provide or reflect new cultural coordinates for the rest of society. Brands like Calvin Klein come to stand for the lighter touch, "just being," rejection of gender stereotyping. Gap reintroduced us to the concept of informality and naturalness. The new or reconstituted meanings become social currency, emanating from one sector or industry but available for appropriation by all. The media at large (i.e., films, soap operas, lifestyle magazines and talk shows), opinion leaders, social observers, designers and architects all add to the maelstrom of meaning transfusion. Then there are the groups like punks and hippies that begin as proponents of radical reform and the overhaul of the established order, happily occupying their space at the margin of society—often only to see their principles adopted into mainstream society.

With cultural meaning constantly in circulation and at the disposition of goods and their manufacturers and consumers, those groups are often left with choices to make when the meaning undercurrents start to shift. Take the case of the iPod, for example and the topic of mainstreaming mentioned previously. As iPods become ever more ubiquitous, they lose the cultural cachet they once held for some of the early adopters. Such people like to see themselves at the vanguard and at the margins, where the value of individuality finds optimal expression. Yet as more and more people acquire iPods, as the little white earbuds become part of an urban uniform, those early pioneers look for ways to differentiate themselves and to reassert their individuality. Simply changing to different headphones may be one approach. Customizing the earbuds may be another. Often individuals will preempt companies in customizing products. Customization is a classic example of the role rituals play in the context of meaning transfer.

Rituals

Meaning is transferred from consumer good to individual through direct consumption and usage and via the process of personal ritual and social interaction. A ritual is a set pattern of behavior—a symbolic action—that provides a forum and context for an individual to affirm, assign, evoke, or revise meanings originally derived from the cultural milieu. In *The World of Goods* Douglas and Isherwood (1996, p. 65) describe how rituals can anchor meaning and the role consumption goods may play within the process:

> The main problem of social life is to pin down meanings so that they stay still for a little time. Without some conventional ways of selecting and fixing agreed meanings, the minimum consensual basis of society is missing. As for tribal society, so too for us: rituals serve to contain the drift of meanings. Rituals are conventions that set up visible public definitions. Before the initiation there was a boy, after it a man; before the marriage rite there were two free persons, after it two joined as one.... To manage without rituals is to manage without clear meanings and possibly without memories. Some are purely verbal rituals, vocalized, unrecorded, but they fade on the air and hardly help to limit the interpretative scope. More effective rituals use material things and the more

costly the ritual trappings, the stronger we can assume the intention to
fix the meanings to be. Goods, in this perspective, are ritual adjuncts;
consumption is a ritual process whose primary function is to make sense
of the inchoate flux of events.

Although it is true that formal ritual has less of a role in today's
society, we still make use of many rituals to mark the commence-
ment of important events (e.g., cutting the tape at store openings,
smashing the bottle at ship launchings); the end of life, or ways of
life (e.g., funerals, retirement parties, bachelor parties); the completion of important tasks, accomplishments, or performances (e.g.,
graduation ceremonies, toasting successful negotiations, throwing
or presenting flowers to opera singers or ice skaters); the transition
from one stage to another through the life cycle or from one role or
position to another (e.g., birthday parties, anniversary celebrations
and religious ceremonies like baptism, bar mitzvah, or confirmation) and so forth. This last category has to do with so-called rites of
passage, a phrase coined by the anthropologist Arnold Van Gennep
(1960) in his book *Rites of Passage.* Unlike some other parts of the
world, there are few rites of passage left in Western society today, as
cultural heritage and traditions have gradually lost their relevance,
have been modified, or have been cast in a new context. Passing a
driving test is a modern-day example of a rite of passage to the extent
that it grants the freedom to travel independently and is usually a
strong demarcation line between parent dependence and nonparent
dependence, that is, becoming more adult.

McCracken (1988) identifies four ritual activities in which meaning may be transferred from goods to individuals: exchange, possession, divestment and grooming rituals.

Exchange Rituals

Exchange rituals can be seen in important international soccer
matches, for instance, when team captains shake hands and exchange
club pennants before the game and players exchange shirts at the end
of the game, also sealed with a handshake. In his classic book *The Gift*
French anthropologist Marcel Mauss (1969) presented his theory of
gift exchange, exploring its religious, social, economic and mythological aspects in different cultures and primitive societies. Mauss
was struck more by the social concomitants of exchange than by its

economic character. He found that a number of exchange practices at the heart of all societies are driven by three universal compulsions:

1. The compulsion to give
2. The compulsion to receive
3. The compulsion to repay, or to reciprocate

When objects change hands, what matters is the relations between people that are affected by the exchange rather than the material value of the object. Exchange is about the construction of social ties, the creation of friendships, the resolution of disputes or rivalries, the assumption of obligations. Depending on the parties involved, their particular culture, the nature of the exchange and the epoch in question, the objects of exchange may be a peace pipe, a ring or precious jewelry, a chest of gold pieces, a woman as bride, or a large chunk of land. The concept of reciprocity behind gift exchange was at the heart of many ancient religions. In ancient Egypt religion was basically a negotiation between the gods and the pharaoh. So long as the gods received satisfactory offerings, Egypt would be protected and would prosper.

Gift giving is a potentially significant process of meaning transfer. Often the recipient of a gift is also the intended recipient of the meaningful properties of the gift that the donor wishes to see transferred to the recipient. As mentioned in the context of greetings cards, sometimes the act of giving a gift can be as gratifying for the donor as for the recipient. The socioeconomic implications of gift giving assume even greater significance when one considers that in the United States, for instance, 10 percent of retail purchases are given as gifts. During the Christmas season consumers spend $4 billion per day. Some 25 percent of the flowers sent in the United States are sent on Mother's Day. Online retailers have been quick to move into the gift business. Although gift giving is universal it is also culturally sensitive. Guide books on doing international business often feature a section on the etiquette of gift giving in different parts of the world. In the corporate world gift giving is a very delicate matter, in light of the possible interpretation or intent of bribery.

Possession Rituals

Possession rituals allow consumers to appropriate the meaningful properties of consumer goods. Personalizing, customizing, decorating, cleaning, discussing, comparing and photographing are some of the activities through which consumers assert possession, not in a materialistic or territorial way but rather in the process of self-definition as they draw from the objects the meaning and qualities with which advertising or the fashion system and media world have endowed them. Through customization and personalization individuals seek to transfer meaning from their own world to newly obtained goods and to encode products with personal meaning. Bespoke tailoring, monogramming of new clothing and custom building new houses are examples. The Internet industry provides further examples whereby users are encouraged to personalize and customize home pages and to configure operational procedures in line with their preferences.

Divestment Rituals

Divestment rituals are used when individuals relinquish possession of objects (to empty them of meaning) or acquire goods which have been previously owned (to erase the meaning associated with the prior owner).

Grooming Rituals

Advertising and the fashion system and media world point to the properties that can be had from goods such as cosmetics and hair-styling products through special grooming rituals. Sometimes it is the good, not the consumer which is groomed. Consider the inordinate amount of time dedicated to certain types of automobiles, for instance.

By transferring meaning from the good to the individual, these rituals act like a microcosmic version of the way advertising and the fashion system and media world move meaning from world to goods. Although such rituals are an important means for the transfer of meaning from good to individual, they are not the only means. As described earlier, most consumption involves the movement of symbolic meanings, be it consciously or unconsciously. Individuals consume things that have particular meaning for them.

The meanings of an individual's possessions may relate to his or her individuality, or they may tend toward desired connections with other people. Special possessions, particularly those regarded as extensions of the self, like some of those referred to in the Csikszent-mihalyi and Rochberg-Halton (1981) study (e.g., pets and memory-laden objects), are usually characterized by idiosyncratic meaning. Heavily advertised branded goods, on the other hand, are likely to carry a widely held set of meanings. It does not follow, then, that everybody who bought the same product did so for the same symbolic meaning, as a product may carry a range of meanings, with different individuals ascribing different cultural meanings to the product. In practice, all goods are invested with varying proportions of meaning types. All goods have some cultural and conventional meaning, since meaning, even at its most idiosyncratic, is a cultural phenomenon. Marketers at times strive to modify subcultural associations between products and meanings. At the beginning of the 1960s Honda succeeded in growing the motorcycle market with its "You meet the nicest people on a Honda" campaign, aimed at communicating that motorcycles were not just for rebels and outlaws.

5

Brand Meaning
Definitions and Directions

> People buy things not only for what they can do, but also for what they mean.
>
> Sidney Levy (1959)

Defining Brand Meaning

It is brand meaning that mediates between products and consumer motivation, thereby determining consumer behavior. A brand's meaning is determined by how the brand is perceived by the public at a conscious level and how the brand resonates with them at a semi- or subconscious level, as shown in Figure 5.1. The term refers to the semantic and symbolic features of a brand, the sum of the fundamental conscious and unconscious elements that compose the consumer's mental representation of the brand. Brand meaning both defines and is defined by the territory where the meaning derived from brand associations corresponds with consumer needs and aspirations. It is where the concrete qualities of the product meet the abstract qualities of the brand. Charles Revlon once famously said, "In the factory we make cosmetics. In the store we sell hope." Cosmetics and hope—Revlon means both.

Like the concept of meaning itself, the overall meaning of a brand, or a brand's meaning structure, is multidimensional. It is therefore important to decode and deconstruct these multilevel brand meanings to ascertain the ways the brand holds relevance for and connects with consumers and how it could do so more potently. Accepting the premise that consumers endow products and brands with meanings

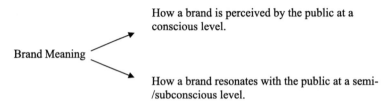

How a brand is perceived by the public at a conscious level.

Brand Meaning

How a brand resonates with the public at a semi-/subconscious level.

Figure 5.1   Facets of brand meaning.

over and above their overt functional value, one important distinction is that between the manifest, salient and conscious aspects of brands and their latent, symbolic and largely unconscious properties. Ostensibly, we conceive of things in practical physical terms and seek functional benefits, but underlying this there is a more profound significance composed of deeper meanings and instinctive ways of defining and shaping ourselves and the world around us. These different concepts and interpretations motivate the choices we make as consumers and the attitudes we form toward brands, as Figure 5.2.illustrates.

The Neuro-Psychological Context of Brand Meaning

There are two important observations with regard to Figure 5.2. The first is that, although practical–rational considerations and emotional–symbolic factors are separated, this is only for ease of

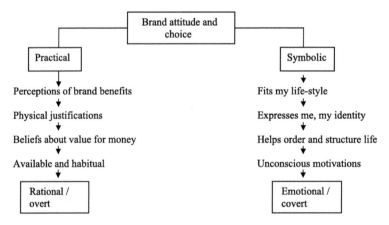

Figure 5.2   Practical and symbolic attitudes to buying brands.

understanding of the diagram. Brand decisions are never wholly rational. In fact, no decision is ever wholly rational. Neuroscientist Antonio Damasio (1996) calls into question psychology's traditional separation of reason from emotion. He states flatly, "Reason without emotion is neurologically impossible." To substantiate his arguments he draws on medical case studies and research into the evolution of the brain itself. In accordance with the triune brain model developed in the 1970s by neuroscientist Paul McLean (1990) the brain is actually a three-in-one brain, consisting of three layers, each corresponding to a different evolutionary stage. The layers evolved cumulatively, each on top of the previous, like an archeological site. The three brain systems, though connected, have distinctive functions and "personalities." Broadly, they are responsible for instinct (reptilian brain), emotion (mammalian brain or limbic system) and reason (new brain or neo cortex).

The important conclusion that Damasio (1994) draws from this evolutionary heritage is that, although the largest, most recent level of our brain, the neo-cortex, is where we perform our rational thinking, this part of the brain is still connected to the older parts. So even when we believe we are making a purely rational decision, we are making that decision via an area that interfaces with our senses, emotions, instincts and intuitions.

Related to this description of brain structure is the second observation regarding Figure 5.2. The elements listed on the left of the diagram have to do with cognitive rational processing. Those on the right side of the diagram are concerned with largely noncognitive responses. Note that noncognitive responses include, but are not limited to, emotional responses. The term *noncognitive* covers feelings, sensations, intuitions and instincts, for example. Moreover, we are not aware of most of our emotional reactions, the majority of which occur in the unconscious. Yet emotions beneath the threshold of consciousness exert a strong influence on what we perceive, how we perceive it and how we react to it. Thus, we may re-present the diagram as shown in Figure 5.3.

Cognitive rational processing is clearly instrumental in defining a brand. Without it consumers would be hard pushed to know why a brand exists in the first place. Indeed, traditional marketing practice is centered on this approach, the strategy being to grab the target's attention and then to persuade him or her through a rational, needs-benefits demonstration that your brand is the one that best meets

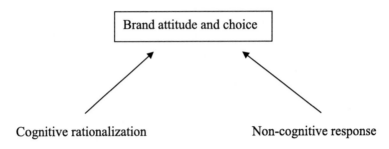

Figure 5.3   Cognitive and noncognitive brand responses.

those needs: "The notion is that positioning is about one salient, over-riding cognitive thought in the mind that will justify engagement and purchase" (Wilson 2002, p. 47). Important though this may be, it is only part of the picture. There is a bigger opportunity still: "To understand more fully how a brand and a person interact we need to understand better what happens at the deeper, more primitive, non-cognitive levels of brain organization as well" (ibid.). For although active, rational processing of brand information goes on with each brand encounter, so too, semi- or unconsciously, does the continu-ous emotional and noncognitive imprinting of the brand.

To quote Gordon (2002, p. 285), "Brands are coded in memory on a cognitive (thinking, analytical, considered) *and* emotional (somatic) basis. These two elements of brand encoding are inextricably linked and it is emotional coding rather than reasoned argument that deter-mines whether or not people take notice of the stimuli related to the brand …." Figure 5.4 summarizes the way these processes work to ultimately generate brand meaning.

We have already seen in Chapter 1 how a brand exists in the brain as a neural associative network, or an engram, and how these asso-ciations are influenced by brand perceptions and determine brand meaning. It is important to remember that a considerable proportion of brand perceptions are acquired under low involvement conditions

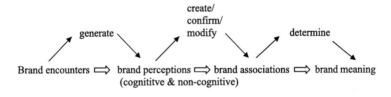

Figure 5.4   Generation of brand meaning.

and thus are not subject to elaborate or even conscious processing by the brain. Brand meaning, like any meaning, is created largely unconsciously as we compare sensory, emotional and cognitive inputs with internalized patterns stored in the brain. The resulting meaning determines our day-to-day experience and influences our memories and behaviors (Marci 2006).

Though we tend to think of brand associations as verbal descriptors of a brand, some two thirds of all stimuli that reach the brain are visual, and there are further modes of representation of brand associations, such as sensory and emotional modes. It is important to keep these different modes of representation in mind when considering associative networks. An associative network involves anything that can be interconnected in our brain with a given concept, including cognitive representations but also connections between a brand, for example and associated emotions, feelings, attitudes and behavioral tendencies or habits (see next section). So many brand associations are in fact stored unconsciously, in nonverbal mode, making them difficult to access from a research point of view.

The brain is designed to store and recall experiences and information of all kinds—for example, cognitive, emotional, motor and social. When we ride a bike, play the guitar, feel our heart race in an empty parking lot at night, or feel calmed by the caress of a loved one, we are using memory. All incoming information sets up neural patterns of activity that are compared against previously experienced and stored patterns. New patterns can modify existing memories or can create new ones. The vast majority of those stored memory templates are based on experiences and interactions that occurred in early childhood. The majority of our memories are noncognitive and preverbal. Furthermore, many of these neural imprints are the result of exposure to storylines and characterizations that come to us in the form of myths, legends, fairy tales, nursery rhymes, parables and religious teachings. This raises the theme of archetypal memories, which is mentioned in Chapter 2.

We also construct throughout our lives what Damasio (1994) calls "somatic markers." He describes somatic markers as particular feelings generated from secondary emotions that have been connected, through learning and experience, to predicted future outcomes. Somatic markers represent the intuitive and emotional feelings aroused in reaction to situations: "When a negative somatic marker is juxtaposed to a particular future outcome the combination acts as an alarm bell. When a positive somatic marker is juxtaposed instead, it becomes a beacon of incentive" (Damasio 1994, p. 174). Somatic markers help us to make rapid, favorable decisions as we go about our lives. They usually function as a warning (i.e., a negative marker). For instance, the emotional shock of nearly having an arm bitten by a lion at a zoo or wildlife park creates a negative somatic marker, which results in our proceeding with caution next time we approach a lion. Physiological changes serve to strengthen the somatic marker: We breathe faster and begin to sweat; our heart rate rises. When we make decisions and behave based on somatic markers we do not necessarily recall the specific experiences that created the positive or negative marker—rather, we are acting from instinct.

These primal responses and feelings can become attached to brand experiences, too, and result in intuitive brand decisions. When elements associated with a brand trigger somatic markers, they can favorably dispose consumers to the brand at an instinctive level. Somatic marking is thus another area of brain activity that contributes to forming the brand engram. Moreover, these types of responses are quicker and more automatic than rational, considered judgments, which often constitute the postrationalization of an intuitive reaction. Brands that manage to connect up with these memories and trigger these markers through their associations do so at a very deep, instinctual and potent level: "… Since the depth of neural imprinting is likely to be much stronger at the non-cognitive level (being older and more heavily used), patterning that occurs here is likely to constitute the most robust and significant aspects of a brand …." (Wilson 2002, p. 49).

Types of Brand Associations

Brand associations may take many different forms. They range from the concrete to the abstract, from the conscious to the unconscious, the direct to the indirect. Direct associations are those that occur directly between two elements without the need or presence of a third, intermediary element. If we see the words *Veuve Clicquot* stamped on the side of a box we immediately think of champagne. Indirect associations are what lead to associative chains, where elements are linked together through one or more intermediary elements. So Veuve Clicquot may generate the following association chain:

Veuve Clicquot → champagne → France → sophisticated

or, alternatively,

Veuve Clicquot → champagne → celebration

A housewife planning for Thanksgiving thinks of turkey. That makes her think of cranberry sauce and then she thinks of Ocean Spray. The diversity in the form and origin of associations underlies the multidimensionality of brand meaning. Moving from the concrete to the more abstract, it is possible to categorize brand associations into three significant groupings: attributes, benefits and attitudes (see Keller 1998, p. 93). In turn, these categories may be further divided in terms of abstractness, according to the association in question.

Attributes

Attributes may be product-related or non-product-related. Product-related attributes refer to the physical composition of a product and those elements, such as ingredients and design features, which affect product performance. Non-product-related attributes are extrinsic attributes that do not have a direct bearing on product performance, though they may be very important in the purchasing decision.

User and usage imagery refers to the type of people who use the brand and in what situations and circumstances they do so. User imagery is more important to a brand like Pepsi than it is to a brand like Duracell. When the values associated with a brand correspond positively with our own value systems, we are likely to identify with that brand. Often we use brands to communicate to others those values we consider important, thus helping to define ourselves in society. This may be part of conforming to the norms and expectations of a certain group or subculture. The topics of impression management and the self-concept are covered in Chapter 2. Price is included as non-product-related attribute as it can be an important association in the formation of brand perceptions, particularly with regard to value and desirability and is a criterion by which consumers often segment their knowledge of a market or category.

Utilitarian considerations such as functional benefits and product-related attributes constitute the more concrete and pragmatic meanings of a brand. These are often a function of what the brand is, what it does and its usage context. Non-product-related attributes and elements that are not factual, objective or instrumental underpin the more symbolic meanings of the brand. It is useful to keep in mind the difference between the two dimensions as well as the interplay between them. They come into play, for instance, in the way people classify and categorize things. As Franzen and Bouwman (2001, p. 92) describe, the classification of items into groups or categories is performed on the basis of their perceived properties, such as the physical manifestation, their functions for us and the deeper (symbolic) meanings we allocate to them:

> On the one hand, the classification is based on natural, objective properties of things (birds have wings, fish have fins); on the other, they emanate from artificial (propositional) meanings they are given by people in a specific culture. Rosch and Lloyd (1978) posit that categories are neither "natural" nor "artificial"; they are rather always the result of an interaction between structural properties of the things as they present themselves to us in the world and our human reactions to them, which for a large part are socially, culturally and situationally determined.

From a very young age we learn to classify objects according to their physical properties. We come to realize that things with four legs and a back that people sit on are chairs, even before we know what the word *chair* means. We then notice that some are wooden and others plastic and start to form subcategories. Traditionally, products and product-related attributes formed the basis for categorization in consumer behavior, particularly given that most brands were monobrands—that is, based on single products or product types— with specific attributes. As umbrella brands and corporate brands become more prevalent, consumers find it more difficult to categorize those brands themselves along purely concrete, pragmatic lines. Virgin is an extreme example.

Benefits

Benefits describe how a brand can solve a problem or offer an opportunity to the consumer or how it can make a consumer's life easier, more fun, more enjoyable, or more meaningful. The differentiating benefits that motivate brand purchase may be functional, sensorial, expressive, or emotive. Strong brands often deliver a combination of these benefit types.

Functional Benefits   Most brands offer functional benefit to their consumers as a result of one or more product attributes and the functional utility they provide.

Some examples are as follows:

- Cleans without scratching the surface.
- Spreads straight from the fridge.
- Leaves your hair more manageable.
- Relieves allergy symptoms without causing drowsiness.

Functional benefits are increasingly easy for competitors to copy, either by imitating the product or by providing the same benefit in a different format. In the oral-care category, besides toothpaste alone, the teeth-whitening benefit is now provided in gels and strips that are applied to the teeth.

Sensorial Benefits   Sensorial benefits are discussed in Chapter 3. They relate to the physical experience of a brand and derive from its sensorial properties—its look, taste, smell, texture and so forth.

Some examples are as follows:

- The pleasure of biting through thick chocolate into smooth ice cream
- The sensation of wallowing in the evocative fragrances of Herbal Essences
- The creamy texture of Boddington's Beer
- The total sensorial appeal—taste, aroma, appearance and even sound—of Bailey's

Expressive Benefits   Expressive benefits allow the consumer to express certain values, contributing to a sense of identity. The expressive benefits of brands help us to express and define ourselves. For instance, a person may communicate and define his or her self-image in the following ways:

- Nonconformist and individualistic by using an Apple Mac
- Rebellious and free-spirited by riding a Harley-Davidson
- Adventurous by driving a Land Rover

- Conscientious and caring by buying Newman's Own or Body Shop products
- Successful by wearing a Rolex

Emotional Benefits   Emotional benefits consist of the positive feelings created in consumers when buying or using a brand. Consumers may be more or less aware of these benefits and their genesis—or rather, of the psychological importance of the benefits. Often, emotional benefits have a deeply symbolic dimension and respond to profound human needs such as the need to be cared for or the need to give and receive love.

Emotional benefits relate to how buying or using a brand makes consumers feel. For example, consumers may feel the following:

- Exhilarated driving a Porsche
- Sexual and feminine wearing Victoria's Secret lingerie
- Important when using or receiving a Mont Blanc pen
- Rugged when wearing Caterpillar boots

The Difference between Expressive and Emotional Benefits   There are similarities between expressive and emotional benefits. Whereas a brand's functional and sensory benefits are based on physical attributes and perceivable elements of the product, emotional and expressive benefits are based on psychological and emotional aspects of the consumer. Expressive and emotional benefits are part of the symbolic appeal of a brand. Though expressive benefits may be similar to emotional benefits, though, they are not the same. Aaker (1996) points out that, in comparison with emotional benefits, expressive benefits focus on the following:

- Self rather than feelings
- Public settings and products (e.g., cars) rather than private ones
- Aspiration and the future as opposed to memories of the past (some brands provide a warm feeling of nostalgia—an emotional, not expressive, benefit. Aspiration and the future usually have to do with the person I would like to be(come), so expressive benefits are more relevant)
- The permanent (something related to an individual's personality) rather than the transitory
- The act of using the product (wearing a cooking apron declares one as a gourmet cook) rather than a consequence of using the

product (the feeling of pride and satisfaction from preparing and serving a well-appointed meal)

Attitudes

Brand attitudes are a function of the beliefs that consumers have with regard to a brand and the degree to which the brand possesses certain attributes or benefits and consumers' evaluative judgment of those beliefs (i.e., how desirable it is that the brand possesses these salient attributes or benefits). Brand attitudes can be seen as consumers' affective responses to a brand. The recognition of the importance of the evaluative and attitudinal component within meaning, in regard to Osgood et al.'s (1957) semantic differential, was discussed at the beginning of Chapter 4. Where attitudes toward a brand are determined in large part by more rational and functional elements, consumers are likely to be more able to verbalize their attitudes and their reasons for them. Where it is the emotional and symbolic elements of a brand that are predominantly generating attitudes toward it, consumers may be less aware of the real reasons for their attitudes and motivations toward the brand. These major categories of brand associations are summarized in Figure 5.5.

Brand Emotions and Emotional Benefits

Strictly speaking, the emotional benefits of a brand refer to the feelings created in and experienced by consumers when buying or using the brand. As such, emotional brand benefits most convincingly accrue from brands in which the underlying products have some connection with these emotions. The emotional benefit corresponds to some emotional aspect of the consumer. So, for instance, driving a Volvo may make somebody feel safe, thus diminishing the fear that person would otherwise feel on taking to the roads.

Alternatively, it is possible for a given emotion to become associated with a brand even when there is no, or only a tangential, relation between the underlying product and the particular emotion. This is not so much about the consumer experiencing the emotion as a consequence of using the brand but rather refers to the cognitive recognition by the consumer that a certain emotion pertains or belongs

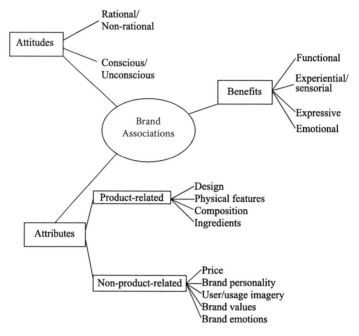

Figure 5.5   Types of brand associations.

to a brand. This is usually achieved through advertising whereby the emotions portrayed in the advertising or invoked in the viewer become linked to the advertised brand. Coca-Cola and McDonald's would be examples. The critical issues are the extent to which the affective response to the advertising transfers to the brand and the credibility with which the brand can claim emotional benefits.

Strength of Brand Associations

The relative strength of brand associations and indeed of any associations, varies considerably. Generally speaking, the more attention that is given to the meaning of brand information during the process of encoding, the stronger the resulting association will be. Another key factor is the structure and solidity of existing brand associations in the memory. Other things being equal, it will be easier for consumers to form an association on the basis of new brand information when a sound and relevant associative structure already exists in the mind. Related to this is the consideration of consistency or congruency with the existing associative network, which will affect the ease of assimilation and integration of new brand information.

Several other determinants have been formulated over time into "laws" regarding the emergence of associations and the likely strength of those associations (Franzen and Bouwman 2001, p. 52). For instance, the law of contiguity states that elements that are perceived together in time (i.e., simultaneously) and space (i.e., in juxtaposition) will become connected. The law of repetition, or frequency, holds that the more often elements are perceived together the more they will be connected. The more often we encounter *Pampers, nappies,* and *dry bottoms* together, the more strongly the connection among the three memory elements is cemented. The law of similarity provides that activating the element of Pepsi, for example, can lead to the activation of Coca-Cola. A further law is that of recency, whereby associations that occurred most recently will be most readily remembered. A corollary of this observation is the gradual waning of connections over time, where associations are left dormant and begin to recede. It is this that allows outdated and no longer relevant brand associations to fade and new associations to replace them, as in the example of Lucozade and its association with convalescence (mentioned later). Finally, the law of vividness holds that the more unique and vivid an association is, the more readily it will be recalled.

It should be noted that, even if a certain association is a strong one, in the context of a purchase or consumption decision it may not necessarily be influential or relevant (see Keller 1998, p. 108). Moreover, the importance ascribed to brand associations may be situation or context dependent (ibid.) and be determined by the specific aims of a consumption situation. Overnight service may be crucial if a deadline looms or less relevant with the luxury of time.

This leads Keller (1998) to propose a sequential structure for brand associations. A robust brand differentiates itself in the first place by the relative strength of its associations, then by the degree to which those associations are evaluated as desirable by consumers and finally by the uniqueness of those associations. The order is significant: In other words, it does not matter how unique an association is unless it is relevant and favorably evaluated, and it does not matter how favorable an association is unless it is sufficiently strongly connected with the brand for consumers to recall it spontaneously. Equally, it does not matter how strong an association is unless it is favorable and relevant and it does not matter how favorable an association is unless it has uniqueness and can distinguish the brand from competing brands.

Core Associations

A brand's core associations, those at the heart of the brand associative network, are those that determine the essential meaning ascribed to a brand and the attitudes developed toward it. Figure 5.6 shows a basic associative network for McDonald's. The core associations would be the restaurants, the meals served there and the people who serve them and, in the case of kids, fun. Note that the brand associative network is a present tense representation of a brand. It depicts how a brand is currently perceived, not how it might be perceived.*

The core of the associative network contains the main primary associations of the brand—the strongest associations that are activated spontaneously when we think of the brand. They would normally include a product or service and a dominant characteristic or property, a product application or usage situation, or more symbolic elements such as user imagery. From this core all sorts of other associations may be triggered, depending on the context within which the brand is encountered and the cues provided.

The Brand Meaning Framework:
Primary Brand Meaning and Implicit Brand Meaning

Primary Brand Meaning

The primary associations previously described constitute the core brand meaning, or *primary brand meaning*. This is the meaning of the brand that would be played back by consumers in research without too much reflection or probing. Gatorade means sports drink. eBay means online auctions. Bayer means aspirin. Starbucks means coffee in different varieties and a nice place to drink it. Primary brand meaning is a summation of the consumer's primary associations and

---

* Note also that the brand associative network shown in Figure 5.6 is, logically, similar in composition to the associative neural network in Chapter 1 (Figure 1.1). The latter is simply introduced from a different—neuropsychological—perspective.

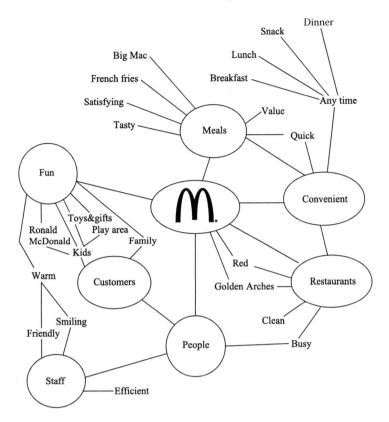

Figure 5.6 Brand associative network—McDonald's.

dominant perceptions about a brand, the snapshot that immediately comes to the mind's eye upon hearing the brand name. Simply stated, it is how consumers spontaneously define a brand.

Given that primary brand meaning tends to be largely influenced by brand attributes and functional consequences, it is likely that it will be correspondingly influenced to some extent by the product category. No product or brand exists in a vacuum and it is probable that perceptions of the category to which a brand belongs (i.e., the context in which it has been placed) and product characteristics found within that category will influence the consumer's definition of a brand's primary meaning. As we will see in later sections, the extent to which this is the case will vary according to the nature of the product (e.g., how important functional aspects are), the stage the brand is at in its own development, as well as the stage the category is at and the brand's communication. Moreover, primary brand meaning is not the domain of solely concrete, palpable product attributes. Abstract product attributes may also inform primary brand meaning. These may be summations of product attributes in catch-all meanings—cars, for example, may be categorized as *family cars* or *sports cars* or defined as *utility vehicles* or *people carriers* (Franzen and Bouwman 2001, p. 208).

Researching primary brand meaning among consumers is essential in that it clarifies and confirms the extent to which the consumers' definition of a brand's essential meaning coincides with the marketer's intentions. An article published in the *Journal of Advertising Research* in late 2000 (Oakenfull et al.), for example, describes how a team from Miami University in Ohio, working with researchers from Pennzoil, conducted research into the meaning of the Pennzoil brand (this in the context of potential brand extensions—we will return to this theme and the research later in Chapter 6). Interestingly, although Pennzoil managers had deemed "protection" to be a fundamental component of the brand's meaning (the word featured in the brand slogan: "We're driving protection"), research results and other company findings indicated that "while protection may be a *property* of Pennzoil, it does not *define* the brand in the public eye" (op. cit. p. 48 author's italics).

Researching the primary brand meaning of Federal Express would probably reveal that it is seen as a delivery service for important documents. It would be interesting to find out if the words *overnight* or *speedy* came up or, indeed, *secure*. Federal Express would hope so: It created a strong point of difference as the fastest and most dependable delivery service around—"When it absolutely, positively has to be there overnight"—becoming market leader in the overnight delivery service category. Of course, it may be speedy, but not as speedy as sending documents digitally. On the other hand, it still has the advantage of offering timely delivery direct to the intended recipient of confidential documents, so security and confidentiality may be elements of its primary brand meaning.

Investigating primary brand meaning among consumers can identify and help eliminate misconceptions about the brand. Dr. Pepper provides an example. In 1969, research indicated that there was a high degree of prompted awareness of Dr. Pepper being a soft drink. However, misconceptions about the brand abounded: that it was made from prune juice, that it contained peppers or pepper sauce, that it was medicinal, that it aided regularity and so forth (Plummer 2000). Indeed, those misconceptions gave rise to a famous advertising campaign for the brand: "Dr. Pepper—America's Most Misunderstood Soft Drink."

The Bic brand offers a salutary lesson to marketers of the consequences of failing to fully understand a brand's primary meaning and to grasp the motivational dynamics and ramifications of that meaning. The French company Société Bic successfully created a market for nonrefillable ballpoint pens in the late 1950s, disposable cigarette lighters in the 1970s and disposable razors in the early 1980s. The company managed to leverage the brand's primary meaning of convenient and inexpensive disposable products across different categories amenable to such a proposition. However, when in 1989 the company tried to extend this primary brand meaning to the perfume market in the United States and Europe they came unstuck. The perfumes (Nuit and Jour [for women] and Bic for Men and Bic Sport for Men) came in glass spray bottles resembling bulky cigarette lighters. The promotional campaign, with the line "Paris in your pocket," featured stylish people using the perfumes. The problem was that through the years consumers had incorporated into their mental definition of the brand an extreme form of detached and impersonal utilitarianism and this was at odds with the very emotive and personal perfume category, even at its lower end.

It is no coincidence that those brands with a clear sense and projection of their most valuable asset, their meaning, are the most successful and enduring brands. Again, Disney is a good example. As mentioned, the Disney brand's primary meaning has to do with fun and wholesome family entertainment—at Disney World, for instance, or through Disney films. When the corporation saw the potential opportunity provided by films suitable for a broader audience it invested in brands such as Touchstone and Miramax, thus preserving the integrity of its Disney heartland.

Besides the more rational and functional associations that contribute to primary brand meaning, a brand's composite meaning may encompass a greater or lesser number of associations of a more symbolic and sociocultural nature. For although the brand associative network is a concept that helps illuminate primary brand meaning, brands are more than just fixed cognitive associations of meanings. To quote Brown, Kozinets and Sherry (2003, p. 31), "Brands mean more than relatively fixed arrangements of associative nodes and attributes. Complexity, heterogeneity, dynamism and para-dox are integral aspects of the consumer-brand relationship." The actual or potential symbolic and sociocultural meanings of a brand are important to understand because such meanings provide two important elements for a brand: differentiation and greater depth. We are here dealing with a second dimension of brand meaning, one that is less manifest, more subtle and ultimately more motivating: implicit brand meaning.

Implicit Brand Meaning

Just as objects, or objects as products, have the potential to be media-tors of deep, symbolic meanings, so too have brands. Implicit brand meaning refers to the ultimate emotional and psychological impli-cations and significance of a brand, to the psychic resonance that the brand has for its consumers. Implicitation represents the vital, visceral dynamic of consumer behavior and choice. Implicit brand meaning is complex. It is highly symbolic, psycho-social meaning, influenced in great measure by cultural norms and values. It may tap into archetypal patterns and may find expression and reinforce-ment though ritual. It evolves from the central truth that bonds the consumer to the product or brand and underpins that bond in a far more vital, deep-seated and enduring way than is the case with other facets of the brand. For example, though on the surface Hallmark is a brand of greeting cards, it is the emotional satisfaction of giving and receiving love that is inherent in the implicit meaning of the brand. Disney is about fun and family entertainment, but its implicit brand meaning resides more in keeping alive the magic and won-der of childhood. To most people, IKEA's primary brand meaning is functional, stylish and affordable furniture. Consumers would not spontaneously talk of democratizing quality design, but projective research techniques may well point to an implicit brand meaning in that area. The laundry category is one of the most fiercely com-petitive arenas in which a brand could choose to compete. Product performance and innovation is and always has been critical to the category. Unilever's long-standing Persil brand in the United King-dom has been no exception to this rule. Yet the brand really evolved through its instinctive understanding of a mother's pride and the caring and nurturing values behind it—again, the subtle distinction between primary brand meaning and implicit brand meaning.

Despite implicit brand meaning being where brand and consumer really connect, marketers often fail to realize this potential meaning of their brands to consumers. A perfunctory appraisal of brand perceptions is inadequate if truly fertile territory is to be identified. To take an example, independence is a value claimed by hundreds of different brands. But how many go farther than the tip of the symbolic iceberg of this value? Independence from what? Or for what? Is it more about a search for something (e.g., a more authentic, rewarding life) than being free from something (e.g., routine, monotony, convention)? Is it about outer seeking or inner searching? Discovering the world, or one's own limitations and possibilities? Is it about making a stand and being heroic, or making a withdrawal and being at peace with oneself? Is there a spiritual element to it? What would be the symbolic significance, for example, of a brand like Jeep Wrangler, with its slogan, "Take your body where your mind has already wandered?"

Value expressiveness is one facet or level of implicit brand meaning. It is where a brand represents, or symbolizes, ideals and values with which the consumer identifies. When Apple Computers declares, "Think different," the brand strikes a chord with consumers characterized by the type of accomplishment/fulfillment, independence/individuation mindset described in Chapter 2. Apple's classic 1984 Super Bowl commercial, inspired by George Orwell's *1984*, featured a totalitarian society with robotic, gray-clad subjects filing into a vast assembly hall. As Big Brother lays down the party line from a huge screen, a young, athletic-looking woman suddenly appears and shatters the screen with a sledgehammer. The announcer then reads the caption: "On January 24, Apple Computer will introduce Macintosh. And you'll see why 1984 won't be like *1984*." Despite only being shown once, the ad had one of the highest audience recall figures in America. A $1.6 million production budget and Ridley Scott's directing talent certainly helped, but beyond the on-screen visual impact, the deep, visceral impact of the commercial lay in its dramatization of what Apple means at a higher-order symbolic level. Consumers choosing Apple computers are endorsing the brand's noncorporate, democratizing stance and empathizing with an ethos of individualism and ground-breaking pioneerism.

Brands such as Apple, Disney and Marlboro exemplify a funda-mental truism with regard to brand meaning: that meaning cannot simply be borrowed or appropriated through a short-term advertising campaign or promotion. Whereas brand personality dimensions, for example, can be altered or recalibrated quite readily through adver-tising and executional devices, brand meaning is about becoming an enduring and consistent expression of a given meaning. It is about how that meaning is sustained in the face of changing times and market conditions, how it is replenished and rejuvenated, how it is leveraged across multiple segments or in different cultures, without contamination, violation or dilution.

The Relationship between Primary Brand Meaning and Implicit Brand Meaning

The principal associations of a brand include both the defining prop-erties on the basis of which the brand is categorized by consumers with similar brands (e.g., Marlboro is a cigarette just like Camel or Lucky Strike) and the often symbolic characteristic properties of a brand that help differentiate it from others in the category (e.g., Marlboro is ruggedly individualstic and invokes the freedom of Marlboro Country). As it taps into deep universal truths and cul-tural values, implicit brand meaning is generally less category influ-enced and more culturally influenced than primary brand meaning. In the automotive category, for example, a Porsche Boxster and a Volkswagen Beetle both have symbolic meaning—but that meaning is radically different from the one (status symbol, executive toy) to the other (from its roots in sixties counterculture, the "Small is beau-tiful" anticar to its present-day playful reincarnation). The theme of brands that develop out of their categories and into the prevailing culture is taken up in Chapter 7 on the evolution of brand mean-ing. At the same time, there may be a symbolic dimension to the category itself, possibly already appropriated by a leading brand. We will explore this theme later in this chapter.

It is worth underlining that primary brand meaning and implicit brand meaning are two distinct concepts, two separate dimensions of total brand meaning, with a greater or lesser degree of interrela-tionship. They are like two different lenses for looking at a brand. Each will bring the brand into focus in a somewhat different manner.

We have seen that primary brand meaning is largely determined by the brand's direct benefits and physical attributes. Brands that establish strong emotional ties with their consumers may possess a less functionally determined primary brand meaning. Similarly, service brands, such as USPS or Avis, are less obviously defined by their physical characteristics and their benefits are less tangible than in the case of packaged goods. Whatever the case, that element, or those elements, that prevail above all others will most readily define the brand in the consumer's mind—that is, constitute primary brand meaning. Primary brand meaning is important to understand because it reveals how consumers perceive a brand.

Implicit brand meaning resides in the extended emotional and psychological significance of brand attributes, benefits and other associations and may tap into deeper category dynamics, higher-order consumer values or archetypal influences. Implicit brand meaning is important to understand because it reveals potentially motivating depth and resonance in a brand. The profundity and robustness of a brand's implicit brand meaning will depend on the way it is understood, interpreted and embraced by the consumer and the extent to which it is cultivated and perpetuated by the marketer. The differences between the two types of brand meaning are illustrated in Figure 5.7.

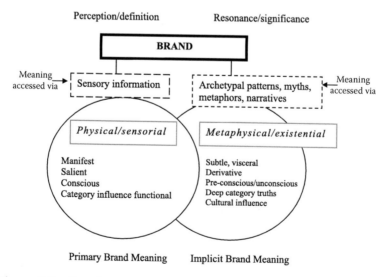

Figure 5.7   Brand meaning model.

Brand managers who are faced with the constant concern of product or service delivery, a reputation for quality, developing new features or line extensions, or appropriating category benefits often lose sight of the symbolic potential of their brands. Not that these marketing considerations are without importance. They are important, and they will largely determine primary brand meaning in the eyes of the consumer. On the other hand, some commentators dismiss the discipline of developing and highlighting unique features and benefits as mundane and uninspiring. The truth is that although appropriating archetypal or cultural high ground affords brands iconic status in the longer term, people usually access brands through their underlying products. So when there is synergy, connection and correlation between primary brand meaning and implicit brand meaning, when actually using and experiencing a product provides cues and triggers to higher brand meaning, that is when total brand meaning is at its most robust and compelling. When you sit astride a roaring Harley, pull on a pair of Nikes, or power up a Macintosh, you are participating in a brand narrative; you are drawing meaning from that experience. That is what brand mystique and brand myth are about.

The Oreo brand provides another example. Introduced in the US in 1912, Oreo has become the most popular cookie in the world (according to Euromonitor International), and is the biggest selling cookie in the US. Consisting of a rich vanilla crème filling sandwiched between two dark chocolate plain cookies, Oreo's primary brand meaning should in theory be quite straightforward. Indeed, the sandwich cookie has remained remarkably unchanged down the years. Despite the multitude of Oreo extensions, for the most part these have been variations on a theme. Chocolate Crème Oreo, Double Delight Oreo with Peanut Butter 'n Chocolate, the vanilla-flavored Golden Oreo, and so forth. Oreo cookies were among the first "interactive" foods, offering consumers different ways of accessing and enjoying them. Consumers are encouraged to use their creativity when eating them, to take ownership of the process and make it an individual experience. There is a traditional ritualistic way to eat an Oreo—twisting the cookies apart, licking the crème and dunking the cookies in milk. This eating experience is portrayed in the global "moments" advertising campaign. At the same time this campaign has consistently nurtured the concept of sharing and connection. Oreo, and its distinctive method of consumption and enjoyment, brings together a son and his dad, or grandpa, or friend, as they share a rewarding moment together. The fact that these moments of connection are often between different generations keeps the tradition alive and relevant for all ages. As stated earlier, a rich implicit brand meaning is not the preserve of substantial, high-priced items, as the example of a simple sandwich cookie demonstrates.

Implicit Brand Meaning in Practice

Gillette is an example of a brand with great depth of brand meaning. Traditionally, Gillette has been about razors and shaving, though the company has sought to expand that meaning to personal grooming with the launch of the Gillette Series line following the success of the Sensor razor. The slogan "The best a man can get" is one of the cleverest slogans ever penned. It evokes the rich dimensions of meaning of the Gillette brand. Its supremacy claim as the best available product is supported by the brand's track record of always being at the forefront of shaving technology. The dynamic look and design of its razors bear testimony to this, with their abundance of silver and black: "What makes this packaging great is not that the shaving system, the handle and blades look pretty, but that the shaver's handle sends a strong message of the best technology any man or woman can get in the world of shaving" (Gobé 2001, p. 113). The other interpretation of the slogan, as the best a man can be(come), alludes to Gillette's implicit brand meaning. On the one hand, the campaign that first introduced the slogan for the Sensor razor depicted a very clearly defined set of masculine values: the well-groomed, fit, successful executive and family man. The somewhat stereotypical portrayal of the ideal American male according to Gillette even passed over into the vernacular, as single women yearned to meet a "Gillette man." On the other hand, at a deeper symbolic level, research reveals that men feel "reborn" when they have just shaved—as if returned to their original pristine state, the way they were when they entered the world. The brand's symbolic meaning thus has both a more conscious, value-expressive dimension and a subconscious psychological dimension. Gillette's previous slogan, by comparison, was the more linear "comfort and closeness."

Levi's provides an instance of a brand that suffered the consequences of a shifting and inconsistent brand meaning. Levi's primary meaning for a long time was original, tough-wearing jeans. In fact, it was the brand that invented the concept of *blue jeans* and defined it for decades. Its move into more general casual clothing diluted and altered this meaning and was not a great success. As fashion changed, Levi's started to lose share to trendy newcomers like Diesel, with baggier, low-cut jeans. Suddenly, contemporary youth started to see Levi's as their parents' brand. Moreover, its symbolic meaning was becoming multifarious and diffuse. To an extent this was an outcome of the brand's rich and far-reaching heritage. Levi's are still the original blue jeans, first riveted for added strength, more than a century ago. The brand's cultural antecedents are rooted in the rugged American West, a symbol of frontier independence and pioneering spirit. For generations, Levi's seemed to catch and represent the mood of the young—never more so than in the 1950s, when Levi's meant jeans and jeans meant youth, particularly rebellious youth. By the 1970s the blue jean was an American icon, ripe for export, and Levi's, along with Lee and Wrangler, were its representatives. Through the rise and fall of the 1980s and 1990s, the brand's implicit meaning has wandered through the symbolism-rich foothills of pioneering independence, freedom, rebelliousness, heroism and sexual confidence, with a bit of humor thrown in for good measure—all while losing touch with the brand's primary target.

It is not unusual for brand meaning to shift and evolve with the passage of time. Consider the earlier example of the Lucozade brand in the United Kingdom. Lucozade is a glucose-rich drink introduced by Beecham Foods (now Glaxo Smith Kline) in the 1930s. It was traditionally positioned as a source of quick and easily assimilated energy in times of sickness. Advertising featured convalescent children and ran with the tag line, "Lucozade aids recovery." The product was packaged in a distinctive 25-ounce bottle with yellow cellophane wrap. Some 20 percent of sales volume went through pharmacists. By the late 1970s volume was trending down and the brand was in decline. New faster-acting, more effective drugs had reduced convalescence periods and many children's diseases were now rarities. The Beecham Foods convalescence drink was losing its way.

The problem, or rather the opportunity, was that to consumers the brand had a somewhat different meaning from that assumed by the company. A "Usage and Attitude" study conducted at the time turned up some interesting findings. Only about 20 percent of the volume was actually being used for convalescence, and only some 30 percent was being drunk by children. A significant proportion of the volume was being consumed in health and by adults. To consumers, the perceived primary brand meaning was shifting toward one of energy boost. Housewives would use it as such during their busy day.

Gradually and cautiously, the company began to embrace this meaning. At first it was framed in the context of an energy boost to help the body regain its normal energy level. With time this evolved into an energy boost to provide extra energy for normal, healthy bodies. The brand's extension into the growing and lucrative sports drink segment provided a natural fit with Lucozade's energy proposition. Today Lucozade is a thriving brand, still marketed on an energy platform. Fundamentally, the underlying product has changed little since its introduction. The sociocultural changes in the environment in which it is marketed have been far more dramatic. Primary brand meaning has evolved from "energy for recovery" through "energy boost to keep me going" to "energy boost to perform." Note how perceptions derived from elements such as packaging cues have consolidated this process—vivid ring-pull cans and smaller, more dynamic portable plastic bottles communicate *energy* in a very different way from the old cellophane-wrapped glass bottles.

Though there has been a linear evolution in the drink's primary brand meaning, it is not hard to understand how its symbolic brand meaning would have undergone a revolutionary transformation. Consider the brand's early associations with convalescence compared with the present casting of energy provision in a more mental-spiritual-attitudinal frame. In brand archetypal terms, the brand has gone from nurturing caretaker to swashbuckling hero.

The General Electric brand, with its former slogan, "We bring good things to life," is an example of a company-generated brand concept and consumer-perceived brand meaning coinciding. Such slogans as this, or Visa's "It's everywhere you want to be," are more than just clever double entendres. By combining functional promise and symbolic connotation, they pave the way for people to perceive the full depth of the brand. In the case of General Electric, a recently introduced product bore perfect testimony to the slogan. The lighting division—another category with great symbolic potential—launched a line of light bulbs called Reveal. According to the company, they filter out the yellow rays that hide true colors, producing a truer, cleaner, whiter-looking light. "The bulb that uncovers the pure, true light," says the sales literature—a product that brings implicit brand meaning to life.

Researching Implicit Brand Meaning

Traditional positioning approaches fall back on the apparent dichotomy of a brand: what in Coca-Cola terminology are sometimes referred to as the *intrinsics* and the *extrinsics,* that is, product-related aspects and non-product-related aspects, or added values. Similarly, it is common practice to divide a brand's appeal into rational–functional areas and emotional areas. This process is an essential part of understanding a brand's make-up but goes only so far in terms of uncovering the full spectrum of brand meaning. Brand marketers usually stop at defining emotional appeal rather than excavating further into the hidden depths of emotional significance. Emotional appeal is frequently derived from facets of the brand personality (e.g., friendly, warm, accessible) and is a strong driver of consumer acceptance. It is therefore a powerful ally to, but not the same as, the brand's emotional significance. Researching a brand's symbolic and metaphorical properties is paramount if we are to understand and harness brand depth.

Yet probing implicit brand meaning is a complex process. Precisely because of its elusive, symbolic nature, this dimension of brand meaning is unlikely to be that at which a brand readily and predominantly defines itself in a consumer's mind. A brand's more immediate, manifest meaning is perceived at a less abstract level. Nobody goes into a supermarket and asks, "Where do you keep your maternal solicitude products?" or tells a car dealer, "I was looking for something in the way of symbolic self-completion."

At the same time, it is often assumed that brands of an overtly functional and rational nature, particularly packaged goods found in a domestic environment, are necessarily bereft of symbolic meaning. Nothing could be farther from the truth: "Packaged goods are as emotionally charged, as laden with symbolism and psychological meaning, as any other, as qualitative research can immediately demonstrate" (Restall 1999, p. 207). You just have to dig a little deeper to find it. For, like meaning itself, symbolic brand meaning is multilayered, its composition ranging from the conscious to the unconscious. Somewhere between these two states are symbolic meanings that lie just below the threshold of consciousness—they are subconscious, or, as they are sometimes called, *preconscious.*

This means that implicit brand meaning can be difficult to access, given the fact that the key drivers of this type of meaning often reside in the deep recesses of the consumer psyche. The more functional and rational associations of a brand will usually be readily communicated in verbal descriptions of the brand. But a large proportion of consumer brand perception is acquired through low involvement processing and many associations are unconsciously stored in a nonverbal mode. Eliciting these nonverbal and pre- or unconscious associations, which often underpin the symbolic meanings a brand holds for its consumers, necessitates a more holistic and wide-ranging approach to research. To encompass the different modes of representation of brand associations (i.e., verbal, visual, emotional and sensory) and recognizing the fact that most associations are unconscious, it is evident that a variety of research techniques is called for to uncover brand meaning in all its subtlety and profoundness.

Such research can be problematical. People are often less willing or able to reveal what is private, highly personal, unspoken and potentially embarrassing. Furthermore, they may not be conscious of their real motivations or may find it difficult to articulate them. Specifically there are three fundamental areas of complication: (1) the problem of access; (2) the problem of representation modes; and (3) the problem of impression management.

Access   The conscious primary associations of a brand are the easiest to elicit in research. Though they are informative in terms of a brand's primary meaning, the risk is that if research does not get farther than these to the less conscious associations, a superficial and lopsided impression of the brand's meaning will emerge. Potentially valuable insights will remain locked away in the consumer psyche and marketers may come to the erroneous conclusion that their brands lack psychological depth.

Representation Modes   Much brand information is not processed rationally, so asking consumers to rationalize about brands is problematical. Moreover, though most human communication is nonverbal, most research information is provided in a purely verbal format. When that research is concerned with less conscious material the situation is even more unsatisfactory. Verbal feedback is usually the result of highly cognitive linguistic rationalization. This is not the ideal way to retrieve impressions represented in visual, sensory and emotional modes or to tap instinctual responses, none of which have been subject to active cognitive reasoning. Moreover, the average person's verbal capacity is simply inadequate when faced with the task of describing in words visual, auditory and other types of sensory impressions. Consider, for instance, how limited our vocabulary is when it comes to describing scents. The risk here, then, is that, even if research manages to access nonverbal impressions and associations, these may not be correctly identified and recorded due to the overreliance on verbal techniques.

Impression Management As mentioned previously, *impression management* is a term introduced by Erving Goffman (1959), who presented the concept in a dramaturgical light in his book *The Presentation of Self in Everyday Life*. Interaction is viewed as a "performance" through which individuals attempt to control the impressions that others form of them, in accordance with the desired goals of the "actor." Whether consciously or not, there is a tendency for people to control the information they provide about themselves. Usually, we process others' impression-relevant reactions to us at a preattentive or nonconscious level. Without consciously considering how other people may be perceiving us, we nonetheless scan the social environment to pick up signs of how others might regard us (Leary and Kowalski 1990). When we are "on show," or the focus of attention, the mechanism of impression management becomes more active and deliberate. Interviews are a prime example, be it a job interview, or a research interview where there is a focus on our self-concept. As a result, respondents monitor and manipulate their responses in keeping with their desired identities and may withhold potentially valuable information. Of course, this possibility exists in any kind of elicitation interview situation.

Tapping the intuitive and unconscious levels of the consumer psyche through the techniques of projection and empathy is essential if we are to understand how consumers relate to brands and their advertising at a deeper level. Ethnographic methods, observation and cultural analysis may also play a role in the more holistic approach required to access symbolic brand meaning. Figure 5.8 illustrates some of the different research methodologies suited to investigating symbolic brand meaning (Lannon and Cooper 1983, p. 204).

METHOD	LAYER	OUTPUT

METHOD				LAYER	OUTPUT
Simple Questioning	PUBLIC	COMMUNICABLE	AWARE	Spontaneous	Immediate, spontaneous response
Asking/ reminding				Reasoned, conventional	Justifications, explanations
Pressing				Preconscious	Detailed elaborations & introspections
Sympathetic probing	PRIVATE	NON-	NON-	Concealed, personal	Personal admissions
Play, drama, non-verbal				Intuitive	Symbols, analogy, imagination
Projective approaches				Unconscious	Repressed attitudes & motives

Figure 5.8   Researching symbolic meanings in brands and advertising.

The type of research methodologies listed toward the base of Figure 5.8 are particularly valuable in uncovering associations and attitudes that, for whatever reason, consumers are reluctant to verbalize and may unknowingly be concealing through the feedback they give. A famous example of this and one illustrating the benefits of projective, psychographic techniques, was an experiment carried out by Mason Haire in the 1940s (see Keller 1998, p. 315). The experiment was conducted to uncover consumers' true beliefs and feelings toward Nescafé instant coffee. A survey had been run to investigate why initial sales of Nescafé had fallen short of expectations. People were asked if they used instant coffee and, if not, what they disliked about it. Most who said they did not like the product attributed this to not liking the flavor. However, Nescafé's management already knew from consumer taste tests that people found the taste of instant coffee to be acceptable when they did not know what type of coffee they were drinking. To get to the truth Haire devised an ingenious experiment.

Haire drew up two shopping lists with the same six items (Table 5.1). The first list included Maxwell House Drip Ground Coffee, whereas the second contained Nescafé Instant Coffee. Each of two groups of subjects, identically matched, were given one of the lists and asked to project themselves into the situation and to characterize the woman who bought the groceries. Two distinct profiles resulted (Table 5.2).

TABLE 5.1   Haire Study Shopping Lists

Shopping List 1	Shopping List 2
Pound and a half of hamburger	Pound and a half of hamburger
Two loaves Wonder Bread	Two loaves Wonder Bread
Bunch of carrots	Bunch of carrots
One can Rumford's Baking Powder	One can Rumford's Baking Powder
Maxwell House Coffee (drip ground)	Nescafé Instant Coffee
Two cans Del Monte peaches	Two cans Del Monte peaches
Five pounds potatoes	Five pounds potatoes

Haire's interpretation was that, for these respondents, using instant coffee was inconsistent with the traditions and mores associated with caring for one's family. Thus, the convenience aspect of instant coffee, at that point in time, was proving to be more of a liability than an asset. It was only when consumers were given a projection exercise that this deeper reason for rejecting instant coffee was uncovered. As a result of these findings a new campaign was developed that highlighted how using Nescafé freed up time for housewives to spend on other important housekeeping tasks.

Projective techniques can help reveal emotional reactions. Because projective questions have no obvious answer and the techniques used are open ended, they can encourage the expression of novel ideas and of fantasy, idiosyncrasy and originality. They can reduce social constraints and self-censorship, leading to respondents being more self-revealing. Such techniques can take many forms, including collages in which respondents are asked to put together a collage using pictures and images from selected stimuli or from magazines and newspapers. Picture completion and psycho-drawing are other techniques. The use of analogies and metaphors is also common in

TABLE 5.2   Haire Study Shopper Profiles

	List 1 (Maxwell House) %	List 2 (Nescafé) %
Lazy	4	48
Fails to plan household purchases and schedules well	12	48
Thrifty	16	4
Not a good wife	0	16

this type of research methodology. A metaphor is the representation of one thought in terms of another. Taken broadly, the term can refer to similes, analogies, allegories, parables and proverbs.

Metaphor Elicitation

Metaphors can help us to interpret what we perceive in the world around us. They can lead us to see new connections and to draw new meanings. Because they can reveal cognitive processes beyond those that mere literal language can identify, metaphors can bring to the surface thoughts that would otherwise go unspoken. Metaphor elicitation and response latency techniques can be particularly effective in uncovering unconscious thoughts and feelings (Zaltman 2003, p. 76). That is why professionals in the fields of clinical psychology and psychiatry are increasingly turning to metaphor elicitation to enable patients to make unconscious experiences more conscious and communicable (ibid., pp. 89–90).

Harvard Business School professor Gerald Zaltman (2003 p. 89) gives the example of consumers' understanding of Chevrolet trucks in terms of a rock, in response to the brand's "Like a rock" advertising campaign. The campaign was developed on the back of metaphor elicitation research with consumers. The metaphor and its subsequent elaboration in advertising reflected the associations already present in the minds of existing loyal Chevy truck owners and communicated them to the broader truck-buying public. The phrase "Like a rock" triggers four basic associations in consumers' minds: "rock" with "take abuse"; "Chevy" with "reliable"; "Chevy" with "rock"; and "take abuse" with "reliable." In making a connection between the idea of a Chevy truck and the idea of a rock, consumers assign certain rock-like attributes to Chevy trucks—like the ability to take abuse—and these are translated into perceptions of reliability and ruggedness. To be able to attribute rock-like qualities to Chevy trucks, consumers have to draw on their existing concepts of rock. The metaphor of a Chevy truck as a rock thus forms a relationship between two different memory structures: that of Chevy trucks and that of rock. The elements of that relationship were already present in the minds of dedicated Chevy truck owners. In the minds of potential first-time buyers, the advertising campaign helped seed the relationship, cause a fusion between the two memory structures and make a connection not previously made.

Zaltman's patented marketing research tool ZMET (Zaltman Metaphor Elicitation Technique) combines projective methodology with in-depth interview. Drawing on neuroscience, semiotics and the ideas of Carl Jung, the technique uses metaphor and visual imagery to uncover the structure of meaning in consumers' thoughts and feelings with regard to a given topic, such as a brand. The technique reconciles the mismatch between the way consumers experience and think about the world around them and the traditional methods market researchers employ to gather this information. Consumers are asked to select images from materials they have at home that represent their thoughts and feelings about the topic under study. In-depth probing by interviewers explores the metaphors, their meaning and their relationship to each other. The emphasis is on probing and not prompting. Effective probing enables respondents to answer in multiple, creative and often unexpected ways, whereas prompting tends to set boundaries and channel participant responses toward the interviewer's own assumptions. The interviews are augmented by developing digital collages of consumer-generated images, which helps summarize many of the ideas discussed and also enables the interviewer to further explore relationships between emerging themes.

Specific steps included in such a session could include the following:

- Storytelling through pictures: Respondents describe how each picture represents their thoughts and feelings regarding the topic.
- Missing pictures: Participants are asked to express thoughts and feelings for which they could not find any images.
- The triad task: Respondents have to talk about similarities and differences among three images chosen at random by the interviewer.
- Metaphor probe: Selected images are explored more deeply to probe for any hidden meanings not yet uncovered. For instance, in "expanding the frame," interviewees are asked to widen the image and describe what they think might be there.
- Storytelling: Participants are invited to tell a story about the images, including plot, characters, emotions and sounds.
- Digital imaging: As described already.

These and other projective techniques are particularly useful for penetrating the human mind to reveal the unconscious constructs of implicit brand meaning. As it is informed more by functional and rational considerations, primary brand meaning can usually be accessed through less sophisticated research methodology and more straightforward, direct questioning. In any case, given the complexity of human thought and behavior, it is always preferable to use a variety of research methods when probing for brand meaning.

Neuromarketing

The new and controversial field of marketing research dubbed neuromarketing measures brain activity to gauge consumer reactions to brands and advertising and to better understand their buying decisions. High-tech tools like functional magnetic resonance imaging (fMRI) enable researchers to map the degree to which certain parts of the brain become activated when exposed to different stimuli. The prospect neuromarketing offers is alluring: the potential to access directly and objectively consumers' thoughts without external interference. Against the backdrop of growing dissatisfaction with focus groups in which people often do not say what they mean or do not mean what they say and in which stimuli are mediated by an interviewer, the idea of getting straight to the source—the brain—is attracting client money. Though still only accounting for a fraction of the $8 billion spent in the United States on market research in 2006 (Park 2007, p. 114), many major marketers are turning their attentions to the techniques of neuromarketing. Moreover, they are doing so with respect to diverse areas of the marketing mix, including new product development and packaging design. In the auto industry, for instance, Daimler Chrysler has invested in neuromarketing research to understand how consumers evaluate car exteriors. Ford recently funded a number of neuromarketing experiments that included monitoring people's brain activity during the viewing of programs interspersed with ads (Wilkinson 2005, p. 22).

Interest in the field was heightened by a version of the Pepsi Challenge performed by neuroscientist P. Read Montague of the Baylor College of Medicine in Houston. Conducted inside fMRI machines, researchers monitored the brain scans of 67 people who were given a blind taste test of Coke and Pepsi. After consuming the colas, all volunteers displayed strong activation of the parts of the brain associated with reward–pleasure and brand preference was about equal.

However, when the experiment was repeated and participants were told what they were drinking, the Coke brand had a dramatic effect: It activated not only the reward–pleasure areas of the brain but also new areas: the memory-related brain regions. The result? Three quarters of the volunteers said they preferred Coke: "This showed that the brand alone has value in the brain system above and beyond the desire for the content of the can," commented Montague (Park 2007, p. 114). In other words, factors other than taste alone, such as the positive associations derived from years of seeing Coke commercials, were so potent that they could override, in Coke's favor, a taste preference for Pepsi.

Neuromarketing has a number of hurdles to overcome before it figures as a mainstream research tool. It remains to be demonstrated in the long run how meaningful its findings are and, in particular, how much they contribute to an understanding of brand meaning. It is very expensive research and is still limited in scale. Then there are the not inconsiderable objections to it from an ethical standpoint. However, as its techniques and applications become more sophisticated and more and more client research money flows into it, neuromarketing looks likely to establish itself as a viable research mode in the years to come.

Sources of Brand Meaning

Brand Experience

As discussed throughout the book, brand meaning is drawn from a number of public and private sources. Advertising is one of the most influential public sources and is discussed at length in Chapter 8. Many marketing professionals still tend to regard advertising and other paid-for communication as the only way to create and maintain brand meaning. Even in the absence of advertising support, though, brands can come to hold vivid meaning for their consumers. The Body Shop is a good example. Famous for creating a niche market sector for naturally inspired skin- and hair-care products, The Body Shop evolved from one small shop in Brighton on the south coast of England selling around 25 products, to become a global network of nearly 2000 stores in 50 countries. The strong meaning of the brand resides in a potent combination of product, sensory experience and a single-minded company ethos, epitomized by founder Anita Roddick and spanning environmental concern, animal rights and humanitarian issues. With its pioneering commitment to tackling global poverty ("Trade, not aid") and its determination to challenge the stereotypes of beauty perpetuated by the cosmetics industry, The Body Shop has come to incorporate a unique set of meanings for its aficionados, the envy of those companies who have tried unsuccessfully to spend their way to brand fame.

With service brands in particular, such as hotels and airlines, experience is likely to be the main source of brand meaning. By way of contrast, with a product like cigarettes, or bottled water, most of the brand meaning comes from the advertising. Direct experience will contribute less to brand meaning. Figure 5.9 illustrates the difference between these two examples. Firsthand experience and advertising are two of the biggest contributors to brand meaning. Their relative importance varies from category to category and brand to brand and is a function of the degree of firsthand experience on the one hand and the amount of advertising consumed on the other.

One of the best examples of an "experiential brand" is Starbucks. Starbucks reinvented the coffee shop and is steadily reinventing a category. Not so many years ago finding a decent cappuccino or a bag of specialty coffee beans was something attainable only by the privileged few who had been initiated into the wonders of *coffea arabica*. Today

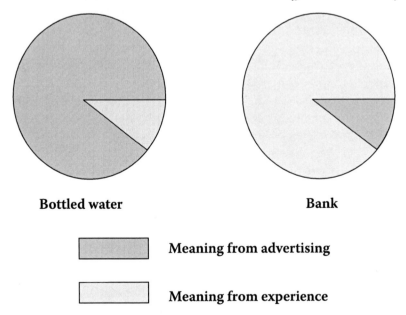

Bottled water   **Bank**

Meaning from advertising

Meaning from experience

Figure 5.9   Sources of meaning compared.

specialty coffee stores and coffee bars are mushrooming throughout our cities and Jamaica Blue Mountain coffee (considered by many to be the finest in the world) can be ordered over the Internet. While visiting Milan in 1983 when he was director of retail operations, Starbucks' chair and chief global strategist, Howard Schultz, had an epiphany about bringing the Italian coffee shop to the United States. He observed the customs of Italian coffee-lovers as they visited any of the country's 200,000 espresso bars and was struck by the environment and the elements of the overall experience.

Schultz's mantra of "retail is detail" finds expression in every facet of the company's operations. The aromas of freshly ground coffee, expertly drawn espresso shots and drip-brewed coffees of the day that greet customers as they enter a Starbucks heighten the anticipation of what is to come. To keep it that way the company banned smoking and asked employees to refrain from wearing colognes or perfumes. Then there is the distinctive color palette cueing coffee in its different stages—the greens of coffee trees and unripe beans, the red of ripe berries, coffee mocha and roasted bean browns. There is a spaciousness and comfortable informality about the shops and their seating areas. The interesting menu boards invite attention. The floors are clean, the packaging attractive and the jazzy, bluesy music easy on the ear. And the baristas will prepare your coffee just the way you want it. Starbucks has turned retailing coffee into an art form, one that appeals to all the senses. It is as much about the sights, sounds and smells as it is about the taste. Starbucks connects with its customers by generating a narrative consistent with their values and preferences. And those customers are involved in the experience, unhesitatingly slipping into Euro-latte Starbucks speak ("Mine's a decaf grande extra cocoa mocha"). What was previously a rather unglamorous beverage to most Americans—an uninspiring cup of joe—has become stylish and trendy thanks in large part to Starbucks—and all with hardly a dollar spent on advertising.

Brand Heritage

Sometimes the brand's own history and the heritage associated with it may be a significant source of its meaning for consumers. Hovis bread in the United Kingdom is a brand with a rich heritage. No other food has been as central to the British diet as the humble loaf of bread. Hovis started out in 1886 as "Smith's Patent Germ Bread." The name Hovis arose from a competition in 1890 and comes from the Latin *hominis vis*, "the strength of man." The original Hovis was a solid wheatgerm loaf. The brand's growth was driven by many successful advertising campaigns, from "Don't say brown, say Hovis" in 1916, to "Have you had your Hovis today?" in 1936 and "Hovis is the slice of life" in 1954. But the most famous campaign for the brand began in 1973 with the "Boy on the Bike" commercial. The ads, set in the early part of the century, were shot against a backdrop of cobblestone streets, rolling hills and country lanes, evocative of the Yorkshire countryside (though actually filmed in Dorset) and accompanied by Dvorak's New World Symphony, with its distinctly old-world feel. The boy on the bike is delivering Hovis loaves. "Last stop on t'round was Old Ma Pegarty's place," he reminisces in a thick northern accent. "It were like takin' bread to top o't'world. 'Twas a grand ride back though…. I knew the baker would have t'kettle on and batches of hot Hovis ready…." The campaign is a classic in nostalgic advertising, oozing the homely, down-to-earth values and goodness of yesterday, going back to the very roots of the brand. It ran for 20 years. It is interesting to ponder whether such a campaign would have the same effect on today's media-savvy, somewhat more cynical audience. Nostalgia, as they say, ain't what it used to be….

Another brand that looked to its roots for meaning was Wrangler, in the European jeans market. The Wrangler name came into being in 1947 when the Blue Bell Overall Company designed a denim jean specifically for professional cowboys (the name itself refers to the job of herding and caring for livestock, particularly horses, on a ranch). In 1993, Wranglers began to be marketed as the "Authentic Western Jeans." It was a credible enough claim, given the brand's history and one that offered the potential, at least, to compete with the Levi's brand, which effectively owned originality in the blue jeans market. But it was not until 1997 that this meaning was really consolidated. The challenge for the brand was to make its Western heritage relevant and attractive to young European consumers. The response was the "Rodeo" advertising campaign. Though largely understated in Europe, in America Wranglers are inextricably linked with the sport of rodeo. They are the only jeans made especially for professional rodeo riders. The jeans often come with a copy of the Professional

Rodeo Cowboys' Association booklet in the back pocket, attesting to the fact that 99 out of 100 rodeo riders wear Wranglers. By presenting rodeo as the ultimate extreme sport, the company managed to avoid falling into the obvious, clichéd Western territory, which would have left young Europeans indifferent.

Brand Names

The selection of an appropriate brand name is one of the most important decisions a marketer has to make in launching a new brand. It can play a critical role in providing cues about brand meaning. For that reason, even if a brand has been in the market for some time, probing consumer reactions to the name can reveal some of the underlying reasons for broader brand perceptions and attitudes. The criteria usually suggested for evaluating brand names are more straightforward than attempts to classify types of names. Desirable brand names (1) can be encoded into, retained in and retrieved from memory with relative ease, thus facilitating recall and recognition; and (2) can favor the creation of images and associations consistent with intended brand meaning. Not all successful brand names meet both criteria. Just as research suggests names with an "x" are particularly memorable—Rolex, Radox, Xerox—there are phonetic reasons why Kodak is an easy brand name to register in the mind and recall, yet there is nothing inherently meaningful about the word *Kodak* to suggest any attribute or category associations.

Kodak is an invented, or *coined*, word. Coined, or made-up, names are just one of the name types usually identified in describing the variety of brand names. Other descriptors include *concrete* (Dove) versus *abstract* (Zest), *real words* (Budget) versus *nonwords* (Avis), *descriptive* (Craftsman) versus *nondescriptive* (DeWalt) and *suggestive* (Pearl Drops) versus *nonsuggestive* (Arm & Hammer). The terms *meaningful* and *nonmeaningful* are also used. Though it is true that some brand names convey no inherent meaning, for the rest it is more practical to think in terms of degrees of meaningfulness, which relates to the two central premises of this book: (1) People are very resourceful in finding and creating meaning; and (2) there is often meaning where, on the surface, little would seem to exist. Even in the case of a nonword brand name, individuals are capable of extracting some meaning (see Chapter 3 on sound symbolism). For example, in a study of computer-generated random brand names as potential candidates for the breakfast cereal and laundry detergent categories, it was found that *Whumies* and *Quax* were more remindful of breakfast cereals and *Dehax* was remindful of a laundry detergent (Peterson and Ross 1972).

There are thus two potential sources of meaning in a brand name: (1) the meaning that may be derived from semantic associations; and (2) the meaning generated by sound symbolism. Take the brand name Viagra, for instance. Viagra rhymes with Niagra, as in Niagara Falls, the famously powerful waterfall. Psychologically, water is linked to sexuality and life. *Vi* suggests vigor or virility and *agra* triggers associations with the fertility of agriculture and the energy of aggression. From a sound symbolism perspective, *v* connotes speed and energy, while the guttural *g* connotes toughness and masculinity. When executives at a well-known naming consultancy saw the handheld wireless prototype developed by Research In Motion Ltd., they thought the little keyboard buttons looked like seeds. The name *strawberry* was thrown up, but *straw-* is a slow, drawn-out sound. *Black* works better; the short vowels in the first two syllables of Blackberry suggest a brisk sprightliness, while the alliteration conveys a user-friendly informality, an impression accentuated by the final *y*, which is a friendly sound often found in nicknames. Semantically, the name suggests accessibility, *while* berry conveys smallness and compactness (Begley 2002 p. B1). Ziplok sounds like a brand that will lock in freshness quickly and effectively and benefits from both sound symbolism and semantic associations.

Other brand names are more inherently and explicitly meaningful. That is, they deliberately cue some aspect of the desired brand meaning. They may allude semantically to the category (e.g., Lean Cuisine low-calorie frozen foods) or to some attribute or benefit of the brand (e.g., Die-Hard batteries, Odor-Eaters, Duracell, Band-Aid). Whereas the most explicitly meaningful brand names, like I Can't Believe It's Not Butter or Gee, Your Hair Smells Terrific shampoo, leave little room for mistake as to what they are, their downside is that such names severely limit future brand extension possibilities— that is, stretching or reframing their meaning. Indeed, this consideration holds true for any brand name with at least some intended meaning. Generally, the more "motivated" (to use a term from semiotics) the meaningfulness, the more limiting it could prove to be in the long run. Compaq was a great name for small computers, but the company has had to invest heavily to facilitate the successful introduction of bigger personal computers. Similarly, Keller (1998, p. 139) gives the hypothetical example of a brand of laundry detergent that is initially given the name *Blossom* and marketed as "adding fresh scent." If it is subsequently felt necessary to reposition the product and add a new brand association, for instance that the product "fights tough stains," this may be difficult to accomplish if the brand name continues to remind consumers of the original meaning the brand holds for them. Rather more literally, when Dell decided it wanted to mean not just your computer but also everything that attaches to it (e.g., printers, projectors), the company had to ask shareholders to approve dropping "Computer" from its name.

High-imagery words are particularly suitable for brand names as they have an advantage in terms of recall over low-imagery words. High-imagery words readily create vivid visual references in consumers' minds. Concrete nouns, with tangible, visual referents (e.g., *mustang*) more easily inspire these mental images than low-imagery, abstract nouns (e.g., *bold*) (Robertson 1989). Blockbuster is a good example of a high-imagery brand name. Originally, blockbuster movies were so named because people would queue around the block to get in to see them. Blockbuster is therefore an excellent name for a company that rents movies. It relates to the category without being generic. JB's Video Rentals or National Video Rentals, whereas descriptive and concrete, inspire less imagery and fewer mental representations, affording the consumer fewer cognitive access points and making the brand names less memorable and distinctive.

Of course, much of the imagery that meaningful, high-imagery brand names elicit is connotative meaning and stored perceptions already existing in the individual's mind for the words used in the brand name. The brand name taps into that existing meaning reservoir. That is the advantage of using a meaningful name as opposed to an invented, nonmeaningful name such as Kodak or Exxon, in which meaning has to be originated from scratch.

Foreign branding can dramatically affect the meanings ascribed to products. By foreign branding is meant the strategy of spelling or pronouncing a brand name in a foreign language (Leclerc, Schmitt and Dubé 1994). Häagen-Dazs may sound Scandinavian, but it is made in the United States and was first served in New York. Klarbrunn water does not originate from mountain springs in the German or Swiss Alps, as the name may suggest; it is American water bottled in Wisconsin. Foreign branding triggers cultural stereotypes and imagery and can influence and enhance product perceptions and attitudes, more than compensating for any initial difficulties in pronouncing and recalling them. The cue *French*, for example, activates a network of associations related to flair, elegance and sophistication (e.g., being *chic* and having a certain *je ne sais quoi*), sensitivity to good aesthetics and appreciation of sensory pleasure, refined taste and an educated palate. In a word, French culture is seen as one of hedonism (ibid.).

Hedonic products afford pleasure—typically sensorial, experiential products—as opposed to utilitarian products, which are evaluated according to their functionality. Thus, hedonism-utilitarianism is both a basic cultural dimension and a central consideration in product perceptions (Robertson 1989). In a series of experiments Leclerc, Schmitt and Dubé (1994) examined the extent to which foreign branding influences product perceptions and evaluations. Focusing on French brand names, they found that, for "hybrid products" with a mixture of hedonic and utilitarian features (e.g., shampoo, toothpaste, deodorant and body lotion), the brands were perceived as more hedonic when the name was pronounced in French than when pronounced in English. French brand names were found to have more effect on attitudes to hedonic products than country-of-origin information. Naturally, country-of-origin information (e.g., "Made in Germany") will add country-specific imagery to the brand associative network, but the apparently stronger cues triggered by foreign branding alone are significant.

Besides the cognitive links that consumers make between brand names and product categories, attributes and benefits are the emotional and expressive connections. Brand names that have strong positive associations, connotations, or symbolism and that stir the emotions and arouse pleasant feelings enjoy enhanced recall. This is particularly so when the product category itself is an emotional one. According to the psychological phenomenon of state-dependent memory, memory of past events is better when those events coincide with an individual's current emotional state (Martineau 1957). Thus, we are more likely to recall happy memories when we are in a happy mood, romantic memories when we are in a romantic mood and so on. So a consumer thinking about brands in an emotional category such as perfumes, colognes, or jewelry should more easily be able to recall emotional brand names, such as *Love, Passion,* or *Happy.*

Brand names, then, can play a fundamental role in the formation of brand meaning. They may carry no inherent meaning, in which case ascribed meaning is provided solely by marketing efforts and consumer responses. Or they may hold a greater or lesser degree of intrinsic meaningfulness. Some names offer little in the way of connotation and are very literal descriptions of the products (e.g., *Shake 'n Vac*), whereas others work less through their denotative meaning than by connecting with the connotative meanings already existing in consumers' minds. Automobile brand names such as Explorer, Mustang and Land Rover are examples. Pierre Martineau (1957) accurately captured the spirit and importance of the brand name more than fifty years ago when he described it as a "psychological label" capable of paving the way for the critical symbolic interpretation of products (Floch 2000).

Brand Logos and Symbols

A logotype consists of the brand name rendered in a distinctive typeface, often combined with a trademark, which is a visual brand device or symbol, such as the Prudential rock. Given that the brain receives and processes pictures more easily than words, visual devices and symbols are potent branding tools and they have proven to be more memorable than words. Often these symbols and visual devices are designed to enhance or reinforce brand meaning in some way. In his book *Marketing and Communication: Beneath the Signs, the Strategies*, Jean-Marie Floch devotes an entire chapter to a semiotic analysis of the IBM and Apple logos:

> Our logo is a great mystery: it is a symbol of pleasure and knowledge, partly eaten away and displaying the colors of the rainbow, but not in the proper order. We couldn't wish for a more fitting logo: pleasure, knowledge, hope and anarchy (Jean-Louis Gassée, ex-chairman of Apple Products. Floch 2001, p. 186).

The logo draws on the story of Eden and the fruit of the tree of knowledge, forbidden to Adam and Eve. Once bitten into, the apple empowered mankind with the gift of knowledge. The reordering of the rainbow stripes connotes free-spiritedness, rebellion and imagination—an appropriate logo for a brand that urges us to "think different." Of course, Apple has since moved away from the rainbow logo (presumably for reasons of practicality, design quality control and modernization), just as it has evolved from flashy colors to predominantly white polycarbonate for its consumer computer lines.

In the late 1800s, Henri Nestlé, a chemist and inventor, devoted several years to the development of Farine Lactée Nestlé, a milk-based food for babies whose mothers could not breastfeed them. At a time of high infant mortality the product saved the lives and health of many infants in Europe. Today Nestlé ("little nest") uses the bird's nest device as a seal of guarantee on all human food products under Nestlé corporate brands. The device is a symbol of the company's ethos of quality nutrition, representing nourishment, security and a sense of family.

Prudential's rock and Legal & General's (United Kingdom) umbrellas are metaphors for solidarity and strength and protection, respectively. The Well's Fargo stagecoach is another example of a meaningful brand symbol, with connotations of the old West, a commitment to make it through and deliver for its customers and the reliable safekeeping of funds.

Relative Richness of Brand Symbols

Incidentally, it is useful to consider the development and employment of visual brand symbols and logos in respect to status symbolism. Status symbolism is the lowest, most basic and most generic level at which implicit brand meaning operates, as well as the most conscious level—where the symbolic value of a brand to an individual amounts to nothing much more than its power as a badge. Designer symbols like the Lacoste alligator merely identify the brand and its wearer. There is little emotional or metaphorical content in the symbol. Similarly, the Michelin man is a symbol that, though it may help create and enhance the brand personality, has no metaphorical meaning. By contrast, the more richly symbolic nature of other brands is often embodied in some physical symbol such as the Harley-Davidson eagle, the Marlboro cowboy, or the Esso tiger. These symbols or icons immediately connote the brand's symbolic meaning regardless of the local language, assuming that the icon and symbolic values have similar currency in the given culture. Whether in the case of the brand itself as symbol (e.g., brand as status symbol), or visual brand symbol (e.g., the Harley eagle), some symbols are clearly more meaningful than others.

One fundamental source of brand meaning that is often overlooked is that of the intrinsic nature of the underlying product and of the product category itself.

Product and Category Significance

Many of the most successful brands have one thing in common: Ultimately, their meaning is grounded in some physical or symbolic truth about the product or category. Kodak, Gillette, Hallmark and Harley-Davidson are examples. The more we probe the nature of the product and its usage, the closer we will come to discovering what the Leo Burnett agency traditionally challenged itself to relentlessly pursue: the "inherent drama" in the product. Bill Bernbach's declaration that "the magic is in the product" was probably more true in his day than today but serves as a useful reminder that sometimes a product has its own story to tell. Returning to the technique of laddering, such an approach, by providing a hierarchy of benefits and values, can offer insight into the symbolic significance of products and categories. For while at one level products and their categories may be fulfilling simple physiological requirements, at another they are often simultaneously responding to more fundamental human needs.

The personal-care category, with its personal wash, grooming and hygiene products, is a case in point. Cleansing may seem like a daily chore, but it is also a ritual that has been associated for centuries and across cultures and religions, with the removal of sin and guilt, the washing away of what makes us feel impure. Ivory soap taps this reservoir of symbolic references. The brand connotes purity, renewal and innocence. From its famous "99 and 44/100% Pure" slogan, arrived at when scientists tested the soap and found that it contained only 0.56 percent impurities, to its ability to float (the serendipitous result of an employee failing to shut off the soap-making machine when he went to lunch, allowing air to get into the soap mixture) and from its product positioning as the more mild and more gentle soap to the name itself, Ivory and its advertising have remained a consistent expression of a brand idea intimately tied to the symbolic nature of cleansing.

Hallmark's brand meaning, mentioned earlier, is founded on the insight that sending cards can actually help us in our everyday relationships. This is a quite different perspective to that of simply fulfilling obligations on special occasions. Moreover, cards are sent not only to benefit the recipient but also because it makes the sender feel good. Recognizing these deeper category motivations enabled Hallmark to take the high ground and at the same time increase card usage—a wonderful example of leveraging category meaning and by appropriation brand meaning, to grow market size and share.

The hair-care market provides an example of untapped potential in this context. By and large the category has completely overlooked the emotional and psychological significance of hair. Deep down (or high up, on the ladder), consumers regard hair as an important indicator of psychological well-being. A good head of healthy, well-kept hair transmits self-respect. Women will often change their hair (by cutting or dying it) after a traumatic experience such as a divorce, the act being a symbolic representation of a break with the past and a new beginning. The Rodgers and Hammerstein song "I'm Gonna Wash That Man Right out of My Hair" from the film *South Pacific* provides a metaphorical variation on the theme. A "bad hair day" is about more than a few wayward curls. Most men, notwithstanding the current trend for baldheadedness, dread losing their hair as they feel it represents a loss of their virility and a kind of unwelcome rite of passage into old age. Yet despite the fact that hair is such an intimate and personal extension of the self, the category has historically treated it as something disembodied and objectified. Most brands are purely functionally driven, treat women as little more than "heads of hair," and never get past clichéd hair shots and stereotypical representations of external beauty. Hair-care brands that reassess category parameters and start to connect with consumers on a different plane will reap handsome rewards.

Guinness, probably Ireland's most famous export, is a brand steeped in tradition. It dominates the global stout category. Arthur Guinness first set up business at St. James's Gate in the heart of Dublin in 1759. Guinness is a stout beer created from four simple ingredients: barley, water, hops and yeast. In its formative years, the brand touted its nutritional properties: "Guinness is good for you," proclaimed early advertising, a reference to its fortifying iron content. In the late 1980s and early 1990s it cultivated a distinctive, individualistic and somewhat mysterious personality through an advertising campaign featuring Rutger Hauer. The commercials were replete with Guinness brand iconography: the blond Hauer dressed all in black suggesting the renowned black and white of the beer's body and head, the fields of barley indicative of its natural ingredients and, above all, the theme of time—for Guinness has become a "graduation beer," a beer that drinkers aspire to and grow into. It takes a while for the palate to become accustomed to its slightly bitter taste.

Furthermore, it takes time and patience to pour and enjoy a pint of Guinness. In fact, Guinness is the only beer you have to wait for. Serving up a perfect pint of Guinness is an art. This from the official Web site:

> GUINNESS® Draught is best served at 6°C (that's 42.8°F), with the legendary two-part pour. First, tilt the glass to 45 degrees and carefully pour until three quarters full. Then place the glass on the bar counter and leave to settle. Once the surge has settled, fill the glass to the brim. It takes about 119.5 seconds to pour the perfect pint. But don't fret. It's worth the wait. (http://www.guinness.com)

During the "surge" phase grayish white clouds billow inside the glass as in some mystical potion. Then, slowly and magically, black and white begin to separate (technically it is a deep ruby color; though it is universally referred to as black, as in, "A glass of the black stuff").

Pouring and savoring a pint of Guinness is a ritual in itself, and this ritualistic pattern of painstaking and dedicated preparation, keen anticipation and rewarding consumption is synthesized into a compelling metaphor in the brand's best commercial to date. *Surfer* (1999) was filmed in Hawaii. Shot in black and white and highly atmospheric, the commercial dramatizes the metaphor of surfers waiting for the ultimate wave representing the anticipation of waiting for a perfect pint of Guinness to be poured. The surfer (not a young actor, but a weather-beaten veteran surfer) waits patiently on the shore for his chance. Finally his patience is rewarded and he launches himself and his board into the ocean to ride with white horses on the long-awaited wave.

The word *diamond* comes from the Greek *adamas*, meaning unconquerable, which passed into Latin and then Old French as *diamant,* with the sense of hardest material (the adjective *adamant* has the same origin). Diamonds are one of nature's miracles, pure crystalline carbon created deep within the earth millions of years ago. Discovered by man more than 4,000 years ago in India, they are valued for being the hardest natural substance on Earth. Diamonds have had a privileged role in history. They have had special powers attributed to them, have been fought over and have even been worshipped. Across time and cultures, the diamond has been associated with invulnerability, lightning, magic, healing, protection and poisoning. The ancient Greeks believed that diamonds were slivers of stars that had fallen to the earth. They were claimed by others to be the tears of the gods. They were originally carried as talismans, before being worn as decorative adornment.

The De Beers mining syndicate promotes diamond jewelry around the world on behalf of the entire diamond industry. The line "A diamond is forever" was conceived in 1947, inspired by the fact that the indestructibility of a diamond makes it the perfect symbol for a lasting relationship. Before De Beers associated the precious stones with eternal love, the diamond ring as the standard token of betrothal hardly existed. Today, cultural differences notwithstanding, the diamond has become the gemstone of choice when people want to express the love they feel for another. This naturally occurring substance, the transparent form of pure carbon, has acquired the most sublime of meanings: the ultimate symbol of love.

Products, then, have the potential to become mediators of deeply motivational meaning. Understanding the context of a product, its original purpose and usage brings us closer to fathoming its fundamental meaning. Brands that succeed in tapping macrotruths about a category or market and its underlying structure and dynamics acquire a larger brand meaning. This transcends simply owning the category benefit. It requires capturing and coming to represent the meaning that lies behind that benefit.

6

Brand Meaning and Brand Strategy

Brand Definition and Differentiation

The meanings that brands have for consumers should become the guiding lights for brand strategy development. A consumer's preference for a given brand, after all, invariably depends on what the brand means to that consumer. We have seen that the process by which brand meaning takes shape is driven by the constructive interplay between marketer/advertiser-generated public sources of meaning (through, e.g., mass media, advertising, product placement) and more personal sources of meaning (e.g., direct experience, consumption patterns and rituals). Hopefully, the way consumers perceive and define a brand will correspond to the vision and intention of the marketer and will be reflected in brand strategy and communication. Any discrepancies between the brand meaning in the consumers' eyes and the framework developed by the marketer need to be taken into account in deciding subsequent brand strategy.

Brand extension, for example, may well alter brand meaning. What is Gatorade's primary brand meaning after the extension into energy bars, nutrition shakes, and Propel Fitness Water? Or that of Alka Seltzer after it was extended to cold and flu relief? Brand extension in the context of brand meaning is discussed later in this chapter. As an example of direct experience and usage influencing brand meaning consider the experience of the Yellow Pages in the United Kingdom. After the British public was introduced to the Yellow Pages in the early 1970s, they became used to turning to the book to find a plumber or electrician at times of burst pipes and flying sparks. The directory was becoming associated with distress and domestic emergencies. The company's response is discussed in

Chapter 8. A more drastic example illustrates how advertising itself can occasionally lead to an unintended brand meaning. In the early 1990s, not long after the collapse of the Berlin Wall, an international brand of antiperspirant was launched in Eastern Europe. The advertising featured tennis player Steffi Graf, demonstrating how effective the product was even for someone engaging in strenuous physical activity. Use of antiperspirant did not enjoy the same penetration levels in Eastern Europe as it did in the West, and the commercial was interpreted quite literally. The brand quickly came to signify a way of preventing perspiration specifically while playing sports until appropriate measures were taken to correct the misapprehension.

Whereas product meanings are more derivative of physical attributes and functional consequences, brands have far greater amplitude of meaning. A brand might have a tangible, concrete appearance, but the real function and value of a brand is as a signifier of meaning, often symbolic meaning. That is why, in the context of international marketing, brand meaning can often cross cultural and geographic borders more easily than product meaning.

We have seen that a brand is defined by its various attributes and associations. These associations can be numerous. Many come with the market territory and may be seen as generic associations, offering little motivational or differentiating potential. Taking the carbonated soft drinks market as an example, *fizzy* and *sparkling* are generic associations apparently offering minimal leverage for brand differentiation. *Thirst* is also a category generic, but some brands have sought to appropriate the association for themselves—for example, Sprite, with its "Obey your thirst" campaign. In years gone by, when the marketplace was less cluttered, Coca-Cola used to "own" the "benefit tripod" of thirst-quenching–refreshing–delicious-tasting. New brands started to compete and move in on associative territory they believed they could occupy more strongly than the market leader (e.g., 7-Up and Sprite in terms of clarity and neutral color and thirst-quenching) or to take advantage of space or gaps (e.g., the "hit" from drinking a full-flavored orange drink like Tango in the United Kingdom—"You'll know when you've been Tangoed."). Some time ago Coca-Cola opened up a new associative thread by splitting refreshment into physical refreshment and mental–spiritual refreshment.

Taking into consideration a brand's primary associations as well as its more abstract and symbolic associations, the resulting cluster of different brand associations is what gives a brand a robust depth of meaning for its consumers. Having a range of brand associations does not imply a lack of focus—either on the part of the consumer or the marketer. As stated, it is precisely the way a brand combines different attributes and associations that potentially gives it uniqueness and enriches the brand meaning. What is important is to be clear about what the key defining and differentiating associations are. Coca-Cola runs tactical advertising linking the brand with food, for example, and the brand has a food association. It is, though, a secondary association and so it is unlikely that food would be a defining or differentiating element of Coke's brand meaning.

Which of a brand's associations most define the brand in the consumer's mind and are they the associations that should define the brand? The aim is to achieve greater brand definition and greater brand differentiation. In fact, brand definition and brand differentiation should go hand in hand. By foregrounding the most relevant associations (across all brand activity), clarity of brand definition will be heightened. The associations that are foregrounded should be the ones consumers perceive the brand as uniquely owning relative to others in the referential framework. Prince is predominantly associated with oversize tennis racquets. As mentioned, FedEx was just another player in the U.S. delivery business in the early seventies. It achieved differentiation and great success when it decided to concentrate on overnight delivery only. *Overnight* became its key association and FedEx meant overnight delivery. Since then the company has gradually moved away from the overnight concept.

Over time, the configuration of associations should evolve in line with changing market circumstances, competitive activities, consumer priorities and the like. The challenge is to maintain the core associations as intact and relevant as possible. In the Lucozade example the central *energy* association was and always has been kept at the heart of the brand, whereas the *convalescence* association has gradually been allowed to recede.

Equipped with a sound knowledge of the competitive and referential framework within which a brand exists and of the mindset and motivations of the consumer, it should be possible to identify associations that are generic to the category and those that the brand has appropriated, or can do so, to its advantage. Over time, market categories develop a range of typical associations and characteristics, which are effectively the cost of entry into the category—a brand has to measure up to these to be able to compete in the category. Yet

often nontypical associations and characteristics allow brands to
achieve success through differentiation. It is important also to identify emerging consumer trends that may presage future desirable
associations. Are there new associations, consonant with the brand's
current meaning, that can become part of the defining set? Once this
is done, attention should be given to the brand's hot points—those
aspects of the brand (e.g., advertising, packaging, product presentation, distribution) that create, consolidate and communicate the
core associations. How effectively do they achieve this? Are there
other brand areas that are unexploited or underused in this respect?
The benefit of undertaking these steps will be an increasingly well-
defined and differentiated brand, with a depth of meaning founded
on relevant and motivating consumer needs and values.

Brand Concept

It should be possible to encapsulate the intended brand meaning in a
strategic brand concept. This can best be described as shorthand for
the meaning the marketer would like the brand to have in the mind of
the consumer. Broadly speaking, the nature of a brand concept may
be functional, experiential, or symbolic. A brand with a functional
concept would be sought by consumers needing to resolve practical
problems and looking for utilitarian benefits. A brand with an experiential concept would fulfill needs for sensorial or cognitive stimulation. A symbolic brand concept may take one of several forms. It
may be concerned with group affiliation or social standing or may
tap into deeper psychological or emotional territory. Although some
product classes lend themselves quite obviously to one of these concept types (at first glance it is hard to think of a spanner or chain-
saw as anything other than functional implements), in theory it
should be possible to assign a functional, experiential, or symbolic
identity to almost any kind of product. Moreover, brands typically
offer a mixture of these different types of benefits. The brand concept should find expression in, or at least be reflected in, for example,
the brand communication, brand name, slogan and other elements
of marketing activity. It is not necessarily intended for literal consumer exposure, for example as a slogan—though slogans often provide a concise indication of a brand concept. Consider, for instance,
"Strong enough for a man; made for a woman," which is a slogan (for

an antiperspirant/deodorant) and "Femininity restored to my skin," which is not (and is more of a brand concept). "Diamonds are forever" is an example of a brand concept that appears as a slogan.

In the early 1990s the Automobile Association (AA), Britain's largest roadside auto service, was losing members and failing to recruit new ones. This was in part due to the recession and in part to competitive activity. Its arch rival, the Royal Automobile Club, had been running a new campaign promoting itself as the "New knights of the road," while new entrants like National Breakdown were undercutting its two bigger rivals. The AA conducted research showing that, whereas its patrol people were considered friendly and helpful, perceptions of the company's professionalism (e.g., reliable, trustworthy) could be improved. The organization came up with a novel and challenging brand concept: "The 4th emergency service." New advertising was developed showing the AA to be a highly professional emergency organization. The slogan encapsulated the brand concept: "To our members we're the 4th Emergency Service," thereby slotting the AA into fourth position in the consumer's mind, behind, but associated with, the fire, police and ambulance emergency services.

Brand Extension

The territories that brands occupy in the minds of their consumers are subject to borders like any other territories. The demarcation lines may be less obvious and more flexible, but the difference between one brand territory and another may be as pronounced as the difference between French and German. Brand extension tests the limits of those territories and the rigidity of their borders. The greater a brand's elasticity or, rather, the greater the elasticity of a brand's meaning, the greater the extent to which it can be stretched to cover new territory in the form of new areas of its existing market or related markets or totally unrelated markets. New-product introduction is an important strategic activity for companies seeking growth. It is, though, not without risk. Estimates of the percentage of new-product failures vary enormously but have been as high as 80 percent (Bragg 1986, pp. 61–62). Line extension uses an existing brand to enter a new market segment in the same product class or category (e.g., Diet Coke, Cherry Coke, Liquid Tide, Miller Lite).

Brand extension uses an existing brand to enter a totally different product class (e.g., Ivory shampoo, Milky Way ice cream, Zenith computers). It is estimated that 95 percent of the 16,000 new products launched in the United States every year are line or brand extensions (Murphy 1997).

With the overall cost of introducing a new brand easily reaching $150 million in some markets (Tauber 1988), the attraction of leveraging an established brand to introduce a new product is strong. It is a highly effective way of reducing the risks and difficulties associated with launching a new product. It offers consumers and the trade, a degree of reassurance through familiarity with the parent brand and may also provide advertising efficiencies. It can even have a positive effect on sales of the parent brand. So what makes for successful brand extensions like Ivory shampoo and Virgin cola, whereas Pillsbury microwaveable popcorn and Levi's Tailored Classics never get off the ground?

Much empirical research has been conducted to try to determine the conditions under which brand extension is likely to be successful. Not surprisingly, given the at times conflicting and divergent results of these studies, their findings have yet to be generalized into a broadly applicable theory of brand extension. Of the several key factors identified, there is perhaps most agreement on two in particular:

1. Evaluations of a brand extension are influenced by the quality and strength of the parent brand (i.e., the higher the perceived quality of the parent brand, the higher the chances for success of the extension).
2. Evaluations of a brand extension are influenced by the fit between brand and brand extension (i.e., the greater the fit between the brand and the brand extension, the greater the chances of success) (For more see Aaker and Keller 1990; Boush and Loken 1991; Park, Milberg and Lawson 1991).

Fit refers to the compatibility of the parent brand with the proposed extension. It has been defined as the extent to which a consumer accepts the new product as a logical and expected extension of the brand (Tauber 1988). Problems arise when there is a lack of fit and the brand is stretched too far, or in an indiscriminate and undisciplined way, as was the case with the Gucci brand. The parent brand may not be seen to add any value to the extension or may receive undesirable associations as a result of the extension. The need for the extension to fit the parent brand again underlines the importance of understanding what the brand means to its consumers in the first place. Ascertaining brand meaning is both the first step in estimating the chances of success of a given extension and a prerequisite for the generation of new brand extension ideas.

A study conducted by a team from Miami University, Ohio and researchers from the Pennzoil Company sought measurement of brand meaning for the Pennzoil brand (see Chapter 4). A categorization-based procedure was used to help identify key elements of the brand's meaning for purposes of extension and, in particular, which elements most defined the brand. When asked what Pennzoil meant, consumers' comments might include *oil, protection, automotive*, and *tough*. Four possible brand extensions were therefore hypothesized, each fitting Pennzoil in some way: cooking oil, wood sealant, windshield washer fluid and work clothes. Fit judgments were based on brand property similarities; so, for example, cooking oil fits the brand through *oil,* and wood sealant fits the brand through *protection.*

The different brand characteristics that were the subject of research thus included what Pennzoil is (oil); what it does, or its benefit (protects); its usage context (automotive); and its image (tough). It was important to gauge the relevance of these different qualities. For instance, windshield washer, wood sealant and cooking oil are all fluids, but this would be of little value unless *fluid* was important to Pennzoil's meaning. Also, negative observations were as important to measure as positive ones. So, whereas cooking oil might have a degree of fit through the oil association, the majority of respondents felt Pennzoil should not be linked with food. The automotive association was found to offer the best opportunities for brand extension.

Extension Effects on Brand Meaning

If the decision is made to extend a brand to a new category, the reciprocal impact of the extension must always be given consideration, as an extension can have positive or negative effects on the parent brand. On the plus side, the extension may clarify, consolidate and reinforce brand meaning. Through their brand extensions Gerber means *baby care,* Nabisco means *baked cookies and crackers,* and Hershey's means *chocolate.* Extensions may also broaden brand meaning. Xerox provides an example. The brand had become virtually synonymous with paper copying in the United States. But its heritage was becoming a liability in the digital age in which electronic copies of documents were increasingly replacing paper copies. Xerox expanded its product line to include digital printers, scanners, and word-processing software. In 1994 the company also launched a new visual identity to underscore its brand evolution. A digital-looking X, with pixilated left arm, signified the increasing movement of documents between the paper and digital worlds, and a new tagline, "The Document Company" heralded its leadership in the document management market.

Incidentally, a decade later, in 2004, Xerox turned to a new, cleaner-looking logo, featuring the Xerox name without the "digital X" over the signature line "Technology. Document Management. Consulting Services." The highly descriptive capabilities line suggests that "The Document Company" was deemed too limiting for Xerox, and indicates that there is still a tendency for the word document to denote paper in customers' minds. The company's product development strategy and marketing activities in the coming years will likely seek to consolidate a brand meaning of document management within the whole life cycle of information flow.

Keller (1998) gives other examples of extensions that have expanded the meaning of their brands (Figure 6.1). The Weight Watchers brand had a very clear meaning to those who followed its weight-watching programs. In 1978 Heinz bought Weight Watchers and transferred

Brand	Original Product	Extension Products	New Brand Meaning
Weight Watchers	Fitness centers	Low calorie foods	Weight loss and maintenance
Sunkist	Oranges	Vitamins, Juices	Good health
Crayola	Crayons	Markers, paints, Pens, pencils, clay	Colorful crafts for kids
Aunt Jemima	Pancake mixes	Syrups, frozen waffles	Breakfast foods

Figure 6.1　Expanding brand meaning through extension.

that meaning to a large range of food products targeted at the weight wary. An interpretation of the meaning of the Caterpillar brand in the apparel arena gave rise to Caterpillar boots. As another example of brand meaning being modified through brand extension, consider how the meaning of the IBM brand changed significantly after the introduction of the IBM personal computer. In general, the more successful the brand extension, the more likely it is to confirm or redefine the meaning of the core brand.

On the negative side, brand extensions can confuse consumers and dilute brand meaning, as Ries and Trout (2001, p. 229) allege was the case with the Scott brand: "The more products hung on the Scott name, the less meaning the name has to the average consumer." This, argue the authors, was a case of Scott Paper falling into the "line extension trap" and overextending the Scott brand as it was expanded to encompass ScotTissue bathroom tissue, ScotTowels paper towels, Scotties facial tissues and BabyScot diapers. In the 1980s Levi's introduced a line of men's suits sold as separates (jackets and trousers) called Levi Tailored Classics. The venture failed because the Levi's brand meaning could not accommodate the concept of quality tailored suits. Incidentally, when, some years later, Levi's introduced its range of khakis, it did so under a different brand name—Dockers (cf. Disney's use of the Miramax and Touchstone brands for its more adult-oriented films, mentioned in Chapter 5).

The brand extension graveyard has a proliferation of famous name headstones. Kodak is a brand that, for all its prowess, has experienced the limitations that brand meaning can put on a brand that seeks to spread itself into associated areas of market opportunity. Kodak means conventional photography. It does not mean videotape, though it has put its name on the product. Neither does it mean instant photography, though it has ventured into that market. Conversely, Polaroid means instant photography, as the company discovered when it tried to get into conventional 35-mm film. Neither, in retrospect, were Jack Daniel's beer or Coors water likely to find consumer acceptance. And if Blockbuster means movie rentals, Blockbuster Music was always likely to confuse consumers. The first impression is that it must be a chain that rents music CDs. Blockbuster's core associations are *movies* and *rental*. Given the name and the strength of the movie association, it can probably get away with retailing movies, but retailing music is a step too far. Besides, if Blockbuster sells music CDs the brand's meaning is diluted, leaving it vulnerable to a new movie rental specialist and trailing those brands that mean music retail, both the bricks-and-mortar and the online variety such as iTunes and Amazon.com.

An interesting recent example of questionable brand extension is the launch of Gatorade energy bars. Gatorade is best known as a sports drink. It therefore does possess an association with sports and people usually associate energy bars with sport and physical exertion. But Gatorade is about rehydration. "The science of sweat" and "Thirst quencher" says its packaging. Conversely, the introduction of Lucozade energy bars in the United Kingdom displays more "fit." The core association of the Lucozade brand is energy. Although Lucozade, like Gatorade, is a fluid, the energy component of the brand meaning makes energy bars a more coherent extension for Lucozade than for Gatorade. Note that from a corporate point of view Gatorade's extension into energy bars made sense, drawing on the strengths of both the Gatorade brand in a sports context and parent Quaker Oats' expertise in grains. What is good for the company, though, is not always good for the brand. Another questionable brand extension was Dannon's decision to put its brand name on bottled water. The Dannon company in the United States is owned by the French Groupe Danone, the world's biggest marketer of cultured dairy products such as yogurt, cheese and dairy desserts. To most people Dannon is yogurt. Brand extensions into other dairy products would not dilute the brand the way an extension into bottled water does.

The Honda brand was originally associated with motorcycles but later extended to automobiles. Today, the Honda brand spans garden power tools and generators as well. The meaning of the brand has thus been transformed over time and has become more abstract. If the original association with motorcycles is replaced in consumers' minds by a concept such as quality or reliability or service and the brand still carries meaning for consumers, then the intervening brand extensions will have simply converted brand meaning into something more abstract. If that is not the case, then the brand will have lost any sense of coherent and cohesive meaning, will have been diluted and will merely serve as a catch-all name on which to hang a set of unrelated products.

An abstract brand meaning does not necessarily infer a diluted brand meaning. Neither is it necessarily a weak foundation for brand extension. We have seen that the primary meaning of a brand is determined by the associations that most define the brand in consumers' minds. Those associations may be functionally driven, or they may be more abstract, based on expressive values, for example, as in the case of Rolex. Staying with the watch category, a comparison of two brands, Timex and Rolex, provides an illustration (Park et al. 1991). Though both belong to the same category, the brands convey very different meanings to consumers: Rolex standing for the concept of prestige and luxury and Timex being associated more with product performance. In the case of status-symbol brands, like Rolex, functionality has a reduced importance ("Who wears a Rolex to tell the time?") and brand meaning is more abstract and subjective. In such cases, the semantic and psychological space between primary brand meaning and symbolic brand meaning is reduced. In the case of Rolex primary brand meaning would presumably be about luxury or prestige, and symbolic brand meaning would fall in the realms of achievement, recognition, or power. The symbolic meaning of a brand like Dettol, by way of contrast, would be quite different from its primary brand meaning (antiseptic disinfectant/germ killer): Its symbolic brand meaning might be expressed in terms of maternal protection, perhaps, or as providing impregnable defense against an unseen evil, or, more metaphorically, as a crusading champion (taking a cue from the sword brand symbol). Its use in a first-aid and medical context and childhood memories of its strong carbolic smell in conjunction with cuts and abrasions, may elicit a different set of symbolic associations.

Brands with a more specific, functionally driven primary meaning may have less latitude in terms of potential extensions and may be more tied to parent category-to-extension category similarity or complementarity. Conversely, brands with a more abstract primary meaning may have more latitude and may be less constrained by category considerations. They do, however, risk having their meaning diluted through indiscriminate extension and instances where consumers can see no particular logic or added value from the extension, which is perceived as simple brand exploitation.

Primary Brand Meaning in Extension Strategy

In the context of brand extension, then, it is invariably primary brand meaning (of the parent brand) in which we are interested. In the case of a brand like Dettol, for instance, it is the brand's antiseptic germ-killing properties (i.e., functional benefit) that define its primary brand meaning—thus providing the fit between the parent brand and extensions into bar and liquid soap, antiseptic cream, relief spray and medicated plasters. Often, primary brand meaning is closely linked to a particular product class or category—Kleenex, for example. Extending outside of that category can be problematical. Though Cadbury's extension to drinking chocolate was a logical one, its association with chocolate was weakened when it produced mainstream food products such as mashed potatoes and soups. Bayer's decision to put the Bayer name on nonaspirin products weakened its grip on the aspirin category in the United States. Clorox means bleach; assigning the Clorox brand name to a cleaning product without bleach entails risk.

In a related context, Clorox challenged Procter & Gamble and Unilever in 1988 when it introduced the first bleach with detergent. Despite heavy investment, Clorox was only able to muster a 3 percent share and eventually, after Procter & Gamble had introduced Tide with Bleach, Clorox withdrew from the market. Clorox's failure was at least partially due to the limiting meaning that the brand had for consumers as essentially a bleach product, which, although powerful, was perceived as caustic and potentially harmful to fabrics. On the other hand, the strength of these associations has enabled Clorox to extend successfully into the household cleaning products category, where the bleach ingredient is considered to be more relevant (Keller 1998, p. 478), creating such products as Clorox Wipes and Ready Mop. Interestingly, the extension may also have failed because, with a product like "laundry detergent with bleach," laundry detergent is seen by consumers as the primary ingredient and bleach as the secondary ingredient. An extension from a brand with laundry detergent as an integral part of its primary meaning is thus more likely to find consumer acceptance than an extension from a brand the primary meaning of which is founded on bleach (ibid.).

In 1988 Seven-Up introduced the brand extension 7Up Gold. 7Up Gold was an amber-colored, spicy, caffeinated drink, flavored with cinnamon, ginger and lemon-lime. The product struggled and was eventually discontinued. As one Seven-Up executive put it, "People had a clear view of what 7Up products should be—clear and crisp and clean and no caffeine. 7Up Gold is darker and it does have caffeine so it doesn't fit the 7UP image" (Keller 1998, p. 471).

Curiously, the executive prefaced this by saying that the product was misunderstood by the consumer. It may be more accurate to say that the brand was not understood by the manufacturer. On the other hand, the Coca-Cola Company has steadfastly withstood the temptation to dilute the primary meaning of its flagship brand. Coca-Cola continues to thrive because the company knows what the brand means at a primary level: brown-colored soda with the taste of cola.

Examples such as that of Clorox, or Chiquita's failure in its attempt to move beyond its strong banana association when it tried to extend to frozen juice bars, illustrate what Franzen and Bouwman (2001, p. 54) refer to as the phenomenon of associative inhibition. They quote the further example of the Dutch brand Biotex, a biological detergent, which is so strongly associated with the meaning of *prewash* that it proved impossible to develop an association with the meaning of *main wash* for a new line extension. Similarly, Bausch & Lomb's unsuccessful venture into Bausch & Lomb branded mouthwash was an illustration that the brand's primary meaning for consumers (eye-based solutions) inhibited the incorporation of liquid products to be put in the mouth.

Brand-Specific Associations in Extension Strategy

Brand-specific associations play an important role in extension strategy. A brand-specific association is simply an attribute or benefit, particular to a brand, that differentiates that brand from competitive brands. For example, Apple is associated with user friendliness, an association not typical among computer brands or the product class as a whole (Broniarczyk and Alba 1994). Though it is true that product category similarity has an influence on brand extension (i.e., generally a brand can be extended more easily when there is similarity between the new category and the original category than when the new and original categories are dissimilar), it is important to understand the interplay between category considerations and brand-specific associations.

A research study by Broniarczyk and Alba (1994) sought to measure the extent to which brand-specific associations moderate the influence of brand affect on extension judgments. It also measured the extent to which, if a brand's specific associations are highly relevant and motivating in the extension category, the brand will be evaluated more favorably than extensions of its original competitors, even if those competitors are more favorably evaluated in the original product class. The study compared two brands: the less preferred (in the original product class) focal brand (e.g., Close-Up); and the more preferred (in the original product class) comparison brand (e.g., Crest). So, for example, Close-Up is evaluated less favorably than Crest in the toothpaste category. Close-Up has a breath-freshening association, whereas Crest has a dental protection association. The breath-freshening association of Close-Up is relevant and motivating in the mouthwash category and the breath mint category. It was therefore predicted that an extension from Close-Up in these two categories would be evaluated more favorably than a Crest extension. On the other hand, it was predicted that a Crest extension in the dental floss category and also the toothbrush category, where dental protection is relevant and motivating, would be better evaluated than a Close-Up extension. These predictions proved correct, with the exception of the mouthwash category, where the Crest mouthwash was interpreted more favorably because subjects interpreted it as an antiplaque dental rinse, which is highly consistent with Crest's dental protection association.

Associative Strength and Directionality

This raises the important matter of the orientation of brand associations. We have seen that brands evoke different types of associations, given the different contexts in which and with which brand information is represented and linked in our minds. For example, brands may be associated with one or more product categories or a usage situation, or product attributes or consumer benefits. We have also seen that brand information is represented in semantic memory as a brand associative network. Associations are formed when nodes in that network link up so that association strength reflects the semantic relatedness between two nodes in a network (Farquhar and Herr 1992). This semantic relatedness may be represented by either a nondirectional relation or a pair of directional relations. Figure 6.2 illustrates both cases for a brand and a given associate, be it category, usage situation, benefit, attribute, or any other association.

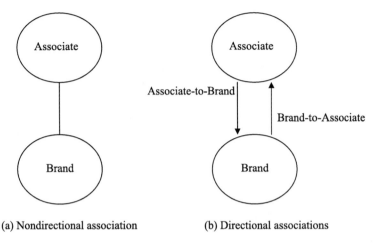

(a) Nondirectional association   (b) Directional associations

Figure 6.2 Nondirectional and directional associations.

In the case of directional associations it is important to distinguish between the following two relations:

1. Brand-to-Associate Relations: directional associations starting from the brand and spreading out toward a category or benefit associate, for example.
2. Associate-to-Brand Relations: the reciprocal associations directed toward the brand. Farquhar and Herr (1992) give the following examples: The product category *greeting cards* is strongly associated with the Hallmark brand; the usage situation *washing windows* likely evokes the Windex brand; the product attribute *baking soda* is at the core of the Arm & Hammer brand; and the benefit of *mildness* is strongly associated with Ivory.

The strength of the directional association between a brand and an associate is called dominance. Directional brand associations would be of less interest if the strengths of the two directional relations were equal—in other words, if asymmetry did not exist (Farquhar and Herr 1992). However, Loftus (1973) demonstrated that the strength of a link in one direction can differ from the strength of a link in the other direction. In the case of brand and category associations, for example, there can be a different probability that a category reference evokes a given brand than the probability that the brand name evokes the product category. These respective dominance patterns are called category dominance and instance dominance:

1. Category dominance is defined as the strength of the directional association from a product category to a brand. Crest and Close-Up are instances of the *toothpaste* category. Category dominance is a measure of the degree to which hearing or thinking of the category (e.g., toothpaste) evokes the brand (e.g., Crest or Close-Up). In research, according to the methodology employed to measure category dominance, a strong category-to-brand association results in a brand being named earlier, recalled more frequently, classified faster and recognized sooner (Farquhar and Herr 1992).

2. Instance dominance is defined as the strength of the directional association from a brand to a product category. It is a measure of the degree to which the brand name evokes the product category, or categories in some cases. If a reference to Gillette immediately cues thought of razors this is an example of high instance dominance (i.e., strong brand-to category association).

Research carried out by Herr, Farquhar and Fazio (1992) investigated the category and instance dominance of several prominent brands. The findings are illustrated in Figure 6.3, which allocates brands to each of four possible combinations of high and low category and instance dominance. The authors point out that, other things being equal, brands with high category dominance are more likely to be selected by potential buyers regardless of whether they have high instance dominance (e.g., Crest toothpaste) or low instance dominance (e.g., Listerine mouthwash). In normal purchase situations the product category is activated before mental brand selection

	Instance Dominance	
	High	Low
High	Crest toothpaste Schwinn bicycles Folgers coffee	Skippy peanut butter Listerine mouthwash White Cloud bath tissue
Low	Peter Pan peanut butter Scope mouthwash Charmin bath tissue	Close-Up toothpaste Huffy bicycles Hill's Bros. coffee

Category Dominance

Figure 6.3 Category dominance and instance dominance for several brands.

(e.g., "I need some toothpaste…"). If category-to-brand association is highly dominant, a brand will be evoked automatically and selected over others. In this case instance dominance has negligible effect on brand choice. Conversely, if category-to-brand association is not sufficiently strong, then other brands will be accessed and enter the consideration set. In this second phase of the search process a brand with high instance dominance gains the advantage. So if, referring to Figure 6.3 for example, no brand of bath tissue has sufficiently high category dominance, then Charmin would prevail over White Cloud, as the former has higher instance dominance.

Incidentally, in rare cases, extremely high category dominance can become problematical for a brand. One aspect of brand awareness and salience is consumer ability to identify a brand as associated with a product category. There is an important difference between simple awareness of a brand name and the ability to associate it with a particular product category. Much brand-building activity is aimed at securing a position whereby a brand owns a category—in which the brand virtually defines its category or subcategory. Slogans like "Bring out the Branston" seek to make a brand synonymous with a (sub)category—in this case with the pickle category, where Crosse & Blackwell's Branston (named after the town in Staffordshire, England, where it was first made) competes with, for instance, Heinz Ploughman's Pickle. If that category is a niche market, this will not pose a problem. For example, at one stage, Cadillac meant *luxury car*, but it could hardly be considered a synonym for *automobile* (Oakenfull and Gelb 1996). However, when it is a broader category that the brand practically defines, the marketer needs to be aware of the potential consequences.

When consumers begin to label a product category with a brand name, it would appear that the marketer has achieved the ultimate in brand notoriety. In the U.K., people use the word *Hoover* to refer to a vacuum cleaner—any vacuum cleaner, be it from Hoover or from Electrolux or any other manufacturer. The word is used as a verb—"to do the hoovering." There is a very thin dividing line between maintaining salience and top-of-mind awareness and becoming generic. When the latter occurs, the courts may decide that a brand name can no longer be considered or used in a proprietary manner. *Escalator, yo-yo, thermos, cellophane and spam* are examples of brands that have lost their name exclusivity and have become generic. The word *aspirin* (acetylsalicylic acid) is generic in the United States, though everywhere else in the world only Bayer can legally use the word. On the other hand, the Rollerblade Company took action to protect its brand name when the media started to use the term *rollerblading* and promoted instead the use of *in-line skating*. Similarly, the Xerox Corporation has run advertising encouraging people to use the term *to photocopy* and not *to xerox*. Although this branding paradox affects relatively few brands, it is perhaps more common than might be thought. Recently, Austria's Supreme Court ruled that, in that country, Sony can no longer claim exclusive trademark rights for the name *Walkman* given that it had passed into common usage once it had been defined in a German dictionary as any portable stereo player.

With regard to brand extension, Herr, Farquhar and Fazio (1992) and others demonstrated that brands with high category dominance, though commanding a significant share of the parent category, find it difficult to extend very far to other categories. This is because the affect associated with a highly category-dominant brand transfers to an extension only when there is a close relation between the target category and the parent category. Highly category-dominant brands thus have more sharply delineated boundaries than less category-dominant brands.

Expanding the Brand versus Expanding the Market

In seeking growth and new business opportunities a company should always ask itself two questions: Should we be in that business? And, if so, should we be in that business with this brand? When Black & Decker, the world's largest power-tool manufacturer, decided to move into professional power tools, it resisted the temptation to call the new range, or line, Black & Decker Pro. Rather, it developed a separate brand altogether, called De Walt. De Walt soon became the second largest power-tool brand, after Black & Decker. When Honda introduced an expensive car it created a new brand called Acura, which soon became the biggest-selling imported luxury car in the United States—likewise with Toyota, when it introduced the upscale Lexus brand.

Yet the urge to extend a brand that has already proved itself in one category is a strong one: "Consider yourself lucky if your brand can own a word like 'safety' or 'driving' or 'thick' or 'overnight.' Many marketers know this and they still look to expand the meanings of their brands.... But what works is not expanding the brand, but expanding the market" (Ries and Ries 2002, p. 26). By making overnight *de rigueur* among hard-pressed business executives, Federal Express multiplied the overnight delivery market and kept its brand meaning sharply focused. Kleenex is such a strong brand because Kimberly-Clark has been disciplined in its development of the brand. Whether as pocket pack, family pack, soft pack, menthol, or scented, Kleenex means tissue. In fact, Kleenex means tissue to such an extent that Kimberly-Clark has to remain wary of the generic trap just described. On its packaging the product is described as "Kleenex brand tissue" in the same way that Xerox has run advertising to remind people Xerox is a brand. Of course, as mentioned earlier, there is another, more strategic, reason that Xerox does not want to be synonymous with photocopying.

If an extension strategy is to be pursued, it is important to think beyond the first extension and to consider fruitful areas of growth from subsequent extensions. Extension strategy should be incorporated in a brand plan with a long-term perspective aimed at optimizing brand leverage but avoiding diluting important brand associations and confusing the consumer. Determining the defining associations and attributes of a brand is of paramount importance in planning extension strategy. Strong brand associations provide a point of differentiation and competitive advantage for extensions. A brand's core associations can be reinforced by extending the brand to other products, but they may equally limit the brand's ability to stretch beyond its existing boundaries. What are the defining brand associations and how will they be consolidated and developed in subsequent extensions? For example, a brand such as Vaseline has a "moisturizer" association that could be extended to soap or face cream (Aaker 1990, p. 55). The brand's medicinal association, however, might be extended to antiseptics, first-aid cream and hemorrhoid cream. The choice of the first extension will strengthen one association at the expense of another. Clearly such a brand plan will be developed in the context of corporate objectives and strategy. If an existing brand from the same company already occupies one of the potential extension categories, it may not be appropriate to extend another brand to the category if the two brands will compete head to head. Such considerations will help guide the brand plan and map out the brand

territory with its borders. Effectively, the brand plan paves the way
for the meaning that the brand will ideally have for its consumers.

Brand Portfolio Management

The result of a succession of brand extensions is a brand portfolio, which will be characterized by greater or lesser brand breadth
(Boush and Loken 1991). Brand breadth refers to the diversity of
product types under a given brand name. Brand breadth is largely
determined by consumer perceptions of how typical and similar successive extensions are. For example, if extensions of the brand are in
the form of new products that closely resemble existing products,
the outcome would be a narrow brand. A broad brand would be the
result if the opposite were the case. In the latter case, a distinct meaning for the brand can still be maintained by focusing on an abstract
dimension that spans the portfolio and can unite and unify the distinct products associated with the brand. It is important to ask what
each member of the portfolio family derives from the parent brand
and what they give back. Does each member reflect the brand meaning and vision of the parent?

Things can become complicated when corporations are managing many subbrands under master brands in different categories.
Increasingly, companies are choosing to have fewer, more clearly
defined strong brands than a proliferation of ill-defined, potentially
competing brands. In 2000, for example, then Unilever co-chair
Niall FitzGerald announced a five-year plan aimed at reducing the
number of brands owned by Unilever from 1,600 to 400, then further
limiting that number and concentrating resources on select power
brands. In the automobile market BMW provides a good example
of a well-structured brand hierarchy and portfolio. The corporate
brand, BMW, with its "The ultimate driving machine" slogan, stands
for style, performance and the driving experience. Under the corporate brand sit its well-differentiated subbrands, the 3, 5 and 7 series,
suggesting a logically designed hierarchy.

Conversely, General Motors' brand portfolio and hierarchy presents some problems of definition and distinctiveness. The five divisions of Cadillac, Oldsmobile, Buick, Pontiac and Chevrolet were
originally established to target distinct market segments. With time,
however, the boundaries have become blurred and there has been

brand overlap. Recently the company has sought to remedy this by giving the brands more focus: Chevrolet as the entry-level value brand, for instance; Pontiac as the younger person's sporty performance-led vehicle. But it has been no easy task. By way of contrast, the 18 different brands of the Swatch Group—the largest manufacturer and distributor of finished watches in the world—are neatly slotted into different price and market segments. On the lowest rung are the Swatch and Flik Flak brands ranging from $25 to $130. The next rung is the $200 to $500 Tissot. Then comes the Longines brand at $750 to $2,000. It is beneath Omega watches, which go for $1,500 to $5,000. Blancpain is next, from $5,000 to $150,000. At the top of the market is Breguet, retailing at between $20,000 and a million dollars. Around these there are the American fashion brands cK and Hamilton and the design brand, Rado. None of these watches competes with another from the portfolio.

Brand Architecture

BMW and GM provide examples of the two extremes of branding strategy. Whereas GM has more than 30 brands, BMW has one. They represent different, but equally valid, approaches to brand architecture. Brand architecture is the organizing structure within a brand portfolio. It determines the way the brands in the portfolio are related to each other and, thus, the respective brand roles. As such, it is inextricably linked to the theme of brand meaning. The increasing attention being paid to brand architecture is a relatively recent phenomenon. In times gone by brand structures were simpler and less unwieldy, with few extensions, subbrands and endorsed brands. Corporate takeovers and acquisitions and market fragmentation have led to a far more complex brandscape, exacerbated by the relentless desire to leverage brand assets in the face of the prohibitive cost of creating new brands.

If the vast majority of products carry (at least) two brand names, the question becomes from where do consumers take meaning? And how does the meaning of one brand affect that of the other? Though brand architecture and the strategies that shape it are company-side concerns, consumers themselves will also subconsciously and spontaneously filter and hierarchize when confronted with a multiheaded brand. Consider, for instance, the complexity of Nestlé's Friskies

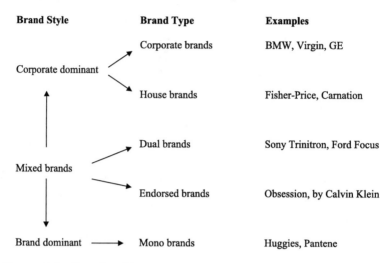

Figure 6.4 Brand architecture spectrum.

Gourmet à la Carte—compared with Mars Bar. Where two or more brand names appear on a pack, the relationship between the brands is governed by the nature of the driver roles that the brands play. Which one of the brands is the primary driver of the purchase decision? Do they share the driver role evenly? What meanings and associations do the different names contribute to overall take-out? In the case of Carnation Slender, for example, which is a meal substitute for dieters, the Slender name denotes weight reduction, whereas Carnation suggests rich creamy products. A contradiction in terms? Or do the names create the impression of a product that is rich and creamy in taste but low in fat calories (Saunders and Guoqun 1997)? Questions of driver roles and meaning content are what should underpin branding strategy. Together, the different potential permutations of branding strategy form a brand architecture spectrum, as illustrated in Figure 6.4.

Corporate Brands

With a corporate brand strategy, the corporate brand serves as the dominant master brand. In the case of Virgin it provides an umbrella for the company's various business operations, which are signaled with generic descriptors (e.g., Virgin Airlines, Virgin Cola, Virgin Rail). It is the Virgin brand meaning that unites the various offerings.

This approach provides the company with great scope to achieve synergies across the different businesses. The potential downside is that if the corporate brand name is spread across many diverse businesses it can end up meaning very little, as in the case of Mitsubishi in Japan, where the name is used by some sixteen different companies, including Mitsubishi Corporation, Mitsubishi Electric, Mitsubishi Motors, Mitsubishi Chemical, Mitsubishi Oil, Mitsubishi Materials, Mitsubishi Paper, Mitsubishi Plastics and Mitsubishi Construction (Ries and Ries 2002).

Besides the synergies and economies of scale that corporate branding offers, playing up the corporate brand is an effective strategy in markets that are very dynamic and in which products may become quickly outdated. If a product line changes or is superseded, most of the subbranding effort and investment will have been wasted. In technology-dependent markets processor speeds, coverage, data storage capacity and the like are subject to constant change and evolution and allying a brand too closely to a particular technology can backfire in the long run.

Corporate brands are often found where the corporate primary brand meaning is synonymous (or at least started out being synonymous) with a product class. Heinz tomato ketchup, Kellogg's cornflakes, Cadbury's Dairy Milk and Quaker oats are examples.

Though stressing the corporate brand allows consolidation of a strong corporate identity, for example in the case of British Airways or Shell, the monolithic structure does have its limitations. In particular, it severely restricts a company's ability to target specific groups or segment markets with subbrands. Companies like Kodak and Levi's have found out to their cost the difficulty of maintaining a single, corporate brand as an umbrella for a wide product line with a large market share.

House Brands

Diversified companies may choose to employ the names of divisions, or houses, for the promotion of products in different markets or specific targeting of market segments. Unilever's ice cream business, for instance, goes under the brand name of Walls in the United Kingdom and Australia. Whereas Quaker uses its corporate identity on cereals, it markets its toys under the Fisher Price brand. Similarly and for reasons of product line incompatibility, Mars uses the Pedigree brand for its pet food business.

Dual Brands

The most common form of branding is where a corporate or house brand is combined with an individual brand name, usually a strong subbrand. The relationship between the two brands is a dynamic and evolutionary one. Where the corporate or house brand is the primary frame of reference the subbrand can enhance, differentiate and stretch the masterbrand by adding or magnifying or modifying associations. Because the relation between the masterbrand and subbrand is a tight one (tighter than in the case of an endorsed brand, for instance), the subbrand can impact significantly on the meaning of the masterbrand.

The masterbrand and the subbrand may have equally important driver roles. In this case the masterbrand is performing more than just an endorser role. For instance, in the case of Gillette Mach3 the meaning and credibility of Gillette in the razor market and the leading-edge innovation represented by Mach3 are both important factors in purchase decision and consumer loyalty. The subbrand may itself become highly robust and meaningful and may eventually become an umbrella brand for a whole family of product extensions. Clairol's Herbal Essences, for example, now has a vast range of hair-care products.

Subbrands allow entry into an emerging low-end segment of a market, though this does come with associated risks: (1) that of cannibalization; and (2) that extending a brand downward may have an adverse effect on the image of the parent brand name. The subbrand should be able to insulate its parent brand from such damage. As for cannibalization, this risk should be reduced by clearly demarcating the territory between the lower-quality and -priced line and the superior line.

Similarly, subbrands can be used to penetrate the high end of a market. Coors Gold and Holiday Inn Crowne Plaza are examples. In some cases the subbrand can improve the perceived quality of the core brand name (e.g., Holiday Inn and Coors). On the other hand, a new premium version may cause less favorable perceptions of the core brand than was previously the case—Coors may seem less appealing in the presence of Coors Gold, for example. Also, the image of the core brand may prove to be a limitation for the premium subbrand as it seeks to compete at the high end. In the case of Crowne Plaza, for instance, the Holiday Inn connection was eventually dropped (see Aaker 1996, p. 288). In any case, the important point is that when subbrands are used they will tend to modify (positively or negatively) perceptions of the core or parent brand, due to the new associations created.

Endorsed Brands

Endorsed brands have more independence than in the case of dual brands. The brand name enjoys prominence but is endorsed by another brand, usually a corporate or house brand. The endorsement may vary in its subtlety and discretion, ranging from the Lever house flash on its household cleaning products or the GE light bulb through to Courtyard by Marriott. The endorser brand serves to support and add credibility to the endorsed brand while at the same time allowing sufficient distance between the two brands for the endorsed brand to take on independent meaning. This also reduces the risk of contamination of brand meaning. Courtyard by Marriott, for instance, is very different from Marriott itself, being less upscale, offering fewer services and representing a dissimilar type of hotel experience.

  Subbrands and endorsed brands, then, allow companies to provide new product offerings without incurring the expense of introducing a totally new stand-alone brand or the risk of stretching an existing brand and potentially diluting its meaning and weakening its franchise.

Mono Brands

This is the branding strategy of choice for large conglomerates in diversified lines such as Procter & Gamble and Unilever. Procter & Gamble markets more than 80 major brands that have very little tie-in to Procter & Gamble or to each other. Rather, these firms have distinct product ranges, each marketed under a different, stand-alone mono brand. It is a strategy that allows companies to clearly position products on functional benefits, with each product line responding to specific consumer needs.

Consider the hair-care market. Most consumers will identify the need for a shampoo to leave their hair *clean, healthy* and *shiny*. Though practically all shampoos will leave hair feeling clean, Procter & Gamble decided to address *healthy* through their Pantene Pro-V brand ("For hair so healthy it shines"; "So healthy you'll love your hair"). Dandruff and dry scalp affect more than 50 percent of the American population at some time (internal P&G study, from Head & Shoulders Web site). Procter & Gamble's Head & Shoulders brand dominates the dandruff shampoo category. The total impact of these two brands (and there are others in the Procter & Gamble hair-care portfolio) would be reduced if, instead of two distinct and differentiated brands, there was P&G Healthy Hair and P&G Dandruff Control under the P&G shampoo brand.

So even though mono brands are expensive to establish and entail sacrificing the synergies and economies of scale that result from leveraging a brand across multiple lines and segments, they do allow a company to dominate those segments individually through tightly focused branded offerings. Mono brands permit the creation of a more single-minded meaning and ownership of a particular association, as with Pantene and its healthy hair proposition. They also offer the corresponding benefit of providing a means of avoiding undesirable associations. Prelaunch research indicated that any association between the new Saturn brand and General Motors could have an adverse effect on the former, so the company deliberately avoided any link between the two brands ("Saturn. A different kind of company, a different kind of car."). Before the launch of Old Navy, management were considering branding the concept as the Gap Warehouse but pulled back from the idea, given the potential for irreparable damage to be done to the Gap brand through an association with lower-priced clothing as well as the obvious risk of cannibalization. Similarly, Volkswagen could negatively affect the images of Porsche and Audi if the brands were connected, and, equally importantly, Volkswagen's own strong brand meaning would be distorted. The other major benefit of a mono brand is its use in announcing and embodying a truly breakthrough new product with distinct new advantages. The impact may be diminished if the new product is introduced under an existing brand.

In practice, most companies mix and match the branding systems they employ. Besides company policy, branding strategy is determined by factors such as corporate history and prevailing market structures. Where a leading brand has held its dominant position for many years, the brand name can often be traced back to the origin of the company and its association with a particular product class. In those early days, company and brand were one and the same and this relation has endured, as with Kellogg's cornflakes. Where companies have grown through merger and acquisition they often display a hybrid brand structure, the result of assimilating a collection of corporate, house and mono brands. Consider the following milestones along the road to what is today Kraft Foods Inc.:

1982: Jacobs Kaffee merges with Suchard-Tobler to form Jacobs Suchard in Europe.

1985: General Foods Corporation is acquired by Philip Morris Companies Inc.

1988: Kraft Inc. is acquired by Philip Morris Companies Inc.

1990: Kraft General Foods International acquires Jacobs Suchard.

1993: Kraft General Foods acquires the U.S. and Canadian ready-to-eat cereal business from RJR Nabisco, including Shreddies and Shredded Wheat.

2000: Philip Morris Companies Inc. acquires Nabisco Holdings, with its cookies, crackers and snacks business. The Nabisco brands are integrated into the Kraft Foods business worldwide.

It is unsurprising, given this complex web of mergers and acquisitions, that there are within the vast portfolio products bearing the corporate brand, like Kraft Singles cheese slices, Nabisco-endorsed brands, such as Oreo, Chips Ahoy! and Ritz crackers and mono brands like Jell-O and Milka.

Distribution issues may also have an influence. To avoid channel conflict and overlap among upscale specialty stores, department stores and drugstores L'Oréal (itself owned by Nestlé) has three brands in the cosmetics market: Lancôme, L'Oréal and Maybelline. This is not uncommon with clothing and fragrance brands. The retailer brand Gap adopts a mono brand strategy for its three principal brands, with Banana Republic at the high end, Gap in the middle and Old Navy at the value end of the market. In a similar vein, when Levi Strauss introduced its new discount Signature line in 2003, it did so through the discount store Wal-Mart, with almost no advertising support, to prevent the line from cannibalizing the more expensive Levi's brands. Signature jeans do not feature the company's famous red tab but do bear the Levi's name. Rolling out through other discount stores has the potential to weaken the Levi's brand further by too closely associating it with discount prices.

Brand architecture, then, is how a company's brands are related to and differentiated from each other in a composite structure. In evaluating new product introductions and brand extensions and in building or restructuring a brand portfolio, it is essential to recognize and respect the parent brand's meaning, vision and parameters of relevance. With each line and brand extension the parent brand is redefined in the consumer's mind, whether imperceptibly, marginally, or more substantially. Gratuitous extension can result in the brand being stretched out of recognition and in having its meaning diluted to the detriment of the other products within the portfolio. Judicious extension, on the other hand, can consolidate and enhance parent brand meaning and represents a highly advantageous way of introducing new products and entering new categories.

Consumption Constellations

Consumption patterns in the form of purchase chains can be logical and intuitive. If a consumer uses a toothbrush regularly, he or she is likely to be a frequent user of toothpaste. Anyone with several pairs of decent leather shoes is likely to be a user of shoe polish. In a similar context, on-line retailers such as Amazon.com will make recommendations to customers based on a title previously purchased and items subsequently chosen by other customers who bought the same title. A man paying a thousand dollars for a new silk suit is unlikely to be content wearing an old tie with it and will probably be in the market for a new tie and maybe a new shirt too. In each case we are dealing with the complementarity among different but related products. It is only the nature of this complementarity and the type of connection among the products that differs. Working with consumer databases, it is possible to predict the probabilities of consumption chains. In some instances the connection between products is primarily functional. In others, the ordering principle underlying consumption patterns is symbolic meaning. In this case the consumption constellation is a cluster of complementary products or brands with a similar symbolic meaning to the consumer.

Baudrillard (1968) refers to "systems of objects" or "object networks", that is, a range of complementary objects or things wherein consumption objects are important not for their specific utility but as a collection of objects in their total meaning. The symbolic differences between product configurations promote affiliation with certain types of people or serve to differentiate oneself from others. Besides the need for self-definition and a sense of self-importance, the key sociopsychological dynamic behind consumption constellations is the human need for order and consistency. The first person to formally record the nature of this need and its consequences with regard to objects or goods was the French Enlightenment philosopher Denis Diderot (McCracken 1988). In a genial essay called "Regrets on Parting with My Old Dressing Gown" he describes how, after receiving a new dressing gown as a gift from a friend, his study, in which he would sit wearing the garment, seemed to be looking the worse for wear. He gradually replaced its contents until it was completely transformed, only to find that he missed his old, well-worn dressing gown that was so in keeping with his untidy but comfortable study and the bric-a-brac that filled it: "Now the harmony is destroyed. Now there is no more consistency, no more unity and no more beauty" (Diderot 1964, p. 311).

The "Diderot effect" occurs when a new good requires that a whole chain of complementary goods be acquired. In McCracken's (1988, p. 125) words, "The drive for consistency that is the motive force of the Diderot effect is insatiable. It is not satisfied until all of the companion goods around it are replaced with new ones that speak as it speaks...." A consumption chain can be triggered with a single purchase (or gift) specific to a particular consumption constellation, or culture of consumption, which has no precedent in a consumer's existing complement of consumer goods. McCracken labels this type of purchase a "departure purchase," as it represents a departure from the consumer's usual consumption pattern.

Another axiom of consumption constellations is that combinations of brands convey symbolic meaning with greater emphasis and resonance than do individual brands in isolation. Being aware of the meaningful aspects of different brands allows marketers to identify potentially potent brand complements (e.g., with a view to joint promotions) and clusters of brands that are likely to appeal to a given group of consumers. The consumption constellation concept, based on convergent symbolic meaning, implies a holistic, across-categories approach to brands, as opposed to the more traditional within-category perspective. The latter is typically centered on differentiation and substitutability, whereas the hallmark of the consumption constellation is meaningful complementarity.

7

The Evolution of Brand Meaning

Brands start off as labels on products and end up as icons of meaning.

Goodyear (1996, p. 113)

Introduction

When a company launches a product, that product will have a number of distinguishing features. It will have a name, a logo, a physical format, distinctive packaging, a certain taste, maybe special design features and so forth. Yet at the beginning these elements lack meaning for consumers. Though they are elements that will contribute to the brand meaning, at the outset they—and by extension the brand—have no real meaning. From a meaning perspective, the brand still does not exist. As consumers become acquainted with and gain experience of the product—purchasing it, using it, discussing it with friends, seeing advertising for it—the primary brand meaning begins to form. More gradually and with the further passage of time, the abstract and symbolic properties of the brand begin to percolate through—qualities that are often provided by consumers themselves. Implicit brand meaning begins to evolve. Though primary brand meaning is likely to remain fairly consistent once it forms, implicit brand meaning, assuming the brand is given depth by manufacturer and consumer alike, will outpace the development of primary brand meaning once the symbolic properties begin to take hold. A potential scenario for the evolution of brand meaning (depending on the brand in question) is illustrated in Figure 7.1.

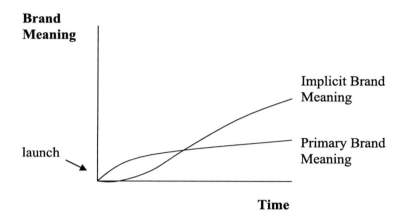

Figure 7.1   Example of evolution of brand meaning.

From Unbranded Good to Brand as Icon

So what stages does the development of brand meaning pass through? The transition from production-led to consumer-driven economies in today's developed countries has brought with it a change in the role and nature of brands. What were once commodities now compete in highly branded, competitive categories. Not so many years ago products such as milk, sugar and eggs were sold unpackaged as commodity items. As competitive market economies develop and with them the need for product differentiation, so brands become more prevalent and instrumental. Essentially, the progression has been from products being perceived as bundles of utilities to brands existing in consumers' minds as clusters of meaning. A useful model has been developed to illustrate how the nature of branding, and of brands, evolves over time (Goodyear 1996). An adaptation of the model is shown in Figure 7.2.

- Stage 1—unbranded goods: In this stage goods are treated as commodities and manufacturers do not attempt or need to differentiate their products. Demand usually exceeds supply. It is a scenario most characteristic of developing economies, though extremely low-interest products in developed economies would also fall under this group.

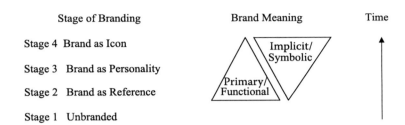

Figure 7.2   Brand evolution model.

- Stage 2—brand as reference: As competition increases manufacturers are obliged to differentiate their products, which they do primarily along functional lines, identifying their utilitarian benefits with a distinctive name. The name is thus used for identification and as a guarantee of quality and consistency.
- Stage 3—brand as personality: As it becomes increasingly difficult to gain competitive advantage through product performance, manufacturers start to build emotional appeal into their brands, endowing them with personalities of their own and fleshing them out in advertising. A closer affinity starts to develop between consumer and brand, with the consumer becoming an active participant in the relationship and the molding of the brand's meaning.
- Stage 4—brand as icon: With time and consistency some brands become meaningful symbols to large groups of people. They become iconic brands. Icons are beacons of meaning within a society. Responding to dynamic motivational drives like loving, winning, or searching, iconic brands tap into the higher-order values of a society, in some cases the global society. Brands can become symbols of freedom or symbols of individuality or rebelliousness or masculinity. By the time this stage is reached, where the brand has come to represent something bigger than itself and its meaning is predominantly symbolic, the brand has effectively become decoupled from the product life cycle as traditionally defined.

Figure 7.3 provides an illustration of the model as applied to the U.S. bar soap market:*

---

* McEnally and de Chernatony (1999) built on the study by Goodyear and proposed a six-stage model of brand evolution, adding a fifth stage of "brand as company" (IKEA is given as an example) and a sixth stage of "brand as policy" (with the Body Shop as an example).

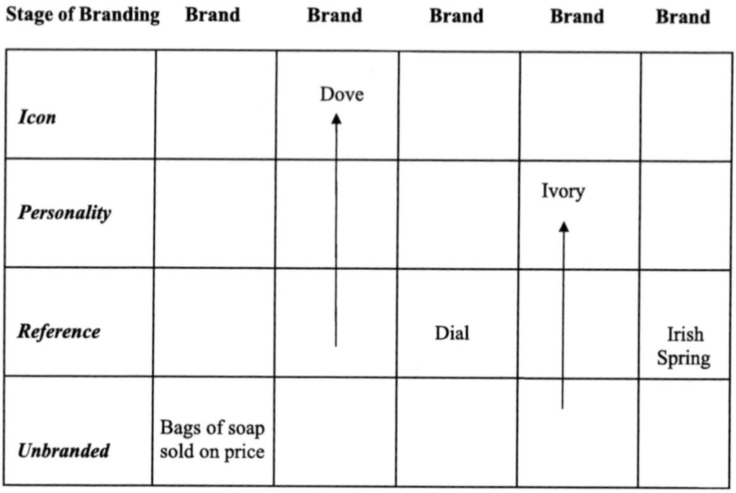

Stage of Branding	Brand	Brand	Brand	Brand	Brand
Icon		Dove ↑			
Personality				Ivory ↑	
Reference			Dial		Irish Spring
Unbranded	Bags of soap sold on price				

Figure 7.3 Example of branding over time in U.S. soap market.

- Bags of soap entered at the unbranded stage and never progressed, the soap being sold on price and as a commodity.
- Dove entered at the reference stage and is steadily evolving into an iconic brand.
- Ivory entered as an unbranded product and has progressed from stage one to stage three.
- Dial and Irish Spring entered at the reference stage and have not progressed.

The model can apply at a macroeconomic level, for example comparing developed economies with developing economies. In the latter case fewer brands are likely to have reached Stage 4, whereas in the case of developed economies a smaller percentage of goods will be unbranded. Or the model can be used to compare one category with another as well as to assess the brand evolution within an individual category as in the aforementioned example. Categories that are more mature and that are composed of high-involvement products, such as cars and banks, will have a larger proportion of their brands at Stages 3 and 4, as consumers will have closer relationships with these brands. So-called low-involvement categories, on the other hand, are likely to have the majority of their brands at Stage 2, with some reaching Stage 3 and only a few, if any, at Stage 4, given that consumers are less likely to invest low-interest products with iconic significance. It should be noted, though, that, even if a category is deemed low involvement today, there is no reason why it must remain so in the future (see the toilet tissue example that follows).

It follows that a category may contain examples of different types of branding at the same time as the brands in the category occupy different stages of evolution. It is not to say, however, that each brand is destined or intended for the next stage up. Depending on corporate objectives, category dynamics and so forth, brands may have reached their apex at Stage 2 or 3 and their managers may be happy to let them settle there. It is even feasible for a brand to fall back to a lower category in the event that the brand is neglected over time and does not receive promotional support. It will gradually lose its consumer franchise and eventually will be reduced, for instance, to brand as reference rather than brand as personality.

By the same token, a brand does not necessarily have to pass through one stage to attain the next level up. New brands can enter the category at any branding stage provided that existing brands in the category have laid a sufficient foundation of consumer understanding and accessibility to facilitate rapid adoption of the new brand. If a category contains symbolic brands a new brand may enter directly at this level if management has the money and vision to establish the brand at a symbolic level. On the other hand, a new brand in a category where its predecessors are brands as reference is unlikely to enter as brand as icon, given the comprehension gap between the two levels and the lack of intermediary consumer priming.

These factors also determine how long it will take for a category to move from being commodity centered to embracing brands as personality, for instance, or how long it takes for a brand to reach symbolic status. Some 70 years ago most British households used ordinary paper, often newspaper, in the bathroom. Today the toilet tissue market is highly competitive and big brands like Andrex and Kleenex are supported with large advertising budgets. Coca-Cola was invented in 1886 by Dr. John Pemberton, an Atlanta pharmacist who mixed the concoction in a three-legged brass kettle in his back yard. Pemberton's bookkeeper, Frank Robinson, came up with the name and scripted it into its famous flowing letters. It was first sold to the public at a soda fountain at Jacob's Pharmacy in Atlanta in May of the same year. One hundred years later Coca-Cola had evolved through brand as reference and brand as personality to become the biggest absolute and symbolic brand in the world.

One of the most remarkable transitions from commodity market to branded market was that of bottled water in the U.K. Given the backdrop of recessionary times in the early 1970s and the fact that ordinary tap water was free and safe to drink, the prospects of a French company's persuading skeptical Brits to pay a pound for a bottle of fizzy water did not look good. An advertising campaign by Perrier in 1974 was dismissed in a *Financial Times* article as a waste of time, claiming that bottled waters would be drunk only by cranks and foreigners. Sales of bottled water totaled 3 million liters in 1976. In just one decade that figure rose to 128 million liters. Perrier went on to spearhead a 600 million pound market, thriving on its award-winning "eau" campaign, which made the brand synonymous with bottled water and French wit. Today, Perrier competes with brands like Evian and Vittel.

Perrier was able to leapfrog the insignificant few brands as reference that existed at the time less because of the precedent established by those brands and more due to the conceptual proximity of bottled water with the overall soft drinks category. Market researchers were never quite sure whether to include the burgeoning bottled water market in their measurement of the soft drinks market or treat it as a separate market. Of course, consumers think less in terms of categories than they do in terms of needs and wants. The measurement criterion of the Coca-Cola Company, "share of throat," captures this graphically and accurately. If on average we have about eight drinks a day, what matters is how many of these are water, Coke, coffee and so forth. Incidentally, given the primal associations of water as the source of life—things, including us, grow and thrive with it and wither and die without it—and its cleansing and purification properties, it is surprising that no brand has managed to extend into the potentially highly symbolic territory that lies beyond the usual clichéd imagery of mountains and springs.

Other recent examples of success in branding what were once considered commodities are Chiquita bananas, Sunkist oranges and the California Milk Processor Board, with its "Got milk" campaign. The no-calorie sweetener NutraSweet turned a commodity into a brand when it made aspartame a household name in the early 1980s. The brand's success persuaded food and beverage manufacturers to use the sweetener in their products, to the extent that, 6 years after it was introduced, NutraSweet was being used in 3,000 different products. This impressive feat was achieved through a strategy of "ingredient branding," where a product, invariably starting life as a commodity, is promoted to the end user in a bid to encourage him or her to look for and even demand the use of the hero ingredient in the host product. At one time computer chips were a commodity item in computer manufacturing. There was no perceived difference in performance among different chips among either consumers or computer manufacturers. With their ubiquitous "Intel inside" campaign, Intel built a brand from what was regarded as a commodity.

If evolving from unbranded commodity to brand as reference, personality, or icon can add millions of dollars to a brand's value, moving in the opposite direction, toward commodity status, has the opposite effect. One of the best examples of a company's rescuing its brand from the brink of commoditization is the turnaround performed by Gillette in the razor market. The 1970s was a period of great product innovation from the company. In 1971 they had introduced Track II, the first twin-blade razor with two parallel blade edges housed in a single, disposable cartridge. Performance was improved in 1977 with the launch of Atra, which featured a pivoting head. Toward the end of the 1970s Bic introduced disposable razors and Gillette found itself embroiled in a tussle for the disposable razor segment. Although Gillette responded with the first disposable twin-bladed razor, Good News, the ensuing battle was anything but. By the mid 1980s disposable razors accounted for fully half of the market. Disposables were dragging razors into a commodity market, where added value had no place and the purchase decision was based purely on price and convenience.

Gillette's next move was a masterstroke. In 1990, after abandoning advertising for its disposables the previous year and following 10 years and $200 million of research and development, the company introduced its Sensor twin-blade shaving system. With blades mounted on springs that enabled the razor to adjust to the contours of the face, Sensor delivered a demonstrably superior shave. Together with the "Gillette. The best a man can get" campaign, supported to the tune of $175 million, the new product extricated Gillette from the disposables quagmire and reestablished its innovation-driven leadership position. It also reversed the market's headlong flight to commoditization and, with the subsequent introduction of Sensor-Excel and Mach 3 (launched in 1998 on the back of a $750 million development budget), endowed the brand with an unassailable mixture of leading-edge technology and global symbolic values.

The commoditization of branded products may come about when a branded patent or technology becomes readily available to other manufacturers and the brand is not strong enough to withstand the onslaught of competition. Drugs that lose their patents are an example. When formulations become widely available, generic versions appear on the market. The product becomes a commodity and can no longer command a premium. The Office of Generic Drugs has estimated that between 2003 and 2010 branded drugs worth more than $20 billion in annual sales will lose patent protection. Similarly, the easy duplication of manufacturing processes and lack of enforcement of copyright protection mean that in countries like China, India and Mexico thousands of products can be produced that are perfect imitations of the European and American-made originals.

The branding level at which a given brand finds itself both determines and is determined by the meaning it has for consumers and therefore their relationship with the brand. In the case of a new brand the functional aspects will be assimilated quite quickly, but it takes rather longer for the more subtle, emotive properties of a brand to evolve. It is easier to win the consumer's head than his or her heart. As mentioned, this process is helped or hindered according to the amount of groundwork undertaken by brands already existing in the category. The meaning to consumers of brands as reference will be very functional, based largely on rational and utilitarian considerations. As managers build a distinctive brand personality, through advertising for example, the brand exerts more of an emotional appeal on consumers. Gradually, the brand's symbolic values evolve and the brand becomes important for what it symbolizes. What are the implications for brand meaning over time—both primary brand meaning and implicit brand meaning—as a brand develops in this way?

From the Category into the Culture

Brands that become truly iconic share certain characteristics. They evoke distinct experiences and feelings in people. They come to represent ideals and deep-seated convictions. They are connected to a culture and a set of values. They may stand for a sense of justice and equality. Or they may embody a spirit of adventure or discovery. These are the types of values discussed in Chapter 2.

Some of the earliest cultural icons were religious, whose iconicity was embellished through storytelling, reference in sacred documents and appearance in holy places. The inexorable development of mass media vehicles—from the early days of print through the golden era of film and broadcast television—and today's phenomenon of instant online information sharing have had a profound impact on the emergence and circulation of cultural icons. This, together with ever more sophisticated marketing by the cultural industries, means that cultural icons can surge into the public consciousness more rapidly and more extensively than ever. Today's new gadget, or newly elected politician, or character in a film release, or sought-after tourist destination may all become tomorrow's cultural icon. The same is true for brands, which may transcend the product categories from which they emerge to attain the status of cultural icon in relatively short measure, if they can become compelling symbols for a set of values or ideals that resonate within a society or culture.

Though iconic brands often capture the mood of the time, what determines the longevity of their iconic standing is the ability to remain contemporary and relevant as time passes. The counterculture Volkswagen Beetle of the late 60s has morphed into the Volkswagen New Beetle in the early 21st century. But brand iconicity is not a one-way ticket and even Volkswagen slipped back into dormant hibernation, at least in the U.S. market. In his book *How Brands Become Icons,* Douglas Holt (2004) points out how Volkswagen's Beetle had become, by 1970, one of the most influential iconic brands in the United States by embodying the bohemian and art world myth of the late sixties era. Yet from 1972 to 1994 Volkswagen lost its iconic value as it failed to respond appropriately to the "cultural disruption" (i.e., socioeconomic or ideological ground shifts) of that period. From the mid 1990s onward Volkswagen managed to rekindle its iconic strength by reinterpreting its original myth in the context of the new sociocultural challenges of the day and embracing the indie myth as the cornerstone of Volkswagen's updated brand narrative (ibid., pp. 129–130).

In similar vein, Holt (2004, pp. 96–124) reviews the ebbing and flowing of Budweiser's iconic value in the U.S. market through the years. Throughout the 1980s Budweiser climbed steadily to iconic stature on the back of its artisan myth. With its "This Bud's for you" campaign, Budweiser lauded and celebrated the men-of-action heroic blue collar workers who, through their selfless dedication to their craft and skilled manual labor, were gradually ensuring America's economic comeback. By the late 1980s and early 1990s economic realities had changed. Recession was followed by a largely jobless recovery and Budweiser's heroic artisan myth had lost traction. The brand floundered with an uninspiring mix of insipid Americana until around 1997 when Bud's myth was radically reinvented and aligned with the emerging slacker myth, pioneered by brands such as Mountain Dew. The slacker myth* was a more cynical, yet affirmative, worldview that poked fun at those who sold themselves and toiled blindly for the corporate dream and instead posited that hanging out with good friends was the route to happiness.

What these examples illustrate is that when a brand's implicit brand meaning—part of which is culturally determined—becomes sufficiently compelling for enough people it can stand shoulder to shoulder with other cultural icons of the period. Yet all too often brand managers fail to understand the nature of that implicit brand meaning and let a golden opportunity slip through their hands as the brand is dragged back into the mire of market share battles, category conflicts, promotional frenzies and price wars. Take care of the meaning and the market share will take care of itself. When Levi's started losing market share in the late 1990s, the trend was generally considered to reflect the company's gradual failure to transcend its products and category and become a free-standing meaning. Yet Levi's had been an iconic U.S. brand in the 1970s, just as Coke was— and just as Volkswagen and Marlboro had been in the 1960s and Nike, Budweiser and Absolut would be in the 1980s. Maintaining iconic status is not easy, as brands such as Levi's, Pepsi and Cadillac have recently shown.

---

* Holt (2004, p. 41) draws a useful distinction between what he calls affirmative myths and myths of resistance. The former endorse prevailing ideology while the latter challenge it. Budweiser's "This Bud's For You" campaign is an example of an affirmative myth, whereas Volkswagen's counterculture Beetle of the 1960s was founded on a myth of resistance.

Brand Communities

Iconic brands form visceral, profound connections with their consumers. Those consumers may have different ages, backgrounds, gender, ethnicities and creeds, but they are drawn together as an extended family through their affinity to a brand. Behind every iconic brand is a committed brand community. Sometimes these brand communities actively organize themselves, as in the case of Harley-Davidson. In other cases they form a looser, more passive association of like-thinking people who share an enthusiasm for a brand. Think Apple, Volkswagen, Starbucks, or Virgin. The term *brand community* refers to "a specialized, non-geographically bound community, based on a structured set of social relations among admirers of a brand" (Muniz and O'Guinn, 2001, p. 412). Brand communities exhibit three traditional markers of community: (1) shared consciousness; (2) rituals and traditions; and (3) a sense of moral responsibility. Shared consciousness arises when "members feel an important connection to the brand, but more importantly, they feel a stronger connection to one another" (ibid., p. 418). Rituals and traditions "represent vital social processes by which the meaning of the community is reproduced and transmitted within and beyond the community.... (These) typically center on shared consumption experiences with the brand" (ibid., p. 421). Muniz and O'Guinn (2001) give the example of Saab owners acknowledging each other on the road by honking or flashing their headlights.

Harley-Davidson: An Icon of Meaning*

When people tattoo a brand symbol on their skin it is, quite literally, a graphic illustration of the meaning that brand has in their lives. The famous Harley-Davidson "bar and shield" is the most popular tattoo in the United States. Besides those aficionados proudly sporting the ink, the brand is imprinted on the consciousness of hundreds of thousands more. If truly iconic brands are about standing for something bigger than themselves, then few would surpass the iconic status of Harley-Davidson. In fact Harley has become such a cultural icon that, to understand the brand, it is first necessary to understand the complex

---

* For this case study I owe a debt of gratitude to Dr. Ross Stuart Fuglsang of Iowa Morningside College and his excellent work *Motorcycle Menace: Media Genres and the Construction of a Deviant Culture* (dissertation, 1997).

sociocultural background that is so much a part of the brand's heritage and meaning.

Although the first Harley-Davidson rolled out of the Milwaukee machine shop run by William Harley and Bill and Walter Davidson in 1903, it was during the late 1940s and 1950s that America's motorcycle culture began to make itself felt in the public conscious. Postwar America was a world of middle-class comfort and conformity on the one hand and increasingly restless youth on the other. The growing youth culture that idolized James Dean, Marlon Brando and Elvis Presley had trouble identifying with what they saw as the blandness of middle-class mainstream. To disaffected and unsettled young men, motorcycling and the culture surrounding it provided excitement and adventure. It also afforded some sense of camaraderie and belonging, as riders came together to form clubs.

Of the nearly 6 million motorcycle owners in the nation today, about 60 percent are between the ages of 37 and 64. Many of these enthusiasts trace their early impressions of bikers and motorcycle culture back to the 1954 classic *The Wild One*. The film, hallmarked with Brando's particular embodiment of virile masculinity, set the precedent for a generation of biker films to come. *The Wild One* was based on Frank Rooney's *Cyclists' Raid,* which in turn owed its plot to a real incident in 1947 when a mob of motorcyclists indulged in a weekend of violence and revelry in the town of Hollister, California. As if the damage done to the biker image by Hollister was not bad enough, the 1950s saw the emergence of the most notorious biker club, the Hell's Angels, who would also eventually become tarnished through violence and organized crime.

The year 1969 saw the release of the iconic *Easy Rider.* The film depicts a search for freedom in a corrupt and conformist America, following the fortunes of its two biker antiheroes, played by Peter Fonda and Dennis Hopper. *Easy Rider* equates motorbikes with the freedom of the open road, adventure and exploration rather than with delinquent and criminal behavior. Although they are involved in drugs, the bikers are presented as harmless outlaws rather than criminals. They exist outside society's norms and conventions. The names of the two main characters, Wyatt and Billy, call to mind the controversial desert lawman and adventurer Wyatt Earp and legendary outlaw Billy the Kid. Indeed, commentators have observed the similarities between the biker film genre and that of westerns. The underlying theme of westerns is "a conflict on the border between two lands or two eras, with a hero divided between the two value systems" (Fulsang 1997, p. 143, paraphrasing Cawelti 1969). Biker films borrow from this idiom. Moreover, they often take place on borders that are both literal and figurative. The Southern

California setting of many biker films places them near a national border as well as the border between civilization and the desert.

Events such as those that took place in Hollister damaged the image of the motorcycle and its devotees. Harley-Davidson tried to disassociate itself from the unsavory aspect of outlaw bikers, but it was not easy and ran counter to business sense at a time when the company was depending on many of these hard-core enthusiasts for its very financial survival. In the early 1960s Japanese motorcycles began to make inroads into the market and in 1968, to evade a hostile takeover, Harley-Davidson was sold to American Machine & Foundry. Despite having its back to the wall, the company gradually began its remarkable recovery. In the face of fierce Japanese competition, Harley-Davidson struggled on as the last bastion of the American motorcycle industry. This served to instill a tremendous sense of pride and patriotism in the brand. In 1981 a group of Harley executives and stockholders bought the company and it was soon back in the black. In 1986 it felt confident enough to support the removal of tariffs on Japanese bikes and it has since gone from strength to strength.

The company's resurgence brought with it a renaissance in the biker myth—albeit a sanitized version that has now been absorbed into the mainstream. The Harley-Davidson company of the 1990s through to today has preferred to accentuate freedom and individual expression with a hint of nonconformity rather than the rebellion of its outlaw roots. Yet the changes of the past 30 years or so have not completely extinguished the biker outlaw image. It is an image that Harley-Davidson would not want to see completely overhauled, as, in truth, it has always been an integral part of its heritage and mystique. The Harley-Davidson myth is inextricably bound with the biker myth. The appeal of the outlaw biker fantasy, rooted in antiestablishment and nonconformity, still holds sway over law-abiding establishment members not immune to the urge to escape, however briefly, the constraints of modern life. From the rich and colorful antecedents just outlined come the Harley values of the 21st century:

Freedom
Adventure
Individuality
Patriotism

Harley owns the category essence. It is synonymous with the freedom of the open road, the ability to break loose and the thrill and exhilaration of the wind in your face. The personal freedom that the brand represents includes freedom from confinement—both "the freedom of the saddle" (as opposed to the automobile) and from four walls—and freedom from mainstream values and social structures (Aaker 1996, p. 138). The macho ruggedness that is part of the brand's personality is equally appealing to the not inconsiderable number of female riders as it is to the wide spectrum of male devotees.

Harley-Davidson exemplifies many of the ways brands become the repositories of vital meaning. It is a case study that illustrates many of the key themes of this book. Harley delivers a very potent mixture of emotional, expressive and experiential benefits. It makes its users feel like the people they want to be and helps them play out their fantasies. It gives them a sense of identity and makes them feel connected with others in their brand community whose values they share. It is the ultimate experiential brand. Harley riders will tell you that there is nothing quite like the look, feel and sound of a Harley—800 pounds of gleaming steel with its trademark styling and a throaty roar as distinctive as a human voice. As any Harley enthusiast will tell you, only a Harley sounds like a Harley.

Even nonowners and nonbikers are drawn to the brand's mystique, as witnessed by the huge volume of officially licensed Harley merchandise the company sells. Wearing a Harley T-shirt or a bomber jacket emblazoned with the bar and shield is one way of drawing meaning from the brand. In terms of the meaning transfer model, as the fashion and media worlds steadily disseminated the outlaw biker story, the biker myth became attached to the Harley brand. Today 45-year-old white-collar professionals and office workers appropriate this meaning when they buy and ride a Harley bike.

There is much ritual surrounding Harley machines, including the customization of bikes and the ceremonial trappings on show at Harley rallies—with their profusion of black leather, weaponry, heavy boots, big beards and ubiquitous tattoos. These rallies are the ultimate manifestation of the Harley brand community. It is a community the company is very careful to nurture—through plant tours, special events, rallies and races. The Harley Owners Group (HOG) unites more than 800,000 members worldwide, organized into well over 1,000 chapters, making it the largest factory-sponsored motorcycle organization in the world. Harley-Davidson takes the concept of extended family very seriously. Says the company's Web site, "Here's the bottom line: We like to think of Harley-Davidson—from the top corporate officer to the newest Harley owner and rider—as one big, happy family" (http://www. harley-davidson.com). This is more than facile marketing speak. Company executives and dealers sponsor HOG activities and ride alongside members at rallies, creating a special bond between organization and customer and affording Harley executives and engineers invaluable feedback and learning.

Few brands have managed to generate the kind of deep visceral connection and unswerving loyalty that Harley has. While the HOG refers to ownership of a Harley machine, the name is also an appropriate metaphor for the group of people who own not just the product but the brand itself: the consumers. As with all iconic brands, Harley executives would happily admit that it is they, the devoted consumers, who own the Harley brand—not the company. It is a state of affairs that has taken many years to come about. Harley-Davidson is the very antithesis of the dotcoms that wasted millions in the late 90s trying to buy brand status overnight with frivolous advertising campaigns. The brand has achieved its iconic status through consistency at every touch point with its consumers. Not many brands have the benefit of more than 100 years of history behind them, but that counts for nothing without a cohesive brand message across advertising, product development, distribution channels, customer service and licensing activity.

In the way that only vigorous brands can, Harley generates a compelling brand narrative. As Jon Howard-Spink (2003, p. 16) writes, "We are at our most loyal when buying the story of the brand … and the opportunity to become part of that story." Blurring the lines between classic brand community and subculture, the Harley brand invokes an enduring myth, situates its adherents in an aspirational and inspirational context and provides them with a vocabulary, code of conduct and a way of life: "Live to ride, ride to live."

As iconic brands develop in the way just described, consistent with the brand evolution model, there are, then, two important dynamics to their evolution that are worth underlining. The first is that these brands break out of their category and into the culture. The meaning and importance they hold for consumers come to reside less in their category context and more in their sociocultural context. Again, the example of the Volkswagen Beetle is a case in point. Brands that become culturally pervasive offer their consumers a vocabulary—both literal and metaphorical, a brand narrative of which they can be a part and an enduring way of life. Buying into a way of life that is provided by an iconic brand is very different from simply buying so-called lifestyle brands. The relationship between consumer and brand in the latter case is far more superficial. These are little more than badge brands, which are soon discarded in favor of the next fad. Brands that make the transition from category players to cultural icons are liberated from comparison with competing brands from

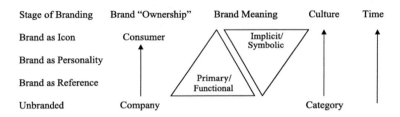

Figure 7.4 Brand evolution model: from category to culture.

the category and instead come to represent more meaningful satisfaction and fulfillment in peoples' lives. Nike makes great sports shoes, but Nike's cultural brand significance (and implicit brand meaning) is that it gives people a sense of accomplishment and makes them feel good about themselves through sport and physical exercise.

The second dynamic of brand evolution from brand as reference to brand as icon is that the brand's center of gravity gradually shifts from manufacturer to consumer. By the time the brand has evolved from category to culture, its passage into consumer ownership is complete. These two dynamics are illustrated in the enhanced brand evolution model shown in Figure 7.4.

Evolution and Consistency

To survive, brands must evolve and sometimes diversify. This does not have to be at the expense of consistency and continuity, but it often is. Brand extension, realignment, cobranding—all can have a direct effect on brand meaning by transplanting a brand from one context to a completely different one or juxtaposing it with a semantically different brand. The ideal brand is one where there is a seamless fusion between product values and brand values and where this unity can be maintained in the long run. Of course, this does not mean that the product or brand cannot undergo change any more than it implies that new advertising campaigns cannot be developed to replace existing ones. Product innovation allows brands to reinforce what they stand for and to contemporize brand meaning. Keeping the brand's values relevant and in line with consumer priorities will necessitate occasional innovation. But that innovation should be evolutionary and consonant with brand meaning. For example, from a business perspective Starbucks, with its huge prime site presence, can easily generate incremental revenue by selling carbonated drinks and sandwiches or can engage in joint promotions. For a long time the company resisted the temptation and instead sought to evolve the brand by mining its brand meaning and by exploring what else coffee can be besides hot and liquid. Just recently, more and more of its outlets are selling other food products, leaving the way open for new specialist contenders to encroach on Starbuck's coffee territory.

Above all, once resonant symbolic meaning begins to emerge for the brand, it should be treated as the precious property it is. Implicit brand meaning should be nurtured and preserved over time, even if primary brand meaning is modified in the interim to keep pace with, or ahead of, the market. Unilever's Persil brand in the United Kingdom, mentioned earlier, began life as a soap powder and remained so for some time, even after much of the market had moved into synthetic detergents. Its slogan from the 1920s to the 1970s was the simple but memorable "Persil washes whiter." Today the brand encompasses a wide range of variants, including the highly successful tablets and has extended into dishwashing liquid. The primary brand meaning has thus evolved significantly; at a technical level the brand today bears little resemblance to that of the 1960s, yet, through all the format and formulation changes, the brand's implicit meaning remained intimately linked to a mother's pride and care for her family.

As a brand develops from brand as reference through brand as personality to brand as icon, its brand meaning footprint will expand. This is inevitable given the passage of time, product innovation and brand extension, successive advertising campaigns and so forth. Indeed, such activities are essential ways of amplifying brand meaning. Brand meaning is embellished when it finds cumulative resonance among consumers. The greater complexity that this gives the brand should make it more robustly meaningful. However, the danger is that complexity becomes confusion and incoherence. A brand-meaning footprint that is expanding is one thing; a brand-meaning footprint that is dispersing is quite another. Trying to be all things to all people has led to the downfall of many a brand. Complexity can and has to be accommodated but should never eclipse the importance of standing for something distinctive and motivating.

8

Brand Communication

Introduction

Before exploring brand communication, it is worthwhile to review some of the precepts and principles of communication in general, as these have important implications for the communication of brand meaning.

What Is Communication?

Communication can be defined as the intentional or unintentional transfer of meaning through messages. The study of communication is the study of those meanings in their sociocultural circulation. Two ideologies of communication have evolved through the years:

1. One sees communication as the transmission of messages and focuses on how senders encode and transmit and receivers receive and decode those messages. It is concerned with the function and mechanics of communication—channels, such as sound waves and light waves and media, like the human voice, the body, television, photographs and so on. A message is essentially construed to be that which is transmitted, as determined by the sender's intention. This has been described as a transmission or transportation view of communication: a process of transmitting messages at a distance, particularly for the purpose of control and persuasion.
2. The other ideology sees communication as the generation and exchange of meanings. It is concerned with how, through sign systems, meanings are created and perceived in sociocultural behavior. This approach uses semiotics as its modus operandi. In

semiotics signs take the form of words, images, sounds, objects and gestures. It is a broad-ranging approach that covers human communication in all its modes (i.e., sound, sight, touch, smell, taste) and in all its contexts (e.g., dance, clothing, film). Semiotics emphasizes the text, which is anything capable of being "read" or decoded, like a page of writing, a painting, an advertisement, or the way somebody is dressed. Semiotics favors the term *reader* over *receiver*, as it stresses the more active role of the reader in creating, or negotiating, meaning from the text.

Paul Watzlawick and the Palo Alto Group expounded five axioms of communication in their book *Pragmatics of Human Communication* (Watzlawick, Beavin and Jackson 1967). First and foremost was the assertion that one cannot *not* communicate. In other words, meaning is inherent in all human behavior. Behavior has no opposite: There is no such thing as nonbehavior. So even if we try not to communicate we are still sending out a message. Ignoring somebody is a form of communication, even if all it communicates is, "I don't want to communicate with you." It is akin to reading a sign that says, "Please ignore this sign." We thus live in a constant flux of communication and negotiated meanings. We engage in communication instinctively, intuitively, often unconsciously.

These observations have particular relevance in the context of brand communication. From the brand perspective, everything communicates. Though we normally think of advertising as the primary form of brand communication, it would be shortsighted to overlook the diverse and less obvious ways a brand communicates with its consumers. Packaging, for example, is a crucial part of the dialogue. Moreover, packaging is a free advertising medium, right there at the point of purchase. Later in the chapter is reviewed how brand communication nowadays stretches well beyond paid for advertising and how it is driven by myriad consumer interactions with the brand. Indeed it is useful to draw a distinction upfront between marcoms (i.e., company-sponsored marketing communications such as paid-for advertising), and brand communication in its broadest sense, of which marcoms are a subset. Before exploring the broader horizon, let us concentrate on the specific way advertising shapes and conveys brand meaning.

Advertising as the Communication of Brand Meaning

By framing, evolving and modifying the associations and meanings attached to a brand, advertising plays a pivotal role in the generation of brand meaning and subsequent consumer behavior. The successful outcome of the process depends both on the advertiser's skill in creating and influencing those meanings and on the way they are interpreted in the light of the target's motivations, values and aspirations.

A couple of examples from the cigarette market illustrate the point. Marlboro cigarettes were originally targeted at women and were sold in a pink pack. When it was decided to relaunch the brand to target men, the symbol of a cowboy was adopted for advertising. For sure, the cowboy was felt to represent a certain rugged, independent type of masculinity. But, as always with truly iconic brands, the adopted symbol did far more than simply provide personality cues. The cowboy was depicted on horseback, invariably alone, working on the range. As McCracken (1993, p. 127) describes, "The meanings of this constellation were clear enough: (a) freedom, (b) the satisfaction of physical challenge, (c) the glory of the great outdoors, (d) release from urban strains and stresses, (e) freedom from industrial labor, (f) freedom from the confines of city life and (g) the 'true grit' of a real male activity. These were the new meanings of Marlboro." Without any change in the underlying product itself, the meanings of the brand changed dramatically. These meanings have been developed and consolidated through the years since the 1955 relaunch: "The Marlboro brand now carries clear and compelling meanings. It does so because advertising put them there" (ibid., p. 127).

The Strand cigarette example mentioned in Chapter 3, where the consumer take-away was the exact opposite of that intended by the advertiser, was a salutary if extreme lesson. In truth, it is rare for such blatant discrepancy to arise between intended brand meaning and consumer-perceived brand meaning. The Strand example, though, does remind us that communication takes place in the ears and mind of the listener, not in the mouth of the speaker and that brand meaning can only effectively materialize in the mind of the consumer.

Given that brands exist in a permanently evolving sociocultural context and that their meaning for consumers is mediated by constant direct personal experience, it is not unusual for meaning slippage or shifts to occur over time.

The U.K.'s Yellow Pages, mentioned in Chapter 6, is a case in point. Since its launch the business telephone directory had become associated with distress calls to help people resolve problems like burst pipes or dry rot. Of course, that was part of the original concept: to group together the telephone numbers of all the services and businesses people might need to contact, whether to fix a leak, send a bunch of flowers to somebody, call a taxi, or find somewhere that could replace a starter motor. It was convenient, practical and time saving because instead of having to traipse around town you could "let your fingers do the walking."

By the early 1980s, however, negative associations were tending to influence consumer perceptions of the brand and the company wanted to endow it with more positive, emotional values. To this end, a new campaign was developed, the first commercial airing in 1983. In it, an affable elderly gentleman, despondent at not having found a copy of a book called *Fly Fishing*, by J. R. Hartley, on a shopping trip, tries the Yellow Pages and starts to phone around. At last, to his delight, he comes across a book shop that has a copy. Placing his order over the telephone, he carefully pronounces his name: "J. – R. – Hartley." As he beams, the voiceover announces, "Good old Yellow Pages. We're not just there for the nasty things in life." Among subsequent commercials, a father uses the directory to find a new bicycle for his son's birthday; a couple use it to find a motorized lawnmower for their loyal elderly gardener; and a cricket umpire manages to find a new hat for an important cricket match at Lords (England's most important cricket ground). The campaign ran until 1995.

U.K. paint manufacturer Crown had seen its market share decline considerably since the early 1980s. Having been almost at parity with its rival Dulux in 1980, by 1995 it was only a third the size of the category leader. Advertising had projected a functional brand character and the brand was seen as old-fashioned and masculine. Furthermore, product proliferation and the introduction of a number of subbrands meant that the meaning of the Crown brand was becoming increasingly diffuse. The company set about rationalizing its product range and looked to a new advertising campaign to reverse its fortunes. The advertising would have to strengthen the Crown brand and to promote the color range (many people still preferred to use "safer," neutral colors like white) as well as to instill some contemporary and emotional values into the brand—all in the absence of any rational advantage.

The new campaign challenged the category's advertising conventions. Whereas traditional paint advertising had focused on the end benefit of beautifully painted homes, the new advertising strategy was to dramatize the use of color as a benefit in itself. Using color was presented as an emotionally uplifting experience. The advertising associated Crown not so much with the transformational benefits of the product on a home but rather with the transformational benefits of the brand on the people who use it. There was not one shot of a paintbrush or a household interior. Crown's value share increased by 40 percent in 2 years. Though the marketing plan had its own category-related targets, the objective of the advertising in terms of brand meaning was clear: to create ownership of "color" for the brand in the minds of consumers, encouraging them to look at color, and by association the brand, in a new light.

So, as mentioned earlier in this chapter, effective advertising works by framing, consolidating and modifying the meanings attached to a brand. We have seen that brands are represented in our memories by engrams—networks of connections in our brains that link together everything we know about brands. Connections between brand associations are reinforced by advertising and other stimuli and they are what ultimately define these brands in consumers' minds. Creativity and consistency in advertising have the effect of strengthening the linkage between the associations and the brand. A well-known example comes from an unlikely product category: toilet tissue. Andrex toilet tissue was first advertised in 1972, in the U.K.'s first-ever TV commercial for toilet tissue. The advertising featured a playful Labrador puppy. Over 100 commercials later the puppy is still used in advertising for the brand. It is one of the U.K.'s longest-running consistent TV campaigns. The puppy has become one of the best-known and best-loved brand properties.

The decision to create an association between a puppy and a brand of toilet tissue was an inspired one. Andrex claims to be soft, strong and long. Often the mischievous puppy is shown becoming entangled in the toilet tissue and then scampering off, unraveling the roll of tissue in the process—a subtle product demonstration of strong and long. The puppy also cues softness and gentleness as well as triggering two other highly relevant markers: *loving* and *family*. An on-pack promotion for the brand offered a toy puppy in return for proofs of purchase and announced that a percentage of sales value would be donated to the Guide Dogs for the Blind Association.

Today, all sorts of puppy merchandise is available and the brand continues to support both the Guide Dogs for the Blind Association and the National Canine Defence League. To the extent that advertising works by strengthening connections between brand associations, the pathways connecting the puppy and other Andrex brand associations have been very well traveled through the years. To any U.K. housewife the mention of the word *Andrex* will immediately trigger access to brand memories, the strongest of which will be the puppy. Similarly, a picture of a Labrador puppy will probably cue brand memories for Andrex.

Brands that can appropriate symbolic meanings and communicate them through their advertising are at a considerable advantage. Advertising resonates more meaningfully and operates more effectively at the symbolic, intuitive level of consciousness. Such advertising often employs emotionally charged images and visual metaphors. On the one hand, memory is strengthened by heightened affect. On the other, it has been shown that visual, nonverbal content (most human communication is nonverbal) has direct access to the subconscious, without being filtered by the conscious. Whereas the conscious mind has only limited recall, the subconscious has permanent memory. Symbolic metaphorical advertising, which elicits an emotional, intuitive response, has the potential to tap into the deepest, most enduring substance of the human psyche.

Advertising the Brand versus Branding the Advertising

From the perspective of advertising as brand communication, the important issue is how people respond to the brand rather than the advertising—or, rather, how they respond to the brand through the advertising, which brings us right back to brand meaning. By helping to shape brand meaning, advertising develops the relationship consumers have with the brand. That relationship is determined by the way consumers interpret brand meaning in the context of their set of values and motivations. Advertising must therefore be relevant for the brand and involving for the consumer (Figure 8.1). It should not get in the way of the consumer–brand relationship, for example by drawing attention to itself at the expense of the brand or creating dissonance, in which the advertising seems to have little to do with the brand.

Crucial to the success of a given piece of advertising is the degree
to which the communication message and the brand are integrated
in the creative content. The advertising concept must be inextricably linked to the brand to establish the desired mental connections.
When there is brand linkage and integration, the advertising triggers the brand associative network, which it may either reinforce or
modify in some way. Where brand linkage and integration is weak,
the creative content may be recalled, but the brand may well either be
misattributed or simply not noticed. Even if there is correct advertising–brand attribution, there may still exist the danger that the brand
is being sustained less by its meaningful properties and values and
more by its advertising halo.

There is a major difference between advertising that is "spon-
sored" by a brand and advertising that is intrinsically branded. It
is a safe assumption that no advertiser in the world would not want
his or her brand correctly linked to its advertising. Yet every year
millions of dollars are wasted on generic or misattributed advertising. We are all familiar with having described, often with a wealth
of detail, a particular television commercial we liked, without the
faintest idea which brand it was supposedly advertising. It is hardly
surprising that this happens. Each day we are bombarded with hundreds of commercial messages. Most of them we screen out. Even if
we see advertising that appeals to us, we can perfectly well enjoy it
without the need for any further mental activity or processing, such
as registering the brand.

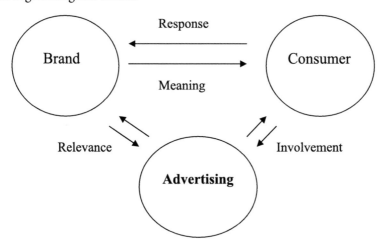

Figure 8.1 Advertising as brand communication.

Tracking data have shown that some ads are more than 10 times more effective than others at generating brand-linked memorability (according to Millward Brown). Branding in advertising entails more than an extended pack shot or displaying the brand name throughout the ad. Here are some of the ways branding is woven more seamlessly into the fabric of the advertising.

Structural Branding

With structural branding any of a number of familiar structural features in the advertising may serve to identify that advertising as being from a given brand. The structure or style of the advertising, ownership of a certain storyline and the inclusion of recognizable characters, be they well-known or simply certain types, all can serve as cues that trigger brand recognition. The important thing about structural branding is that it works throughout the advertising.

Advertising and Brand Properties

Specific, physical elements relating to the brand or its advertising work in a similar way. An existing brand property may be employed in the advertising (e.g., when part of the logo device comes to life), or an element used consistently in the advertising may become a brand property. An example of the latter would be the use of the Labrador puppy in advertising for Andrex toilet tissue. When the property used pervades the advertising, as in the case of the Andrex puppy or the Exxon tiger, it is a form of structural branding.

Nescafé Gold Blend provides an example of the difference between structural branding and the simple use of an advertising property. Up to 1987, advertising in the U.K. had concentrated on the product itself, using the mnemonic device of a gold bean to suggest product superiority. The gold bean thus became a brand-advertising property. In November 1987 new advertising broke, based on the campaign theme of "sophisticated romance," reminiscent of upmarket television series like *Dallas*, *Dynasty* and *Moonlighting*, which were popular at the time. The advertising had a distinctive style and format, mimicking the conventions of these series. There were suspense-filled endings. Each new burst would begin with a reminder of the previous episode. And in each episode the two protagonists drew closer and closer to a romantic liaison. Through its use of structural branding the advertising became instantly recognizable and the "Love over Gold" campaign became synonymous with the Gold Blend brand.

Brand Protagonism

Advertising in which the brand plays a central, protagonistic role is more likely to lead to brand recognition and recall than advertising in which the brand is somewhat incidental. In the classic 1979 Coca-Cola commercial called "Mean Joe Greene" the pivotal moment is when Mean Joe, at first grouchy as he limps down the players' tunnel injured, finally relents and accepts a bottle of Coca-Cola from a young fan. After taking a drink, the mood changes and he reciprocates by throwing the boy his jersey. The Nescafé Gold Blend campaign started with the man calling on his female neighbor to ask if he can borrow some coffee, and they get to know each other over a cup of Gold Blend coffee.

Several research companies have diagnostic tools, such as Millward Brown's Interest Trace, which are an electronic measure of a respondent's level of involvement as he or she watches a commercial. Such measures are valuable in understanding how people react to the scenes in an ad. They usually display peaks and troughs, with a high point at some stage in the commercial. In the context of branding it is useful to ascertain and compare the level of brand protagonism at the moments of greatest consumer involvement, as this is likely to influence the extent to which the brand is noticed and recalled.

Unfortunately, many commercials are only tangentially branded. Some are little more than a joke, philosophical statement, or fuzzy moment brought to you by Brand x. Others are unwitting instances of borrowed-interest advertising. A case in point was provided by Chrysler. In 2003 Chrysler learned some hard lessons about the pitfalls of celebrity endorsements, or personality associations. In a bid to take the brand upmarket—the "path to premium" strategy—the company cut a three-year, $14 million deal with singer Celine Dion to feature her and her music in advertising for the brand, beginning with the Pacifica hybrid SUV. The commercials were lavishly produced, highly stylized affairs, shot in black and white and carrying the tagline "Drive & Love." They proved to be disastrous. Not for Celine Dion, though—besides her lucrative contract, Chrysler also sponsored her Las Vegas show, "A New Day," which opened on March 25 of that year. With her voice and person dominating the heavyweight campaign, her new album, *One Heart,* had sold over 2 million copies by the end of April. Meanwhile, despite projections of 60,000 Pacifica sales in the first year, dealers had sold only 4,828 in the first 3 months on the market. By year end, adjusted for restructuring costs, Chrysler Group reported a loss of $47 million.

What went wrong? First, the celebrity eclipsed the vehicles and overshadowed the brand. Second, the use of the celebrity did practically nothing to define the brand. There was little meaningful connection between Celine Dion and Pacifica or Chrysler. She did not bring expertise, authority, or connotations of innovation. Any intended metaphor was completely missed by the buying public. To redeem itself, the company has taken the wise move of going back to basics and using the product to define the brand once more. Perhaps the biggest oversight of the ill-conceived campaign was the simple truth that effective advertising always has to be effective brand communication.

Semiotic Analysis of Advertising

The study of the production of meaning from primarily visual communication, such as advertising, has suffered from the lack of a structured approach to analyze and categorize visual communication cues and how they generate meanings. In recent years the field of semiotics has begun to gain acceptance as a credible tool for the research and interpretation of meaning in advertising. Semiotic analysis can be applied to television advertising, posters, ads in newspapers and magazines, direct mailings—anywhere that signs are used within socially shared systems of codes and meanings. It is important to bear in mind that signs within a semiotic context never exist in isolation but always as part of a sign system. Their meaning is derived from the structural relationship they share with other signs in that system.

As discussed earlier, according to Ferdinand de Saussure's ([1916] 1983, p. 67) model, a sign is divided into the signifier (i.e., the form it takes) and the signified (i.e., the concept the signifier represents, or the meaning). A contemporary of Saussure, the American philosopher C. S. Peirce (1931–1935, 1958) categorized the patterns of meaning in signs as iconic, symbolic and indexical. An iconic sign resembles or imitates the signified—that is, it looks like what it represents. A picture of a car, for example, can be considered highly iconic because it looks like a car. Portraits, onomatopoeic words and sound effects in a radio play are examples. In the case of a symbolic sign there is no natural relationship between the sign and its meaning, between the signifier and the signified. The meaning of a symbolic sign is determined by convention. It means what it does because we have agreed and learned through experience that this is the meaning. Languages, numbers, traffic lights and national flags are examples. An indexical sign is one in which the signifier is directly connected in some way—physically or causally—to the signified. This connection or correspondence can be inferred or observed. Thus smoke is an index of fire. Footprints are another example. Peirce himself (1931–1935, 1958) gave the examples of measuring instruments such as a weathercock, a barometer and a sundial.

Though it is common to refer to Peirce's three forms as types of signs, in reality they are not mutually exclusive. Signs often operate on several levels and can be any combination of an icon, a symbol and an index. Indeed, when conducting a semiotic analysis we are usually addressing a hierarchy of meaning in addition to categories and components of meaning.

Given its visually compelling and largely nonverbal nature, advertising like Apple's "1984" commercial for the introduction of Macintosh is particularly accessible to semiotic analysis. The commercial is described in Chapter 5. Moriarty (1995) investigated how meaning is produced in the commercial: What are the dominant visual images? How do the communication elements operate in terms of semiotic meaning: iconic, symbolic, indexical? How do these elements differ in their frequency of mentions and their impact on viewers' perceptions? The most dominant element of imagery was the woman. This figure operates on several semiotic levels. On the iconic level she is clearly a woman runner. However, she represents much more on the symbolic level, being seen as a symbol of a new age and way of life, as a symbol of resistance–rebellion–revolution and also of freedom, innovation and individuality. As such, she is closely associated with the Apple brand and its values—something reinforced by the Apple logo on her clothing.

The sledgehammer was next in terms of frequency of mention. On the simplest level of representation it carries iconic meaning as a sledgehammer. On the symbolic level it carries various meanings, the most prevalent being the destruction of a totalitarian order or the breaking of rules and boundaries. The TV screen elicited a similar number of responses as the sledgehammer. Although it may appear to be a straightforward iconic sign, several more symbolic interpretations emerged, such as the power of the media or the influence of a powerful, controlling government. The next most frequent mention was of the genderless people. It was difficult to identify a common iconic meaning for these figures, as they are presented in a very abstract way. The symbolic meaning attributed to them tended to center on some kind of mind–media control, or brainwashing, or even on inmates under the control of some authority.

Interestingly, though more iconic message elements were mentioned, the ones that had most impact were more symbolic in their meaning—the woman and the genderless people, for instance. Advertising that operates at a symbolic level and presents imagery that is open to interpretation tends to draw in the viewer or reader and to generate involvement through the attempt to interpret the advertising content. A fine balance has to be struck between engaging the viewer or reader's interest and involvement with a somewhat ambiguous advertising message on the one hand and making the message sufficiently clear that that same viewer or reader does not either lose interest or miss the point of the advertising. In the case of "1984" there is no overt sales message. Yet the impact of the commercial, both in terms of sales and development of Apple/Macintosh's brand meaning, was unprecedented.

From IMC to an Expanding World of Touch Points

Though the demise of the 30-second TV commercial may have been exaggerated, and notwithstanding the important role that well-conceived and produced advertising continues to play in the context of brand meaning, there is little doubt that the primacy of traditional advertising is on the wane. It has been a gradual process that has begun to accelerate of late. The 1990s saw the emergence of integrated marketing communications (IMC). In essence, IMC is the attempt to combine, integrate and synergize elements of the communication mix consistent with a one-voice communication strategy. This heralded a trend toward greater media neutrality and in part to the eventual allocation of budgets away from predominantly mass media. But what has radically shifted the landscape of brand communication has been the staggering proliferation of media and other channels, driven by seemingly inexhaustible advances in available technology.

To an extent we have always encountered and experienced brands via multiple channels—media and otherwise. Even the most basic campaign might involve advertising, a salesperson and some element of sales promotion at the point of sale. However, multichannel marketing has entered a new era of ever greater complexity and sophistication. Though existing channels of advertising and sales promotion have remained, they have been fragmented. On the one hand, technological advances have altered existent customer interaction points such as in the case of digitally tailored direct mail or offshore call centers. On the other, the explosion of new media, in particular of mobile and digital media platforms, has changed the way we experience brands. We now live in both an information and an entertainment age. Our insatiable appetite for both means we spend a significant proportion of our time accessing a plethora of digital media platforms such as mobile phones, video games, ipods, DVRs and, of course, the Internet. The broad pattern of media use has shifted. We now read our newspapers on line, watch favorite TV shows on our iPods and check the weather forecast on our mobile phones.

Marketers and media companies alike are following the trends. A long-standing champion of leading-edge television advertising, Pepsi recently relaunched its PepsiOne brand without television. Marketers such as Anheuser-Busch, Procter & Gamble and DaimlerChrysler are following suit. As they rebalance the mix of media channels they use, such companies are redirecting money and attention to digital media. In 2006 Heineken announced it was launching its $50 million "Premium Light" beer with ads on Yahoo, MSN and ESPN.com, among other Web sites. Within months of Apple Computer's October 2005 introduction of its video iPod, ABC, NBC, MTV, ESPN and the SciFi Channel were among the television networks making shows available for download. Also in 2006 ABC announced it would make four of its most popular prime-time shows available free on the Web.

Our Changing Use of Media

The implications of all this are far-reaching. For one thing, the migration of content and the merging of media have undermined the traditional sequence of exposure to media (Carlin 2005). Rather than the limitations of the old sequential exposure to one media at a time, media consumption today is characterized by multiplicity and simultaneity of exposures across different platforms and different sensory dimensions. We have become multitaskers par excellence as we surf the Net while sending instant messages and listening to our MP3s. "The new Treo™ 750 now lets you talk and work simultaneously," runs the copy of a recent ad. "Take multitasking to the next level. Introducing the Palm® Treo™ 750 smart device." Furthermore, time demarcations have become blurred. Gone are many of the old patterns of daypart segmentation. In a 24/7, always-on world, peak time is not what it used to be. It is often commented that with the Internet there are two peak times—during the (work) day and evening.

Then there is the inbound versus outbound dichotomy (Greenberg 2006, p. 11). Outbound represents the old media-driven world of communications where marketers reached out to consumers with interruptive and sometimes invasive messages. But today's consumers have embraced new inbound worlds—media platforms and devices that they choose to visit of their own free will. Mobile applications and on-demand content delivered via iPods and DVRs are examples, but so is an interactive experience delivered at retail via digital signage. It is the consumer who wields the technological power to access these inbound messages—or to filter outbound messages.

Defining Touch Points

These developments serve to highlight the relentless expansion of the multiple touch points an individual has with a brand, which go way beyond the proliferation of new media platforms. A touch point may be defined as each and every interaction a customer has with a brand. Every occasion on which that person comes into contact with the brand—and all that is associated with the brand—is a touch point. Using the product or service is the main touch point. Advertisements, Web sites, direct mail, delivery vans, sales calls and comments about a brand from friends or colleagues are other touch points. It is through these touch points that people experience brands. Customer relationships with brands are driven by these touch points. Above all, through every touch point something about the brand is being communicated. To repeat the earlier point, a brand is never *not* communicating. This is brand communication in its broadest, all-inclusive sense and it is what, over time, determines brand meaning.

The configuration of a brand's touch points will vary according to the nature of the brand itself and its underlying products or services. Neither is it possible to be too prescriptive about the chronology of touch points. Someone buying a brand of room spray may do so on the basis of its packaging. This may be the first point of contact with the brand if that person has not seen advertising for the brand or read about it in a magazine. On the other hand, someone who is in the market for a new car and has a particular brand in mind will likely pass through many touch points—online research, advertising, word of mouth, showroom visits—before making a purchase. After sales service and the touch points that involves (e.g., invoicing, customer satisfaction surveys, service appointments) will then become important. In the case of a low-cost item such as a soft drink, important touch points are more likely to be part of the ongoing dialogue between brand and customer—promotions communicated on the package or via mobile messaging, advertising, in-store signage, event sponsorship and so forth.

Moreover, each touch point will influence differing levels of perception and emotion and will provoke differing reactions, either positively or negatively. The air travel and financial services industries provide some examples. Charles Schwab, one of the world's biggest discount brokers, has been successful in actively managing customer touch points (Lindstrom 2007). While other brokers were busy closing down their branch offices and putting their efforts behind on-line trading, Charles Schwab was establishing storefronts. The results suggest the company made a smart decision. Of all new accounts, 80 percent were opened face to face in Charles Schwab offices. Of these new customers, 70 percent were then happy to have their accounts managed via the Internet from their very next contact with the company. For these customers it was important to experience the company via a human representative in the first instance. Once human interaction had taken place and trust was established, customers were comfortable to move to the relative impersonality of the on-line environment to experience the convenience and time and cost efficiency of online trading.

Consider how we have become accustomed to organizing our air travel directly over the last decade or so. Airlines such as Delta and American Airlines have Web sites and arrangements with other providers' Web sites that allow customers to book flights on line with options such as seat selection and online check in. The intermediary of the high-street travel agency—previously an important touch point for the air travel market—is bypassed when we can search for the lowest fare available and book within a few minutes on line. In the case of air travel the importance of human interaction comes into play from the moment of arrival at the departure lounge through the inflight service to arrival at the terminal. Indeed, in an age where technology is equally available to competing companies, personal service—the very human element of a brand's touch point configuration—is often what differentiates one airline brand from another, as carriers such as Singapore Airlines understand.

Another key observation with regard to touch points relates back to the earlier sections on brand architecture and brand portfolio management. When customers interact with brands they may be doing so at the product brand level, for instance—as in the case of mono brands—or at the house-brand or corporate-brand level. Thus, just as different touch points affect perceptions and emotions toward brands in different ways, so too it is important to ask which level of brand architecture a given touch point is impacting. Manufacturers must decide whether to include in advertising and on packaging brand names such as Nestlé or Nabisco.

Context and Customization: Engagement

Again, it is instructive to consider touch points from an integral, outside-in, customer-centric perspective. The customer is at the heart and is viewed whole, not just as the purchaser of a certain product or brand. The focus is on the customer's life and on the brand in the context of the customer's life experiences rather than on the brand per se. Advertisements, for example, are for the most part encountered in the course of viewing or reading media content. So the actual contact with the customer is formed by the advertisement for the brand and the surrounding media content—in other words, the media context. The more appropriate the media context, the more of an engaging experiential contact is likely to occur with the customer (For a broader review see Calder and Malthouse 2005). For similar reasons certain manufacturers are keen on securing brand exposure within the rapidly expanding video games market. Modern mobile technology allows brand managers to send marketing messages not just to specific users but also to specific users in specific locations—a good example of contextual messaging and of customization.

These days it is becoming easier and easier to design your own computer or your own sports shoes or your own car. Customization of products and services and of brand communication is becoming more prevalent. In the latter case, customization was less important when there was no practical way to target individuals as opposed to groups. But the current communications revolution has moved the market from masses and segments to niches and individuals. On the surface this may seem paradoxical. On the one hand, there has been rampant media and audience fragmentation, growing segmentation of consumer tastes and preferences and diminishing user attention levels. This would suggest dissipation and elusiveness. Yet these very elusive customers are becoming more and more accessible thanks to technological advances such as those that are driving the mobile platform.

This all conforms to the new working definition of engagement announced recently by the Advertising Research Foundation (Wang 2006, p. 355): "Engagement is turning on a prospect to a brand idea enhanced by the surrounding context." Engagement plays a critical role in brand communication and impacts on advertising recall, message involvement and message believability. From an advertising perspective, engagement may be defined as a measure of the contextual relevance in which a brand's messages are framed and presented based on its surrounding context (ibid.).

There are, though, two caveats with which to close this chapter and the book. One has to do with the phrase *permission marketing*. The fact that new technology makes customers more accessible to marketing messages does not mean those customers will always be amenable to such messages. We live in a consumer-controlled media world where people expect to be able to consume media when, where and if they want, on any platform or device. It is today's consumers who have been empowered by new technologies and they are more averse than ever to intrusive, unsolicited communication. E-mail has struggled to take off as a marketing tool due to its early contamination by uncontrolled spam. Telemarketing has been regulated and do-not-call lists have been established to prevent unwanted calls. Companies that use short message service and multimedia messaging service messaging, for instance, will need to bear these experiences in mind.

The other consideration concerns what exactly is communicated. Customization of brand communication is one thing; fragmentation of brand communication is another. The response to media proliferation and audience atomization should be the former and definitely not the latter. The danger is heightened by the extent to which "media in general have disconnected from the overall marketing communication collaborative (creative plus media) over the past decade or so. We cannot forget that somewhere behind all of those artfully planned and implemented messages across all possible media delivery platforms there does exist a Brand and a (creative) story about it" (Carlin 2005, pp. 2–4).

The customization of brand communication means customizing the same brand idea to different consumers and allowing individuals and subsegments to experience the brand in a more individualistic and idiosyncratic way. Companies that use direct marketing contacts such as direct mail and e-mail have long been able to customize these contacts—think of financial institutions such as banks and insurance companies or Amazon.com, respectively. But the same is now true for companies using advertising contacts that have traditionally been oriented to a mass audience. Digital printing, for example, makes it possible to customize the ads that a particular subscriber receives in a magazine or newspaper. Yet ultimately customization is still about the communication of a coherent brand concept. And brand communication, in its broadest or narrowest sense, is still about the creation, communication and interpretation of brand meaning.

References

Aaker, D. A. (1990). Brand Extensions: the Good, the Bad and the Ugly. *Sloan Management Review* 31, 47–56.

Aaker, D. A. (1996). *Building Strong Brands.* New York: The Free Press.

Aaker, D. A., and Biel, A. L. (1993). *Brand Equity and Advertising: Advertising's Role in Building Strong Brands.* Hillsdale, NJ: Lawrence Erlbaum Associates.

Aaker, D. A., and Keller, K. L. (1990). Consumer Evaluations of Brand Extensions. *Journal of Marketing*, 54, no. 1, 27–41.

Anonymous (2007, March 10). How Touching. *Economist Technology Quarterly.*

Asquith, M. (1934). More or Less about Myself. New York: Dutton.

Barthes, R. (1987 [1957]). *Mythologies.* New York: Hill & Wang.

Barthes, R. (1964). *Eléments de Sémiologie.* Paris: Editions du Seuil.

Barthes, R. (1977). *Image—Music—Text.* London: Fontana.

Batra, R., and Ray, M. L. (1986). Affective Responses Mediating Acceptance of Advertising. *Journal of Consumer Research*, 13, no. 2, 234–249.

Baudrillard, J. (1968). *Le Système des Objets.* Paris: Gallimard.

Begley, S. (2002, August 26). StrawBerry is no BlackBerry: Building Brands Using Sound. *Wall Street Journal*, p. B1.

Belk, R. W. (1988). Possessions and the Extended Self. *Journal of Consumer Research*, 15, no. 2, 139–168.

Bourdieu, P. (1984). *Distinction: A Social Critique of the Judgement of Taste.* London: Routledge & Kegan Paul.

Boush, D., and Loken, B. (1991). A Process-Tracing Study of Brand Extension Evaluation. *Journal of Marketing Research*, 28, 16–28.

Bragg, A. (1986). Back to the Future. *Sales and Marketing Management*, 137, 61–62.

Brewer, W. F. and Treyen, J. C. (1981). Role of Schemata in Memory for Places. *Cognitive Psychology* 13, 207–30.

Broadbent, S. (1992). 456 Views of How Advertising Works—and What, If Anything, They Tell Us. *Admap*, 27, 17–20.

Broniarczyk, S. M., and Alba, J. W. (1994). The Importance of the Brand in Brand Extension. *Journal of Marketing Research*, 31, 214–228.

Brown, S., Kozinets, V., and Sherry, J. F., Jr. (2003). Teaching Old Brands New Tricks: Retro Branding and the Revival of Brand Meaning. *Journal of Marketing*, 67, no. 3, 19–33.

Calder, B. J., and Malthouse, E. C. (2005). Managing Media and Advertising Change with Integrated Marketing. *Journal of Advertising Research* 45, no. 4, 356–361.

Campbell, J. (1973). *The Hero with a Thousand Faces*. Princeton, NJ: Princeton University Press.

Carlin, I. (2005). A Vision of Media Planning in 2010. *Journal of Advertising Research* 45, no. 1, 2–4.

Cawelti, J. (1969). *Six-Gun Mystique*. Bowling Green, OH: Bowling Green University Press.

Csikszentmihalyi, M., and Rochberg-Halton, E. (1981). *The Meaning of Things*. Cambridge, UK: Cambridge University Press.

Damasio, A. (1994). *Descartes' Error: Emotion, Reason, and the Human Brain*. New York: Grosset/Putnam.

De Bono, E. (1990). *Lateral Thinking for Management*. London: Penguin Books.

de Chernatony, L. and Riley, F. D. (1997). The chasm between managers' and consumers' views of brands: The experts' perspectives. *Journal of Strategic Marketing*, 5: 89–104.

de Saussure, F. ([1916] 1983). *Course in General Linguistics* (trans. Roy Harris). London: Duckworth.

Diderot, D. (1964). *Rameau's Nephew and Other Works by Denis Diderot*, trans. Jacques Barzun and Ralph H. Bowen. New York: Bobbs-Merrill.

Donaghey, B. (2002). Feel States. Conference paper, Market Research Society Annual Conference.

Douglas, M., and Isherwood, B. (1996). *The World of Goods: Towards an Anthropology of Consumption*. London: Routledge.

Edell, J. A., and Burke, M. C. (1987). The Power of Feelings in Understanding Advertising Effects. *Journal of Consumer Research*, 14, no. 3, 421–433.

Farquhar, P. H., and Herr, P. M. (1992). The Dual Structure of Brand Associations. In D. A. Aaker and A. L. Biel (Eds.), *Brand Equity and Advertising: Advertising's Role in Building Strong Brands* (pp. 263–277). Hillsdale, NJ: Lawrence Erlbaum Associates.

Fiske, J. (1982). *Introduction to Communication Studies*. London: Routledge.

Floch, J.-M. (2001). *Semiotics, Marketing and Communication: Beneath the Signs, the Strategies*. New York: Palgrave.

Franzen, G., and Bouwman, M. (2001). *The Mental World of Brands*. Oxon: WARC.

Fuglsang, R. S. (1997). Motorcycle Menace: Media Genres and the Construction of a Deviant Culture. Ph.D. dissertation. University of Iowa.

Gengler, C. E., and Reynolds, T. J. (1995). Consumer Understanding and Advertising Strategy: Analysis and Strategic Translation of Laddering Data. *Journal of Advertising Research*, 35, no. 4, 19–32.

Gergen, K. J. (1991). *The Saturated Self: Dilemmas of Identity in Contemporary Life*. New York: Basic Books.

Giddens, A. (1991). *Modernity and Self-Identity: Self and Society in the Late Modern Age*. Cambridge, U.K.: Polity Press.

Gobé, M. (2001). *Emotional Branding*. New York: Allworth Press.

Goffman, E. (1959). *The Presentation of Self in Everyday Life*. Garden City, NY: Doubleday Anchor.

Goleman, D. (1995). *Emotional Intelligence*. New York: Bantam.

Goodyear, M. (1996). Divided by a Common Language: Diversity and Deception in the World of Global Marketing. *Journal of Market Research Society*, 38, no. 2, 105–122.

Gordon, W. (1994). Taking Brand Repertoires Seriously. *Journal of Brand Management* 2, no. 1, 25–30.

Gordon, W. (2002). The Darkroom of the Mind—What Does Neuro-Psychology Now Tell Us About Brands? *Journal of Consumer Behavior* 1, no. 3, 280–292.

Gordon, W., and Ford-Hutchinson, S. (2002). Brains and Brands: Rethinking the Consumer. *Admap*, 37, part 1, 47–50.

Greenberg, B. (2006, April 24). Shifting Distinctions. *ADWEEK*, p. 11.

Gutman, J. (1982). A Means-End Chain Model Based on Consumer Categorization Processes. *Journal of Marketing* 46, no. 2, 60–72.

Hayward, S. (1996). *Key Concepts in Cinema Studies*. London: Routledge.

Heath, R. (2000). Low Involvement Processing—A New Model of Brands and Advertising. *International Journal of Advertising*, 19, no. 3, 287–298.

Heath, R., and Howard-Spink, J. (2000). "And Now for Something Completely Different"—Current Thinking about the Brain Means We Need to Change the Way Brands Are Researched. Market Research Society Conference.

Hebdige, D. (1979). *Subculture: The Meaning of Style*. New York: Methuen.

Henley Centre (1999). Planning for Consumer Change. Consumer Survey.

Herr, P. M., Farquhar, P. H., and Fazio, R. H. (1992). Using Dominance Measures to Evaluate Brand Extensions. Working Paper, The Claremont Graduate School, Claremont, CA.

Hoffman, D. D. (1998). *Visual Intelligence—How We Create What We See*. New York: W.W. Norton and Co.

Holbrook, M. B., and Batra, R. (1987). Assessing the Role of Emotions as Mediators of Consumer Responses to Advertising. *Journal of Consumer Research*, 14, no. 3, 404–420.

Holt, D. (2004). *How Brands Become Icons*. Boston, MA: Harvard Business School Press.

Howard-Spink, J. (2003). Who Is Your Brand? And What Is Its Story? *Admap*, 443, 15–17.

Jung, C. G. (1967–78). *Collected Works*. Princeton, NJ: Princeton University Press.

Keller, K. L. (1998). *Strategic Brand Management: Building, Measuring, and Managing Brand Equity*. Upper Saddle River NJ: Prentice Hall.

Kerenyi, K. (1976). *Hermes, Guide of Souls*. Dallas: Spring Publications.

Kernan, J. B., and Sommers, M. S. (1967). Meaning, Value, and the Theory of Promotion. *Journal of Communication*, 2, 109–135.

Kleine, R. E., and Kernan, J. B. (1988). Measuring the Meaning of Consumption Objects: An Empirical Investigation. *Advances in Consumer Research*, 15, 498–504.

Lannon, J. (March 1992). Asking the Right Questions—What Do People Do with Advertising? *Admap*, 11–16.

Lannon, J., and Cooper, P. (1983). Humanistic Advertising. *International Journal of Advertising*, 2, 195–213.

Leary, M. R., and Kowalski, R. M. (1990). Impression Management: A Literature Review and Two-Component Model. *Psychological Bulletin*, 107, 34–47.

Leclerc, F., Schmitt, B. H., and Dubé, L. (1994). Foreign Branding and Its Effects on Product Perceptions and Attitudes. *Journal of Marketing Research*, 31, 263–270.

Lévi-Strauss, C. (1983). *The Raw and the Cooked: Mythologiques*, vol. 1. Chicago: University of Chicago Press.

Levy, S. J. (1959). Symbols for Sale. *Harvard Business Review*, 37, no. 4, 117–124.

Lindstrom, M. (2005). *BRAND Sense*. New York: Free Press.

Lindstrom, M. (2007). Cross Channel Branding. http://www.martinlindstrom.com/.

Loftus, E. F. (1973). Category Dominance, Instance Dominance, and Categorization Time. *Journal of Experimental Psychology* 97, 70–74.

MacLean, P. D. (1990). *The Triune Brain in Evolution: Role in Paleocerebral Functions*. New York: Plenum Press.

Marci, C. (2006). A Biologically Based Measure of Emotional Engagement: Context Matters. *Journal of Advertising Research*, 46, no. 4, 381–387.

Mark, M., and Pearson, C. S. (2001). *The Hero and the Outlaw: Building Extraordinary Brands through the Power of Archetypes*. New York: McGraw-Hill.

Martineau, P. (1957). *Motivation in Advertising*. New York: McGraw-Hill.

Mauss, M. (1969 [1925]). *The Gift* (trans. I. Cunnison). London: Cohen & West.

McBurney, D. H. and Collins, V. (1984). *Introduction to Sensation/Perception*, (2nd ed.), Englewood Cliffs, NJ: Prentice Hall.

McCracken, G. (1986). Culture and Consumption: A Theoretical Account of the Structure and Movement of the Cultural Meaning of Consumer Goods. *Journal of Consumer Research*, 13, no. 1, 71–84.

McCracken, G. (1988). *Culture and Consumption: Markets, Meanings and Brand Management*. Bloomington: Indiana University Press.

McCracken, G. (1990). Culture and Consumer Behavior: An Anthropological Perspective. In *Journal of the Market Research Society* 32, no. 1, 3–11.

McCracken, G. (1993). The Value of the Brand: An Anthropological Perspective. In D. D. Aaker and A. L. Biel, Eds., *Brand Equity and Advertising: Advertising's Role in Building Strong Brands*. Hillsdale, NJ: Lawrence Erlbaum Associates, 125–139.

McCracken, G. (2005). *Culture and Consumption II: Markets, Meanings and Brand Management*. Bloomington: Indiana University Press.

McEnally, M., and de Chernatony, L. (1999). The Evolving Nature of Branding: Consumer and Managerial Considerations. *Journal of Consumer and Market Research*, 2, 1–40.

McQuarrie, E. F., and Mick, D. G. (1992). On Resonance: A Critical Pluralistic Inquiry into Advertising Rhetoric. *Journal of Consumer Research* 19, no. 2, 180–197.

Moriarty, S. (1995, August). *Visual Semiotics and the Production of Meaning in Advertising*. Washington, DC: Visual Communication Division of AEJMC (Association for Education in Journalism and Mass Communication).

Muniz, A., and O'Guinn, T. C. (2001). Brand Community. *Journal of Consumer Research*, 27, no. 4, 412–432.

Murphy, J. (1997). What Is Branding? In S. Hart and J. Murphy (Eds.), *Brands: The New Wealth Creators*. New York: New York University Press, 1–12.

Oakenfull, G., and Gelb, B. (1996). Research-Based Advertising to Preserve Brand Equity but Avoid "Genericide." *Journal of Advertising Research*, 36, no. 5, 65–72.

Oakenfull, G., Blair, E., Gelb. B., and Dacin, P. (2000). Measuring Brand Meaning. *Journal of Advertising Research* 40, no. 5, 43–53.

Ogden, C. K., and Richards, I. A. (1923). *The Meaning of Meaning: A Study of the Influence of Language upon Thought and of the Science of Symbolism*. London: Routledge and Kegan Paul.

Ogilvy, D. (1983). *Ogilvy on Advertising*. London: Pan Books.

Ortony, A. and Turner, T. J. (1990). What's Basic about Basic Emotions? *Psychological Review*, 97, no. 3, 315–331.

Osgood, C. E., Suci, G., and Tannenbaum, P. (1957). *The Measurement of Meaning*. Urbana: University of Illinois Press

Oswald, L. (1996). The Place and Space of Consumption in a Material World. *Design Issues*, 12, no. 1, 48–62. (quoted in Valentine and Gordon, 2000).

Park, A. (2007, January 29). Marketing to Your Mind. *Time Magazine*, 114–115.

Park, C., Milberg, S., and Lawson, R. (1991). Evaluation of Brand Extensions: The Role of Product Feature Similarity and Brand Concept Consistency. *Journal of Consumer Research*, 18, no. 2, 185–193.

Peirce, C. S. (1931–1935, 1958). *Collected Papers of Charles Sanders Peirce*. Vols. 1–6, Charles Hartshorne and Paul Weiss (Eds.), Vols. 7–8, Arthur W. Burks (Ed.). Cambridge, MA: Harvard University Press.

Peterson, R. A., and Ross, I. (1972). How to Name New Brands. *Journal of Advertising Research*, 12, no. 6, 29–34.

Pettigrew, S. (2002). Consuming Alcohol. In S. Miles, A. Anderson, and K. Meethan (Eds.), *The Changing Consumer—Markets and Meanings* (pp.104–116). London: Routledge.

Plummer, J. T. (2000). How Personality Makes a Difference. *Journal of Advertising Research*, 40, no. 6, 79–83.

Plutchik, R. (1980). *Emotion: A Psychoevolutionary Synthesis*. New York: Harper & Row.

Rapaille, C. (2004, November 9). The Persuaders. http://www.PBS.org.

Restall, C. (1999). Multinational Brand Marketing. In D. Cowley (Ed.), *Understanding Brands*. London: Kogan Page, 199–216.

Reynolds, T. J., and Gutman, J. (1988). Laddering Theory, Method, Analysis, and Interpretation. *Journal of Advertising Research*, 28, no. 1, 11–31.

Ries, A., and Ries, L. (2002). *The 22 Immutable Laws of Branding*. New York: HarperBusiness.

Ries, A., and Trout, J. (2001). *Positioning: The Battle for Your Mind*. New York: McGraw-Hill.

Robertson, K. (1989). Strategically Desirable Brand Name Characteristics. *Journal of Consumer Marketing*, 6, no. 4, 61–71.

Rokeach, M. (1973). *The Nature of Human Values*. New York: Free Press.

Sapir, E. (1934). Symbolism. In *Encyclopaedia of the Social Sciences, vol. 14* (pp. 493–494). New York: Macmillan.

Saunders, J., and Guoqun, F. (1997). Dual Branding: How Corporate Names Add Value. *Journal of Product and Brand Management* 6, no. 1, pp. 40–48.

Schachter, D. (1996). *Searching for Memory*. New York: Basic Books.

Schlenker, B. R. (1985). Identity and Self-Identification. In B. R. Schlenker (Ed.), *The Self and Social Life* (pp. 65–99). New York: McGraw-Hill.

Schmitt, B. H. (1999). *Experiential Marketing.* New York: Free Press.

Schwartz, S. H. (1992). Universals in the Content and Structure of Values: Theory and Empirical Tests in 20 Countries. In M. Zanna (Ed.), *Advances in Experimental Social Psychology,* vol. 25 (pp. 1–65). New York: Academic Press.

Schwartz, S. H. (2003). "A Proposal for Measuring Value Orientations across Nations." In *Questionnaire Development Report of the European Social Survey.* http://www.europeansocialsurvey.org.

Schwartz, S. H. (2007). Value Orientations: Measurement, Antecedents and Consequences across Nations. In R. Jowell, C. Roberts, R. Fitzgerald, and G. Eva (Eds.), *Measuring Attitudes Cross-Nationally: Lessons from the European Social Survey.* London: Sage, 167–200.

Slater, D. (1997). *Consumer Culture and Modernity.* Cambridge, U.K.: Polity Press.

Slotkin, R. (1998). *Gunfighter Nation: The Myth of the Frontier in Twentieth Century America.* Norman: University of Oklahoma Press.

Solomon, M., Bamossy, G., and Askegaard, S. (2002). *Consumer Behaviour: A European Perspective* (2d ed.). Upper Saddle River, NJ: Prentice Hall.

Szalay, L. B., and Deese, J. (1978). *Subjective Meaning and Culture: An Assessment through Word Associations.* Hillsdale, NJ: Lawrence Erlbaum Associates.

Tarte, R. D. and Barritt, L. S. (1971). Phonetic symbolism in adult native speakers of English: Three studies. *Language and Speech* 14, 158–168.

Tauber, E. (1988). Brand Leverage: Strategy for Growth in a Cost-Control World. *Journal of Advertising Research*, 28, no. 4, 26–30.

Toynbee, A. (1976). *A Study of History.* London: Oxford University Press.

Travis, D. (2000). *Emotional Branding: How Successful Brands Gain the Irrational Edge.* Roseville, CA: Prima Publishing.

Ulrich, D., Zenger, J., and Smallwood, N. (1999). *Results-Based Leadership.* Boston: Harvard Business School Press.

U.S. Census Bureau (2001, June 29). "America's Families and Living Arrangements: March 2000." http://www.census.gov/prod/2001pubs/p.20–537.pdf.

Valentine, V. (1995). Opening Up the Black Box: Switching the Paradigm of Qualitative Research. ESOMAR (European Society for Opinion and Marketing Research) Qualitative Research Seminar, Paris, December 6–8.

Valentine, V., and Gordon, G. (2000). The 21st Century Consumer: A New Model of Thinking. *International Journal of Market Research*, 42, no. 2, 185–206.

Van Gennep, A. (1960 [1909]). *Rites of Passage* (trans. M. B. Vizedom and G. L. Caffee). London: Routledge & Kegan and Paul.

Veblen, T. (1899). *The Theory of the Leisure Class*. New York: Macmillan.

Wang, A. (2006). Advertising Engagement: A Driver of Message Involvement on Message Effects. *Journal of Advertising Research* 46, no. 4, 355–368.

Watzlawick, P., Beavin, J. H., and Jackson, D. D. (1967). *Pragmatics of Human Communication*. New York: W.W. Norton.

Weaver, R. M. (1974). *A Rhetoric and Composition Handbook*. New York: Quill.

Wicklund, R. A., and Gollwitzer, P. M. (1982). *Symbolic Self-Completion*. Hillsdale, NJ: Lawrence Erlbaum Associates.

Wilkinson, A. (2005) February 3. Neuromarketing: Brain Scam or Valuable Tool? *Marketing Week*, 22–23.

Wilson, J. (2002). Whole-Brain Branding. *Admap*, 431, 47–49.

Yorkston, E., and Menon, G. (2004). A Sound Idea: Phonetic Effects of Brand Names on Consumer Judgments. *Journal of Consumer Research*, 31, no. 1, 43–51.

Zajonc, R. B. (1980). Feeling and Thinking: Preferences Need No Inferences. *American Psychologist*, 35, 151–175.

Zaltman, G. (2003). *How Customers Think*. Boston, MA: Harvard Business School Press.

Appendix

Gestalt Principles of Perception

Besides the principles of simplicity and of closure mentioned in chapter 3, a number of other perceptual tendencies are identified in Gestalt psychology:

The principle of proximity is illustrated by the following figure:

The closer objects are to one another, the more likely we are to mentally group them together. So in this example we are more likely to see three pairs of lines that are fairly close together and a single line on the far right than three pairs of lines that are more distant from one another and a single line on the far left. Here is another classic illustration:

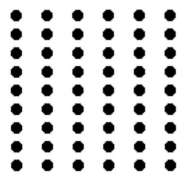

In this figure we do not see just a square made up of dots but rather a series of columns of dots, whereas in the following figure we see a series of rows of dots.

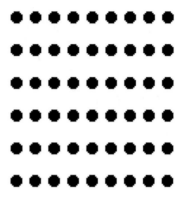

According to the principle of similarity, objects that share similar characteristics such as shape, size, color, or orientation will be grouped together perceptually. Look what happens when we introduce some squares:

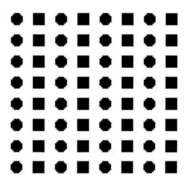

Notice that the circles and squares are the same distance from each other, so the principle of proximity is not influencing how we see the figure. Rather, it is the principle of similarity that causes us to see separate columns of circles and squares. In the context of branding, consumers are more likely to link product line extensions to the parent brand when they have certain physical features in common, such as packaging design and graphics.

The principle of continuity refers to the fact that people tend to see lines as continuing in a given direction rather than making abrupt turns or changes of direction. In the following figure we tend to see lines a–b and c–d crossing one another rather than seeing a–c or a–d as lines, for instance.

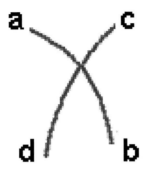

Credits

Chapter 2

Table 2.1 reprinted from Rokeach, M. (1973, p.28, Table 2.1) with permission of The Free Press, a division of Simon & Schuster Adult Publishing Group. Copyright © 1973 by The Free Press. Copyright © renewed 2001 by Sandra Ball-Rokeach. All rights reserved.

Table 2.2 and Figure 2.3 reprinted from Schwartz (2007, p.166, Table 9.1 and p.167, Figure 9.1 respectively) © 2007 SAGE Publications, Ltd., with permission.

Figure 2.5 reprinted from Reynolds, T.J., and Gutman, J. (1988, p.12) © 1988 Advertising Research Foundation, with permission of ARF.

Figure 2.6 with permission of Unilever PLC.

Table 2.3 adapted from Ortony, A., and Turner, T.J. (1990, p.316) © 1990 American Psychological Association, Inc. with permission of APA, Inc.

Table 2.4 adapted from Goleman, D. (1995) © 1995 Daniel Goleman, with permission of Bantam Books, a division of Random House, Inc., and with permission of Bloomsbury, UK.

Figure 2.7 reprinted from Donaghey, B. (2002) with permission of Market Research Society.

Chapter 3

Table 3.3 and Figure 3.4 reprinted from Lindstrom, M. (p. 152, Table 6.5 and p. 153, Figure 6.5 respectively) with permission of The Free Press, a division of Simon & Schuster Adult Publishing Group. Copyright © 2005 by Martin Lindstrom. All rights reserved.

Figure 3.2 with permission of Metropolitan Police Force.

Figure 3.3 with permission of Imperial Tobacco Limited.

Table 3.4 reprinted from McBurney & Collins (1984, p.11) 2nd Edition © 1984 McBurney & Collins, with permission of Pearson Education, Inc., Upper Saddle River, NJ.

Figure 3.5 Shell trade marks by permission of Shell Brands International AG.

Figure 3.6 IBM logo courtesy of IBM Corporation.

Figure 3.8 FedEx service mark used by permission.

Chapter 4

Figure 4.1 adapted from Osgood, C.E., Suci, G., and Tannenbaum, P. (1957) copyright © 1957 by Board of Trustees of the University of Illinois; renewed 1985 by Charles E. Osgood, George J. Suci, and Percy H. Tannenbaum. Used with permission of the University of Illinois Press.

Figure 4.9 adapted from McCracken, G. (1988, p.72) © 1988 Grant McCracken with permission.

Chapter 5

Figures 5.2 and 5.8 adapted from Lannon, J., and Cooper, P. (1983, p.202, Fig.2 and p.204, Fig.4 respectively) © 1983 *International Journal of Advertising* with permission.

Figure 5.6 McDonald's logo used with permission from McDonald's Corporation.

Tables 5.1 and 5.2 reprinted from Keller, K.L. (1998, p.315) 1st Edition © 1998 by Prentice Hall, Inc. with permission of Pearson Education, Inc., Upper Saddle River, NJ.

Chapter 6

Figure 6.1 reprinted from Keller, K.L. (1998, p.459, Fig 12.4) 1st Edition © 1998 by Prentice Hall, Inc. with permission of Pearson Education, Inc., Upper Saddle River, NJ.

Figure 6.2 reprinted from Farquhar, P.H. and Herr, P.M. (1992) in Aaker, D.A. and Biel, A.L. (1993, p.266, Fig.17.2) copyright © 2003 by Taylor & Francis Group LLC, with permission of Taylor & Francis Group LLC.

Figure 6.3 adapted from Herr, P.M., Farquhar, P.H., and Fazio, R.H. (1992) in Aaker, D.A., and Biel, A.L. (1993, p.273, Table 17.2) copyright © 2003 by Taylor & Francis Group LLC, with permission of Taylor & Francis Group LLC.

Chapter 7

Figures 7.2 and 7.4 adapted from Goodyear, M. (1996, p.114, Fig. 2) © 1996 *Journal of Market Research Society* with permission of JMRS.

Figure 7.3 adapted from McEnally, M. and de Chernatony, L. (1999, p.9, Chart 3) © 1999 *Journal of Consumer and Market Research* (now *Academy of Marketing Science Review*), with permission of Academy of Marketing Science.

Color Insert

iPhone ad © Apple Inc. Used with permission. All rights reserved. Apple and the Apple logo are registered trademarks of Apple, Inc.

Author Index

Subject Index